CW00959657

DAVID I

THE KING WHO MADE SCOTLAND

DAVID I

THE KING WHO MADE SCOTLAND

Richard Oram

TEMPUS

Cover picture: Illuminated initial from the Kelso Charter depicting David I.
Courtesy of the Trustees of the National Library of Scotland.

First published 2004

Tempus Publishing Limited
The Mill, Brimscombe Port,
Stroud, Gloucestershire, GL5 2QG
www.tempus-publishing.com

© Richard Oram, 2004

The right of Richard Oram to be identified as the Author
of this work has been asserted in accordance with the
Copyrights, Designs and Patents Act 1988.

All rights reserved. No part of this book may be reprinted
or reproduced or utilised in any form or by any electronic,
mechanical or other means, now known or hereafter invented,
including photocopying and recording, or in any information
storage or retrieval system, without the permission in writing
from the Publishers.

British Library Cataloguing in Publication Data.
A catalogue record for this book is available from the British Library.

ISBN 0 7524 2825 X

Typesetting and origination by Tempus Publishing Limited
Printed in Great Britain

Contents

Acknowledgements

My thanks go to Justine, who once again set me on the track to write this book after years of dithering. Thanks, too, to Jonathan Reeve at Tempus, whose persistence that I should write a book on David finally paid off. Special mentions go to Alasdair Ross, whose research on Moray very gently pulled away the carpet from under my feet on several major issues, but who very generously helped me back up afterwards, and to Alex Woolf, who, as ever, has helped me work through some of the more tortuous areas of debate. Mike Penman deserves a special mention for patience above and beyond the call of duty in listening to me extol the virtues of the 'other' King David, and for his unstinting efforts in helping me to obtain some of the more obscure articles and essays which bulk so large in the bibliography. A special thank you also goes to my colleague Michael Penman for rescuing me from a hole into which I had dug myself and producing the index for this book at very short notice.

I would like to dedicate this book to the memory of my grandparents, Duncan and Marjory Malcolm, who took me as a child to visit many of the abbeys and cathedrals which David I founded, and who fostered and encouraged my developing interest in medieval Scotland.

Introduction

It is nearly twenty years since I first wanted to write a book-length study of the king who changed the whole thrust of Scotland's development and who had such a profound impact on the history of the British Isles. I had been fascinated since childhood by this man who, if the guidebooks were anything to go by, had single-handedly built so many abbeys, castles and burghs, personally wrote the nation's first coherent law code while ministering to the sick, the poor and the aged, and brought a rough-edged and barbarous kingdom face to face with the cultured smoothness of European civilisation. Scotland's medieval history, it seemed, started with this man. Before David was darkness and disorder, things violent and primitive; after him came the new Scotland, a fully-fledged member of the European brotherhood of states, punching well above its weight, confident and complete. Or so my teachers at primary school in 1960s Dundee taught me.

Revision has been a characteristic of Scottish history for most of the last fifty years. It started with the monumental assault mounted against the traditional historiography by the generation of 'angry young academics' led by Geoffrey Barrow and Archie Duncan, with the former's prodigious output of research into the origins of Scottish 'feudalism', underpinned by his formidable charter scholarship, laying the foundations of an altogether new construct: 'feudal' Scotland. The works of Professors Barrow and Duncan, although differing profoundly on the significance – and indeed the meaning – of the 'feudal' innovations evident in the charters, agree that something revolutionary occurred in Scotland during the reign of David I.

Exactly what that revolution was, however, is something that has continued
to be debated and revised ever since, for David has been presented as a
Janus-like figure who both looked forward to the new and back to the old,[1]
with differing degrees of emphasis on the interplay of continuity and
change present in his reign. In Archie Duncan's assessment, David's achievements were made 'without wholesale expropriation of native landowners,
without intensive settlement by Anglo-French landholders throughout the
whole kingdom, and without significant diminution of the resources of the
king'.[2] Certainly, short of a war of conquest against his own Gaelic subjects,
it is difficult to see how David could have forced through far-reaching
change other than by carrying those same magnates with him. Perhaps it is
even more important to recognise that, where there was neither the opportunity nor the need to introduce change, David left well alone, and even
where such opportunity did arise – as in northern Scotland from the 1130s
onwards – David would as readily employ the traditional forces of the
Gaelic magnates as introduce his Anglo-Norman dependants. His style of
government and the developments which he instituted were far more
richly and subtly textured than the simple black-and-white image offered
by the continuity-versus-change mantra.

     In large part, our perception of David's reign as marking a time of decisive
change is a product of the sudden development of large-scale record keeping
on parchment from the second quarter of the twelfth century. Written
records were hardly a new phenomenon, but what was different was the
volume of material produced and, more importantly for modern historians,
the volume which has survived. Historians may wring their hands in anguish
at the scale of what has been lost to us, but that still does not prevent them
from building elaborate theories based on a few surviving scraps of parchment. We are, however, coming increasingly to recognise that much of what
David achieved was carried through on the back of developments begun in
the reign of his elder brother and predecessor, Alexander I (1107–24), especially in terms of Church reform, and that cultural change, with influences
from both the Scandinavian north and the Anglo-Saxon south, was underway throughout the eleventh century. Nevertheless, recognition of the
earlier origins of many of the trends which have been presented as characteristic of David's reign must not be used to downplay the scale of what was
achieved under his governance. The foundations may have been laid already,
but David carried forward the substantial building work.

     Where the greatest caution must be exercised is in tone. David was nei-
ther a betrayer and destroyer of his Gaelic heritage nor a single-minded and

far-sighted creator of a New Jerusalem, yet it is possible to find him presented as both. As will be explored in the study of David's reputation that comes at the end of this book, the presentation of the king as demon and/or deity depends more on the particular personal axe which the modern observer has to grind than on the reality as presented by the evidence. Neither David nor his mother before him, for example, destroyed either Gaelic culture or the native Church in Scotland, or delivered an independent Christian tradition in their kingdom into the clutches of Rome. David's religious reforms were undertaken within the context of a Scottish Church that was already a full member of a western European tradition, and the conflict between 'Celtic' and 'Roman' traditions was simply a local manifestation of a general move towards uniformity of practice within the Church in the course of the later eleventh and twelfth centuries. That is not to say that his policies were universally popular in Scotland with either ecclesiastical or lay communities, but as the better-documented contemporary reform movement in Ireland should warn us, the resistance was more often than not driven by personal political and economic determinants than any principled religious stance. Lay appropriation of Church land – and office – was as much a feature of 'Roman' Anglo-Saxon England and the Frankish continent as it was in 'Celtic' Scotland and Ireland, yet there the reformers' assault on what was widely perceived as a sinful and utterly corrupt practice has not been presented as an inter-cultural conflict.

Full exploration of these wider cultural issues requires a different kind of study than what is being offered here. There will be some who will criticise and lament the absence from this book of a detailed analysis of the whole continuity-versus-change debate, particularly in the areas of David's investments and wider crown-magnate relations, but that is not what this book was aimed at. A full assessment of the colonial movement under David I, his patterns of patronage, and the roles played by both native and newcomer in the construction of his regime must await further study. The focus here is the king, his achievements and his failures. The book is not, nor was it intended to be, an attempt at a definitive study of Scotland in the reign of David I, for that would require a far larger work than is intended for this series.

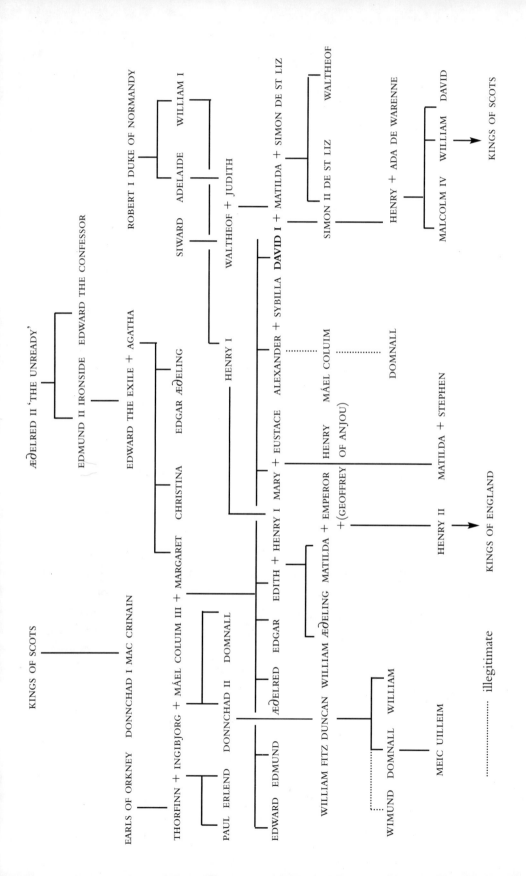

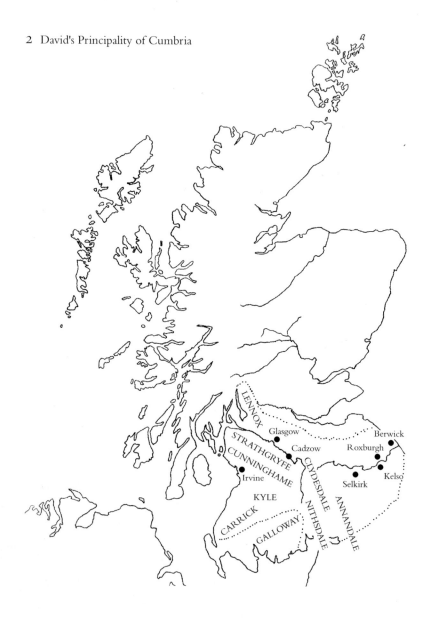

ORKNEY

CAITHNESS

Dornoch

Ross

Duffus

Rosemarkie Forres Elgin

Inverness BUCHAN

ARGYLL OF MORAY

MORAY MAR

BADENOCH Aberdeen

Stracathro

ATHOLL

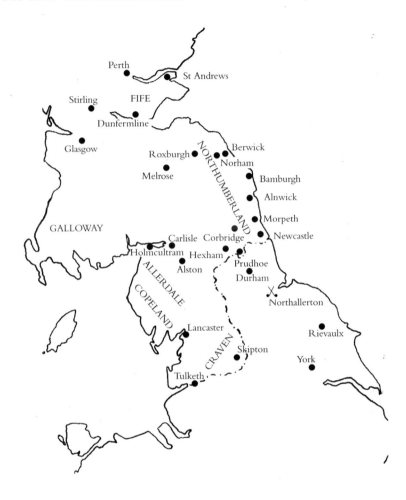

CHAPTER ONE

Máel Coluim mac Donnchada, Margaret and the Founding of the Canmore Dynasty

To understand the reign of David I and the kingdom which he made it is necessary to first understand the later decades of the eleventh century, for in those decades patterns were established in political, social and cultural relationships both within and outwith Scotland that were to drive it down particular avenues of development. The Scotland of David I had been shaped by forces at work over a quarter of a century – and indeed far earlier still – before his birth. For thirty-five years after 1058, one man held the kingship of the Scots. Máel Coluim mac Donnchada, better-known today as Malcolm III or, wrongly as it transpires,[1] Malcolm Canmore, is portrayed commonly as one of the most successful of Scotland's pre-twelfth century rulers, although in both later medieval and modern traditions he is overshadowed greatly by the powerful image of his second wife, Margaret, queen and saint. When asked to evaluate Máel Coluim's achievements as king, however, there are probably few people who could cite with confidence his reign dates, let alone provide a *curriculum vitae*. Some might remember him as the son of the kindly old man murdered by Shakespeare's Macbeth at Cawdor, who plays a cameo role in the early scenes of the play and disappears from Act II Scene 1 to reappear only in Act IV Scene 1. Others might remember him as the founder of Dunfermline. To a few, he is the progenitor of the line of kings labelled by modern historians as the Canmore dynasty, which ruled Scotland from 1058 until the extinction of its direct male line in the person of his great-great-great-grandson Alexander III in 1286. It would be wrong to claim that the foundation of a line of kings that was to rule Scotland for nearly 230 years was Máel Coluim's greatest achievement, but it did represent one of the most significant changes wrought by this ruthless and opportunistic king. The success of Máel Coluim mac Donnchada and his descendants in monopolising control of monarchical power in Scotland laid the foundations for the transformation of the old Gaelic kingdom of Alba from a marginal power on the periphery of Europe into one of the two mature medieval kingdoms contending for the domination of the British Isles.

At the start of his reign, the auspices for his long-term success or survival were not good. The traditional picture of him is as a returning exile, who since 1040 had lived in obscurity at various courts around Britain, dependent on the support of foreign kings and ambitious magnates but lacking any real reservoir of family strength in Scotland. We have no firm contemporary evidence for his movements during the period of nearly two decades after the death of Donnchad mac Crinain, but some modern authorities have suggested that there is evidence in his later actions to suggest that Máel Coluim had lived at the court of the Jarl of Orkney, Thorfinn Sigurdsson. Others would point to the possible evidence that he had spent his exile at the courts of Edward the Confessor, King of England, and his powerful Earl of York, Siward, for proof of his installation on the throne as their protégé. During this time his father's killer, Mac Bethad mac Findlaech, had faced other attempts to depose him, the first in 1045 mounted by Máel Coluim's grandfather, Crinan, Abbot of Dunkeld, and the second in 1046, mounted by Siward of York on the orders of Edward the Confessor. Both had failed, and by 1054 Mac Bethad's grip on the throne seemed secure. Yet, there was always the threat from Donnchad's children, Máel Coluim and his younger brother Domnall (known as Domnall Bán, 'the Fair'), who were growing to adulthood and forging networks of friends and alliances with foreign powers who cherished ambitions to bring the Scots into a dependent relationship with them. For the English king, the establishment of a dependent client in the north would bring stability to a frontier which had proven to be dangerously ill defined for over a century.

Traditionally, it has been believed that the man identified in 1054 by Edward the Confessor as his candidate for that job was Máel Coluim mac Donnchada. This tradition is based on a series of disjointed eleventh- and twelfth-century chronicle accounts which have been strung together to form a fluent narrative, but it has recently been argued strongly that the scenario thereby constructed is fundamentally flawed.[2] The earliest element in the narrative is an entry in the *Anglo-Saxon Chronicle* under 1054, which reports that Siward of York invaded Scotland with both a land and a naval force, defeated Mac Bethad (who escaped safely) and obtained rich plunder, but in the battle on 27 July he lost his own eldest son and several members of both his own bodyguard and the king's huscarls.[3] The battle was recognised widely at the time in Gaelic sources as a great slaughter,[4] but Mac Bethad escaped the carnage and clearly continued as king despite his defeat. Some seventy years later, however, new elements had begun to creep into the tradition as set out by William of Malmesbury in his *Gesta Regum Anglorum*, where he presents Siward as slaying Mac Bethad and installing 'Malcolm, son of the King of the Cumbrians' in his place at the behest of Edward the Confessor.[5] Given that Siward died in 1055 and Mac Bethad lived until 1057, key elements in William's narrative are patently false, but his statement concerning the establishment in his place of *a* Máel Coluim has in the past been accepted uncritically as referring to Máel Coluim mac Donnchada, particularly since the reference to the insertion of 'Malcolm, son of the King of the Cumbrians' (but not the slaying of Mac Bethad) is corroborated by William's contemporary annalist, John of Worcester.[6]

In an effort to accommodate the evidence relating to the 1054 invasion and establishment of 'Malcolm, son of the King of the Cumbrians', with Máel Coluim mac Donnchada's killing of Mac Bethad in 1057, a staged recovery of his father's kingdom has been proposed for the exiled prince, which saw him first recover southern Scotland before going on to kill the usurper and his stepson to secure the northern districts and the undisputed kingship.[7] That scenario, however, is still founded on the assumption that the man installed in 1054 in some part of Scotland was the man who, in 1057, killed Mac Bethad, and still works on the premise that the establishment of Máel Coluim mac Donnchada on the throne was an act of English royal policy. Oddly, however, at no place in the English accounts is it said that 'Malcolm, son of King Duncan' was made king. It is only in the works of the contemporary continental annalist, Marianus Scottus, that specific reference is made to Máel Coluim mac Donnchada's governance of Scotland, and the year given for its start is 1057 or 1058.[8]

These internal contradictions in the evidence led Archibald Duncan to undertake a systematic re-evaluation of the accounts, in which he has stripped away later generations of gloss placed on the basic eleventh- and twelfth-century narrative.[9] The result is a convincing new interpretation which proposes that the 'Malcolm, son of the King of the Cumbrians' installed in 1054 was just that: perhaps a son of the otherwise last known

king of Strathclyde or Cumbria, Ywain map Dyfnwal, or Owen the Bald,
who disappears from historical record in 1018. Ywain's predecessor had been
his elder brother, Máel Coluim, which offers some support for the possibility that this name would have been passed to a scion of the Strathclyde royal
line.[10] If we accept this interpretation, then it appears that what Edward the
Confessor instructed Siward to do was revive the kingdom of the
Cumbrians as a puppet satellite state, and re-establish English domination of
at least the western portion of the Southern Upland zone of Scotland
through this new vassal. Given Edward's aggressive expansion of English
power into Wales at this time, this is not an unlikely reconstruction of
events.[11] The English king was seeking to regain a dominant position on a
vulnerable frontier which his stepfather, Knútr the Great, had recognised as
vital for the security of the whole north-western flank of England. Such a
scenario has profound significance for our understanding of the role of
David as 'Prince of Cumbria' some half a century later.

Where, then, does this new interpretation leave Máel Coluim mac
Donnchada? The simple answer is that we cannot be sure except on one
point: he was not being installed into Scotland as a protégé of Edward the
Confessor, backed by an English army. That Mac Bethad was killed at
Lumphanan, a few miles north of the river Dee in Aberdeenshire, and that
his stepson and successor, Lulach mac Gilla Comgain, was killed the following spring at Essie in Strathbogie, a few miles further to the north, has been
paired with the traditional interpretation which places Máel Coluim in
southern Scotland in 1055–57 to suggest that he was fighting his way north
into his enemies' Moray-based political heartland and that they had per-
ished attempting to repel his attack. That Lulach, however, was able to be
installed and recognised as king after Mac Bethad's death suggests that he
had relatively easy access to the royal inauguration site at Scone, something
that one assumes would be difficult if Máel Coluim mac Donnchada was in
possession of the southern part of the kingdom. Unless we assume that the
battle in which Mac Bethad was killed was actually a victory for the northerners, who then swept down at least as far as Scone to place their man on
the throne before being driven back into their northern fastnesses and final
defeat the following spring, the only viable alternative is that Máel Coluim
was making his bid for power from the north and his rivals had advanced
beyond the Mounth to challenge him.[12]

Given what we know of Máel Coluim's later career, we need not consider him to have been anyone's protégé imposed on Scotland with the
intention that he be a compliant puppet. Certainly, if he had been in any

way beholden to Edward the Confessor, he soon kicked over the traces, for he appears to have been active in raiding into English territory by 1058–59. These raids are usually assumed to have been directed chiefly against the land controlled by Tosti Godwinsson, Earl of Northumbria from 1055 to 1065, but they may have been aimed at recovery of Strathclyde, for nothing more is heard of the 'son of the King of the Cumbrians' and Máel Coluim mac Donnchada was certainly in possession of Cumbria by 1070.[13] Earl Tosti is said to have been engaged in protracted fighting which contained and wore down a Scottish enemy into submission, and this enemy is identified often as Mac Bethad.[14] In 1059, however, it was reported that Earl Tosti, together with the Archbishop of York and Bishop of Durham, escorted Máel Coluim to Edward the Confessor's court.[15] There, he may have made some kind of formal submission to Edward, and we can perhaps be permitted to conjecture that Edward recognised Máel Coluim's *fait accompli* and acknowledged his possession of the Cumbrian kingdom in return, and it was presumably at this time also that the Scottish king became the 'sworn brother' of Earl Tosti. From all of the foregoing, it appears that Cumbria was only loosely attached to the kingdom of the Scots down to the middle of the eleventh century and that the process of its integration into Scotland had only really begun in the course of Máel Coluim mac Donnchada's reign. What had so recently and easily been attached could as easily be detached, as would happen for David after 1107.

Although he had made his peace with Edward the Confessor in 1059, in 1061 Máel Coluim is reported to have ravaged the earldom of his sworn brother, Tosti, plundering even the sanctuary of Lindisfarne.[16] *Prima facie*, this attack was a piece of shameless opportunism, for it was made during Tosti's absence from Northumbria on pilgrimage to Rome, and was intended simply to win plunder. Opportunistic it may have been, but its aim may have been far more significant, and here we must bear in mind the references to Máel Coluim's earlier raids into Tosti's earldom. If we accept that Máel Coluim's objective in 1058–59 was a restoration of his kingdom to the limits of authority exercised by Mac Bethad, Donnchad mac Crinain and Máel Coluim mac Cináeda before him, then the attacks on Tosti's territory could indicate that some part of what had until recently been Scottish land had been detached from the kingdom and returned to Northumbrian rule. The eastern frontier between Scotland and England had only been fixed at the Tweed line in 1018 following Máel Coluim mac Cináeda's victory over Uhtred, Earl of Northumbria, at Carham.[17] When Earl Siward intervened in Scotland in 1054, or even earlier in 1046, it is very probable that he had·

taken back into his northern earldom at least the district between the river Tweed and the Lammermuirs. It may have been this district which Máel Coluim mac Donnchada sought to recover in 1061.

Máel Coluim was no mere opportunistic warlord; he was equally opportunistic as a politician and diplomat. Just like the Anglo-Scottish border, the northern frontier of Scottish royal authority was very poorly defined in the eleventh century, with the Norse jarls of Orkney giving only occasional and grudging recognition to the claims of Scottish kings to overlordship of their extensive mainland Scottish earldom of Caithness. Scottish weakness in the north had been compounded by the pretensions of the rulers of Moray, vassals and agents of the Scottish kings but themselves with dynastic links that encouraged them to seek the Scottish kingship for themselves.[18] The defeats of Mac Bethad and Lulach in 1057 and 1058 had seen Moray's pretensions humbled, and Máel Coluim may have established some form of rapprochement with Orkney during his long years of exile. It cannot be proven, but it may have been from Orkney or with Orcadian support that he had launched his bid for the throne in 1057. Certainly, during his reign there is no indication of a continuation of the Orkney-Scottish conflicts which had been regular occurrences in the tenth and earlier eleventh centuries.[19] Thorfinn Sigurdsson, Jarl of Orkney's ambitions, in large part, were diverted towards a reconstruction of his father's maritime empire in the west, but he and his predecessors had also voiced strong claims to a substantial dominion on the northern mainland of Scotland. These claims may underlie the rather garbled accounts of conflict between Thorfinn and a ruler who may be Mac Bethad preserved in the Orkney sagas, but the contest had been resolved in the Orcadian's favour probably before 1050. During Máel Coluim mac Donnchada's reign, the northern portion of the kingdom appears to have been remarkably peaceful.

Tranquillity in the north may have derived from the greater stability in the region gained in around 1065 when Máel Coluim married Ingibjorg, Thorfinn's widow.[20] This, for the Scottish king, was a highly significant union, for Ingibjorg was no ageing widow but a highly marriageable and politically well-connected woman. She was the daughter of the powerful Norwegian nobleman Finn Arnison, while her cousin, Thora, was the wife of Haraldr Hardrádi, King of Norway, and mother of the Norwegian kings Magnus and Óláfr Haraldsson.[21] Through her, Máel Coluim was to establish diplomatic connections with the Norwegian king, one of the several would-be claimants to the English throne who would emerge in 1065–66. Closer to home, the marriage also brought Orkney into a tighter relationship with the Scots, and for as long as Ingibjorg's sons, the joint earls Paul and Erlend, ruled there, peace prevailed between the Scots and the earldom. Little is known of Máel Coluim and Ingibjorg's relationship other than that it possibly produced two sons, Donnchad and Domnall.[22] The date of her death is unknown, but it appears to have been by about 1069, when the king started to consider the possible benefits of a marriage to a new and even better connected prospective bride.

In 1068, Máel Coluim found himself the host of an important group of Anglo-Saxon refugees fleeing from England. This group comprised key Northumbrian lords, led by Earl Cospatric of Northumbria himself, but the nominal leadership of the party was held by none other than the teenage heir of the West Saxon dynasty, Edgar Æðeling, whom many of the English regarded as their rightful king.[23] With Edgar were his mother, Agatha, and sisters, Margaret and Christina. The exiles hoped that Máel Coluim would aid them in their rebellion against William of Normandy, which aimed to drive the Conqueror into the sea and place Edgar on the English throne. Máel Coluim, however, had played a very cautious role in 1066, offering shelter and protection to Earl Tosti after his subjects had driven him out and he had failed to re-impose his rule after an invasion of his former earldom, but refusing to be drawn into direct intervention.[24] Likewise, Máel Coluim cannot be shown to have taken any direct part in Haraldr Hardrádi of Norway's great invasion in the late summer of 1066 in which Tosti and Máel Coluim's stepsons Paul and Erlend participated. Even in 1068, while the Scottish king may have recognised the potential benefits to him of providing support for the exiles, he chose instead to make peace with William.[25] In 1069, the Northumbrians rose against the garrisons that William had planted in their territory and succeeded in breaking the Norman hold over the country north of the Humber.[26] It is unknown how deeply involved in the early stages of the rebellion Cospatric, Edgar and the other exiles were, or if Máel Coluim himself had finally decided to take a hand in the affair, but they had remained under his protection in Scotland over the winter.[27] As the rebellion spread, Edgar and his associates re-entered England, joining with Waltheof, son of Siward, who had held York under Edward the Confessor.[28] For a while they enjoyed some success, even securing support from King Svein of Denmark, but there is little evidence that Máel Coluim threw his weight behind them at this stage.[29] By late 1069, however, William's counter-attack was gaining momentum and, faced with the ravaging of their lands, Cospatric and Waltheof submitted to the Normans. Edgar and his little band of followers, however, appears to have eluded

William and maintained the semblance of revolt against the occupiers, possibly sheltering with the Danish force that Svein had sent to England.

Traditional accounts present the rising in England as having failed before the end of 1069, but William's position in early 1070 in England generally, let alone north of the Humber, was still highly precarious. The Danes in particular still posed a potent threat, for Svein himself had now joined with his sons and had forced the citizens of York once more into submission;[30] a large Danish fleet was based in the Humber and contingents of the Danish army were in possession of large tracts of Yorkshire and northern Lincolnshire. Perceived Norman weakness, a powerful foreign ally entrenched in eastern England and the continuing unrest elsewhere in England, then, provided the context for what seems otherwise like a curiously mistimed and violent invasion of northern England by Máel Coluim.[31] According to the Durham-based chronicler Symeon, the Scottish king invaded *through* Cumberland – a phraseology which indicates that he did not actually control Cumberland – and, crossing the Stanemore route, entered Teesdale and Cleveland, which he proceeded to ravage. From the area around Hartlepool he turned northwards through the properties of the Durham community, but did not approach Durham itself – possibly reflecting the veneration for St Cuthbert which Máel Coluim and his family later displayed – before coming to Wearmouth. There, by chance suggests Symeon, but more probably by design, he encountered Edgar, his mother and sisters, whom he invited to return with him to Scotland. The invitation, however, appears to have been declined. While Máel Coluim and his army, now laden with booty, began its withdrawal homewards, Earl Cospatric and his men, by then restored to King William's peace, launched a counter-attack through Cumberland. In retaliation, the Scots ravaged the coastlands of eastern Northumbria, where Cospatric's estates were concentrated, before returning to Scotland. At some point after this, Edgar Æðeling and his family took ship with the Bishop of Durham, supposedly intending to find safe refuge on the continent, but they were instead driven northwards.[32]

What had been Máel Coluim's aim in 1070? It has been suggested that his attack was simply an opportunistic plundering raid, or, at best that his plan was simply to detach Northumbria from England and add it to his own kingdom.[33] That, however, ignores the wider situation in England at the time, for, far from withdrawing from England in the spring as they had agreed in winter 1069, the Danes, now reinforced by the arrival of Svein in person, had shifted their focus to a new centre of rebellion against William. Moving south from the Humber, Svein entered the Wash and landed part of

his army, which pushed deep into Cambridgeshire where it seized and fortified the Isle of Ely. There they were quickly reinforced by the local
Anglo-Saxon leadership, including Hereward 'the Wake', a south
Lincolnshire thegn.[34] The coincidence of Máel Coluim's attack with this
renewed Danish onslaught is too fortuitous to be entirely unplanned, and it
is possible that both Scots and Danes were united in their efforts. The meeting with Edgar Æðeling at Wearmouth is likely to have been part of an
attempt to co-ordinate operations and, possibly, to reach agreement on
objectives. Why, then, did Máel Coluim turn north instead of prosecuting
his advantage as Edgar must surely have hoped? The answer is the lack of
progress that was being made in the south by Svein and William's willingness to reach a settlement with the Danes. The failure of the rising to spread
more widely, even among the Anglo-Scandinavian population of East
Anglia, may have persuaded Svein that he had embarked on a venture that
would be costly to him in terms of manpower and resources to pursue.
When William offered to negotiate, Svein was ready to come to terms and,
probably having swallowed another substantial cash bribe, the Danish king
withdrew his men and left England.[35] Together, the Scots and the Danes
might have succeeded, but Máel Coluim was unwilling to take his chances
alone. It was probably news of Svein's treaty with William that prompted
the Scottish withdrawal and, presumably, was also the factor which decided
Edgar on flight to Europe.

The arrival of Edgar, his mother and sisters once more in Scotland late in
1070 may not have been entirely the accident that Symeon recorded. Máel
Coluim was the only one of Edgar's former associates who had not come to
terms with William, and the exiled prince may have attempted to persuade
him to maintain his support for his cause. According to traditional accounts,
most of which were recorded in the late eleventh or early twelfth centuries,
Máel Coluim 'began to yearn' for the elder of Edgar's sisters, Margaret.[36]
The *Anglo-Saxon Chronicle*'s version of Máel Coluim's pursuit of Margaret,
which probably derives from a later hagiography of Margaret,[37] presents
Edgar, his men and his sister as opposed to the marriage proposal, Margaret
on the grounds that she wished to become a nun. Máel Coluim persisted in
his pursuit of the arrangement until Edgar eventually agreed, and Margaret
yielded shortly afterwards, supposedly won over to what was a divine plan
to 'direct the king from his erring path'. The marriage, it seems, was cele-
brated before the end of the year.[38]

The significance of the marriage of Máel Coluim and Margaret was
immense. It immediately changed the nature of Scottish interest in the

continuing efforts of the exiled Anglo-Saxon lords to regain the English throne for Edgar, for so long as the prince remained unmarried and childless it raised the possibility that any children of the marriage would stand as heir to their uncle's claims. It is probable that the naming of Máel Coluim and Margaret's children was made with an eye towards the longer-term recovery of the English throne for a descendant of the West Saxon kings, to make them more acceptable to their Anglo-Saxon subjects, for their four eldest sons were named Edward, Edmund, Æðelred and Edgar after Margaret's paternal ancestors from father to great-great-grandfather and the switch to classical or biblical names for their two remaining sons, Alexander (the greatest pagan ruler) and David (the Hebrew epitome of Godly kingship), was perhaps brought about because the next West Saxon name in the sequence would have been Edmund once again, then Edward. The naming of the first four sons may reflect a period when Donnchad or Domnall (Máel Coluim and Ingibjorg's sons) were expected to succeed to the throne of Alba and that the 'Margaretssons' were intended to replace the Normans when the revolution came south of the border. The switch to Alexander was necessary on one level because the next person in the pedigree would have been another Edmund, but it may also reflect a recognition that all realistic hopes of reversing the Norman conquest of England had ended, perhaps after the execution of Earl Waltheof of Northumbria in 1076. This switch in naming styles over to the wholly alien cultural forms of the Anglo-Saxons can also be read as marking a decisive shift in the cultural influences at work on the king in the early part of his reign. Down to around 1070, Máel Coluim's outlook appears to have been shaped strongly by Scandinavian influences, which were possibly a legacy of his years of exile and were certainly strengthened through his marriage to Ingibjorg. After 1070, Máel Coluim's horizons widened vastly as Margaret introduced her own ideas and experiences into a still conservative, Gaelic kingdom.

There is a wide divergence of opinion as to the degree of the queen's influence over her husband and his policies. Medieval commentators saw her as a civilising power who exercised a tremendous influence over her doting but culturally uncouth and unsophisticated husband. Post-Reformation her reputation declined sharply, as Margaret was seen as the instrument through which the supposedly malign influence of the Roman Catholic Church was imposed on the allegedly simpler and purer traditions of the native 'Celtic' Church, a sinister role which was used as a weapon in the religious controversies of nineteenth-century Scotland where various brands of Protestantism tried to claim the heritage of the Church that Margaret had

supposedly been instrumental in destroying. In the twentieth century the
controversy surrounding Margaret took a new twist as historians debated
the significance of her alleged reformist programme in the Scottish
Church.[39] Margaret has been presented as something of a religious revolutionary, who introduced into Scotland the full force of the great reformist
movement that was sweeping through the western European Church, but
her behaviour shows no clear attachment to the reformist trends that were
emanating from Italy and Burgundy in the later eleventh century. She had,
however, been brought up amidst the spiritual fervour of recently converted
Hungary, where the western European missionaries were still actively pros-
elytising for Christ amidst the Magyars, and had personal experience of the
religious regeneration on the continent that was driven by the supporters of
the great abbey of Cluny in Burgundy. Always bearing in mind that our
principal source of information for Margaret's career in Scotland, and especially as a religious reformer, was produced by her own former chaplain and
confessor, Turgot, who identified himself firmly with the cause of reform
and who would go on to be Bishop of St Andrews in the early twelfth century,[40] it is evident that the queen took an active role in ecclesiastical affairs
that went beyond what was expected of a woman at this time. Turgot's *Vita
Margareti*,[41] written at the request of her daughter, Henry I of England's
wife, Matilda, who was herself taking a very high profile role in the religious
reform movement in early twelfth-century England and was seeking guid-
ance on queenly behaviour in the example of her mother, reveals a certain
eclecticism on Margaret's part in her religious tastes. Margaret, it tells us,
found much that she saw as backward and inadequate by continental standards, but also found much to venerate and support in Scottish traditions,
especially the eremitical and ascetic aspects, and she became a noted bene-
factress of the centre of the native Church at St Andrews.[42] The image
which emerges is hardly that of a scheming revolutionary set on the
destruction of native traditions in the Church.

   Turgot's record of Margaret's direct involvement in the reform process is
limited to a rather brief account of a single council of the leading clergy of
the Scottish Church, which she assembled with her husband's aid.[43] Máel
Coluim, Turgot notes, acted as her interpreter during the assembly.
Although Turgot reports that she organised many such councils, he only
gives details relating to this one occasion and the report that he offers has
been treated with some suspicion as its programme reads very much like
the business with which he was involved as Bishop of St Andrews after
1107.[44] The matters discussed may seem rather trivial today, but at the time

were clearly issues of great controversy, as they diverged from the uniformity of practice which was being imposed on the western Church at that
time and which would eventually see the drawing together of regional and
national traditions into a single code of canon law practice. Margaret's
reforming councils must be seen in the context of this trend.

Margaret has also been assigned the distinction of pioneering the reform
of the monastic tradition in Scotland as part of her overall aim of reforming
the Church. This is a rather ambitious claim to make, for, as mentioned
above, she displayed a strong personal attachment to several aspects of the
native monastic traditions which she encountered, and the alternative that
she encouraged was small-scale and did not survive her death in 1093. She
did, however, with Máel Coluim's support, write to Archbishop Lanfranc at
Canterbury to request his aid, possibly recognising that the wider reform
of the Scottish Church required an injection of outside influence rather
than depending entirely on any reformist trend within the native Church.[45]
Margaret's letter does not survive, but Lanfranc's reply does.[46] In it, it is made
clear that Margaret had written to Lanfranc, reporting on the reforms being
undertaken in Scotland but also pointing to the limits on what she could
achieve without aid. In response to her request for assistance, Lanfranc dis-
patched Goldwine and two other monks from the Benedictine priory
attached to his cathedral. These, it emerges from later accounts, formed the
basis for a new Benedictine community attached to the church of the Holy
Trinity at Dunfermline.[47] In the past, some historians have taken a rather
dismissive view of the significance of this foundation, presenting it as small-
scale and unimaginative.[48] That view, however, fails entirely to see the
context within which this first colony of Benedictines in Scotland operated
and, while it did not perhaps take root in the manner in which Benedictine
monasticism and its reformist principles had in England,[49] the fact that
Margaret made a direct appeal to the most eminent reformist clergyman at
whose cathedral one of the key centres of Benedictine reform was based
demonstrates a keen awareness of the profound changes underway south of
the border.[50]

Much has been made of the failure of Margaret's personal efforts in support of the reform movement to become established and their quick demise
in the upheavals which followed Máel Coluim's and her death in 1093. In
response, it has to be said that her real legacy was in the work of her surviving children, all of whom in some way demonstrated a deep and enduring
personal commitment to religious reform and strong personal piety, and
who re-established and expanded greatly upon their mother and father's

earlier foundation. As Turgot makes clear, Margaret literally had the fear of God thrashed into her children:

> She gave no less care to her sons than to herself, so that they should be brought up with every attention, and instructed as far as is possible in honourable ways. And because she knew that it is written, 'he who spares the rod hates his son,' she had directed the steward of the household to restrain them himself with threats and whippings whenever they erred in infantile naughtiness, as is young children's way. Through this scrupulous care of their mother, as children they excelled in uprightness of manners many who were more advanced in age: they were ever kind and peaceful among themselves, and the younger everywhere showed honour to the elder. Thus, even at the celebration of mass, when they went forward after their parents to the offering, the younger by no means ventured to go before the elder; but in order of age the elder used to precede the younger.[51]

One of her sons, Æðelred, may have been destined from his early years for a career in the Church, becoming Abbot of Dunkeld. Edmund ended his days as a Cluniac monk in Somerset. Edgar was a noted patron of the church of Durham and supporter of the Benedictines. Yet it was the two youngest boys, Alexander and David who brought to fruition the programme set in place by their parents in the reforms which they instituted in the period 1107-1153 (see below chapter nine). David, the youngest, may have been least exposed to his mother's influence in terms of time, but her personality may have made an even more powerful impression on him given the traumatic upheavals which engulfed the young prince with the death of both of his parents in November 1093. Nor should the religious roles of Máel Coluim and Margaret's two daughters be forgotten, although these only influenced Scotland indirectly through their inspiration to David. The family had a remarkable commitment to the reformist programme.

This focus on Margaret's impact on the religious life of Scotland after 1070 should not obscure the fact that her influence extended into many other areas. The events after her death, when there was a strongly hostile reaction to the foreign cultural influences which she imported, have tended to lead to an exaggeration of their extent but not of their significance. Margaret's arrival in Scotland represented part of an important refugee movement which may have been small in number, but which had an altogether disproportionate impact in terms of influence. Although the numbers of high-status refugees from England were small, their concentration at

court and in southern Fife and Lothian probably gave them regular access
to the king and manifold opportunities to restructure his household and its
organisation. Margaret, of course, had unique access to her husband, but
Máel Coluim was not unwilling to embrace the cultural innovations which
she brought. It is clear that Máel Coluim was no fool, and he understood
well the opportunities for an extension of Scottish power which his marriage to Margaret brought. He was probably very keen to see his children
educated in his wife's cultural traditions, for this would have no doubt made
them more acceptable to their potential subjects in England, as would their
Anglo-Saxon names. Turgot indicates that Máel Coluim venerated
Margaret's every act and supported her efforts to introduce the sophistication of the Old English monarchy to the warrior household of the Gaelic
king of Scots.[52] Those efforts may have included encouragement to foreign
traders to bring their exotic finery and rich goods to Scotland, thereby providing an early stimulus to Scottish trade, for the fine materials and artefacts
to which she was used were not available readily in Scotland.[53] With these
new imports she brought a semblance of the richness of the continental and
English courts at which she had been raised, and they were used to support
the elaborate ceremonial, based on English models, which had surrounded
the Old English monarchy. This elaboration extended into the very presentation of the food at ceremonial banquets and in the manners of those
serving at table, although native Gaelic officers such as the *rannaire*, or
divider of the meat, continued to hold their place into the middle of the
twelfth century. In dress and fashions, too, she attempted to remodel her
husband and his court, introducing continental clothing styles and hairstyles
for the king and his courtiers. All of this may seem to be little more than
cosmetic tinkering, but it was tinkering that many among the Gaelic
nobility found too much to swallow. When the king and his wife were dead,
the fashionable aura of the court and the exotic clothing of the royal household were among the most obvious casualties of the conservative Gaelic
reaction.

Down to 1070, the Normans had lacked the extended military reach to
strike against Scotland, and, for as long as Máel Coluim showed no inclina-
tion to indulge in anything other than plundering raids into territory
which William himself lacked any effective hold over, they had little cause
to launch an offensive while so much of England was still only loosely controlled. The marriage of Máel Coluim and Margaret changed all that, for
William must have readily understood its implications for his control of
England. Máel Coluim had to be either neutralised or contained. In 1072,

William advanced on Scotland by land and sea, crossed the Forth and advanced into the heartland of Alba. At Abernethy on the Tay, the two kings met and discussed peace terms. Having received Máel Coluim's homage (or Máel Coluim would have at least become William's 'man' in the way that earlier kings of Alba had accepted the superiority of the West Saxon kings), and having taken important hostages including Donnchad, the king's eldest son by his first marriage, the Conqueror withdrew from Scotland.[54]

William appeared to have achieved much at the limited cost to himself of a few vills granted for the Scottish king's maintenance when he attended the English king's court. Máel Coluim had been neutralised as a threat, at least for the time being, thereby depriving Edgar Æðeling of strong external support for another bid on the throne. Norman power, too, had been projected far to the north of York and William felt able on his homeward journey to deprive the fickle Gospatric of his earldom of Northumbria.[55] Gospatric, who was Máel Coluim's cousin in the paternal line and a great-grandson of King Æðelred II of England (Margaret's grandfather), was eventually received in Scotland and granted Dunbar and extensive estates in Lothian which had originally formed the northern portion of his own lost earldom of Northumbria.[56] In his place in Northumbria, William installed Waltheof, son of Siward, the representative of the alternative line of northern earls, whom he was to bind closely to the royal house through marriage to his niece, Judith.[57] Gospatric's return from Flanders may have been in the hope of enlisting Scottish help against this interloper, and in 1074 Edgar Æðeling also returned to his brother-in-law's kingdom, apparently against the terms of the 1072 treaty, and worked hard to persuade him to launch yet another attack on England.[58] Although he and Margaret received Edgar with great honour, Máel Coluim was not to be persuaded; he had seen Norman power and understood its potential, but had also secured a settlement which had probably recognised his possession of the territory that he had recovered in Lothian and Cumbria in the 1060s. These were gains not to be thrown away lightly. Instead, at Máel Coluim's urging, Edgar sailed for France to accept an offer of a lordship from which he could attack William's territory but, shipwrecked on his way, he lost most of his men and equipment and barely escaped back to Scotland. On Máel Coluim's advice, Edgar set out once again, but this time for Normandy, where he made his peace with William.[59]

For William, it must have seemed that Edgar's submission at Máel Coluim's urging demonstrated the effectiveness of his settlement in 1072, and signalled an end to his concerns over the security of his grip in northern England. On both counts he was to be proven badly mistaken, for around the same time that Edgar was entering William's peace, the king's most recent attempt to resolve the perennial question of the government of Northumbria was beginning to unravel spectacularly. Before the end of 1074, Earl Waltheof was in open revolt, linked with a rebellion by the Norman earls of East Anglia and Hereford and expecting aid from a Danish fleet – but not from the king of Scots.[60] It was a rising that depended on close co-ordination between the allies, but when their planning began to break down, the whole rebellion fell apart and Waltheof threw himself on William's mercy. After at first making conciliatory gestures, William ordered Waltheof's arrest, forfeiture and imprisonment, before finally having him executed in 1076. Although he had been stripped of Northumbria, his widow Judith had been allowed to keep his great Midlands earldom of Huntingdon and Northampton, which passed eventually to Waltheof and Judith's daughter, Matilda. In 1076, few men could have foreseen that this child would marry an as yet unborn son of Máel Coluim, king of Scots, and his wife Margaret who would use Matilda's paternal claim as an excuse to launch a war that would extend the Scottish border southwards to the Tees and, for a time, almost to the gates of York.

Máel Coluim evidently played no part in the rebellion in England, either in support of the rebels or as William's 'man'. Nor does William appear to have expected him to do anything, perhaps, other than to maintain his inaction. In 1079, however, Máel Coluim finally broke his peace with the English king and launched a devastating raid deep into Northumbria, penetrating as far south as the Tyne.[61] The raid had, perhaps, been timed to perfection, for William was engaged in a war against his rebellious eldest son, Robert, in Normandy, and his appointee as Earl in Northumbria, Walcher, Bishop of Durham, evidently lacked military leadership skills to conduct an effective defence. Unlike his experience in 1070 when Gospatric had harried his plunder-laden men on their homeward journey, Máel Coluim's army penetrated deep into English territory and withdrew without encountering any serious opposition. Bishop Walcher's failure to defend his earldom may have been the major factor in turning the Northumbrians against him. Having alienated his subjects by ordering the assassination of his erstwhile Northumbrian right-hand man, the bishop and his followers were massacred by the kin and supporters of the dead man on 13 or 14 May 1080 at Gateshead.[62] It was this outrage rather than Máel Coluim's raids that William set out to punish in summer 1080, but the Scottish raids could not go unanswered. While William's uncle, Odo, the warrior-bishop of Bayeux, harried Northumbria, William sent his son, Robert, with whom he had been newly reconciled, into Scotland to bring Máel Coluim to heel.[63] The chronicle accounts are fairly dismissive of Robert's achievement in Scotland, but it appears that in a meeting at Falkirk he and Máel Coluim agreed a renewal of the 1072 treaty. The Scottish king had escaped once again without suffering any significant check to his power.

As he returned to the south, Robert ordered the construction of a fortress on the north bank of the river Tyne opposite Gateshead, where Bishop Walcher had been killed the previous year. This stronghold – the New Castle on Tyne – quickly established itself as one of the key fortresses of Northumberland, control of which would become essential for any would-be lord of the province. Although Robert's campaign was dismissed as ineffectual, the building of Newcastle to control the lowest crossing-point of the Tyne represented a significant northern extension of Norman power, quite literally establishing a bridgehead in the rebellious earldom and a bastion of royal authority in the district between Durham and the chief seat of the earldom at Bamburgh. It also became a springboard from which further advances were made, and in the course of the 1080s Norman lordly settlement of the country north of the river Tees and east of the Pennine Hills proceeded apace, much of it directed by the new Norman earl to whom Northumberland was entrusted, Robert de Mowbray.[64] Although the consolidation of the king's hold over Northumberland would take until the 1120s to secure, under Earl Robert's direction, Norman knights were settled on Northumbrian estates and the beginnings were made to a network of castles that would greatly strengthen the conquerors' hold on this northernmost extremity of the kingdom. Should Máel Coluim invade again, he would find the military landscape transformed.

Máel Coluim did adhere to the peace for over a decade, refusing even to attempt to capitalise on the political uncertainty in England which followed the death of William I and the accession of William II Rufus or the rebellion in favour of Duke Robert of Normandy in 1088. There is, moreover, no sign that Máel Coluim offered any submission to the new English king: he was not William Rufus' 'man' in the way that he had been for William the Conqueror. This failure by the Scottish king to renew his submission cannot have been welcome to William Rufus, but so long as Máel Coluim did not intervene in the crisis in the north that erupted in 1088 he was ready to accept the situation. Máel Coluim, too, may have adopted a 'live-and-let-live' attitude, willing to maintain the peace provided he was not provoked. He cannot, however, have been comfortable with the steady tightening of the English king's grip on the northern parts of England after 1088 which had seen new lordships established west of the Pennines to bring Norman power into the Lakeland fringe. There are, however, reports of growing friction between the two kings, which led to quarrels and a breakdown of the rapprochement which had been established in the latter part of William I's reign.[65] The friction may have come from a change in policy on William Rufus's part similar to that on the Welsh March, where his nobles were authorised to expand their territory at the expense of the Welsh princes. The final catalyst, however, may not have been any action in northern England, but William Rufus's abrogation in 1091 of his father's settlement with Edgar Æðeling, confiscation of Edgar's Norman properties and Edgar's subsequent flight to Scotland.[66] It was only then, in May 1091 when William Rufus was still absent in Normandy, that Máel Coluim launched his assault on the north of England.[67] This attack appears to have been more than merely an opportunist plundering raid, for the Scots seem to have settled down to besiege Durham, probably rightly identifying the bishop's castle there as the key to control of the country north of the river Tees.[68] This was a new policy for the Scots and it suggests that the king recognised that the enhanced position of the Normans in the north was more than just an inconvenience: it had become a threat. The invasion of 1091, therefore, should perhaps be seen as a bid to take control of the region between the rivers Tweed and Tees, thereby placing a broad buffer between Norman power in Yorkshire and the heartland of the Scottish kingdom.

Máel Coluim's invasion was viewed as being sufficiently serious for William Rufus to hurry back from Normandy in late August accompanied by his brother, Duke Robert, and a major army and fleet.[69] News of the approaching army forced Máel Coluim to abandon his siege of Durham in early September and withdraw towards his own kingdom.[70] William Rufus, however, was not to be deterred from securing a more satisfactory outcome to his own campaign and, despite the loss of his fleet in an equinoctial storm on 29 September, continued his advance. Unlike in 1072 and 1079, Máel Coluim chose to advance to meet the English king in Northumberland, but there was to be no fighting on this occasion either. Instead, Edgar Æðeling and Duke Robert brokered a fresh peace between the two kings, whereby Máel Coluim became William Rufus' 'man' and made oaths of submission to him, while in turn William Rufus promised to restore to the Scottish king the land in England which Máel Coluim had held before. Edgar Æðeling was also reconciled with William Rufus, which may have been his main objective in stirring up the conflict in the first place. Peace had been restored and all parties appeared to have gained from the new treaty, but the English king's duplicitous and mercurial character must have raised the question in the minds of some observers of how long the settlement would last.

Already by the early months of 1092 there were indications that William Rufus was reneging on the bargain, and the issue appears to have been the land that he had promised to restore to Máel Coluim. Traditionally, the reason for the final breach in the relationship between Máel Coluim and William Rufus has been presented as the English king's failure to honour the 1091 treaty through his seizure in 1092 of Carlisle, his building of a castle there and his plantation of an English colony in the surrounding district.[71] This view is predicated on the assumption that Máel Coluim controlled this portion of Cumbria, which came to be known subsequently as Cumberland, in the years down to 1092.[72] There is, however, no evidence to support the view that the ruler of Carlisle expelled by William Rufus in that year had been either an appointee of, or in some way dependent upon, Máel Coluim, and there is no suggestion in any contemporary account that the Scottish king was aggrieved by the English seizure of the place. Certainly, when Máel Coluim made his approach to William Rufus in summer 1093, the purpose of his embassy is stated explicitly to have been the honouring of the terms of the 1091 treaty.[73] Although William Kapelle identified the restoration of twelve vills in England that had been held by Máel Coluim in the time of William I and which probably represented properties intended to support the Scottish king when he came on his occasional visits to the English court, he failed to link these estates with the broken agreement referred to in 1093. Instead, he suggested that the twelve vills, possibly an error for shires, was in fact Cumberland, and that Máel Coluim had expected to be given back control of that territory which he had somehow lost at an unspecified date after 1070.[74] There is no need, however, to construct so elaborate a scenario, for Máel Coluim was simply seeking the implementation of a part of the 1091 peace. What led to the dramatic breakdown in the negotiations between the two kings was William Rufus's unyielding stance with regard to the vills and his supposedly insulting treatment of Máel Coluim.[75]

There is little in the evidence we have for the events of the second half of 1093 to indicate that the year would end in violence and bloodshed. Máel Coluim had sent messengers to William Rufus to ask that he honour the agreement between them and, as we shall explore in chapter three, possibly to press the English king on other diplomatic issues. William Rufus does not appear to have been planning any rebuff and his behaviour seems to have been genuinely conciliatory.[76] The English king summoned Máel Coluim to a meeting at Gloucester in August, sending hostages as surety for Máel Coluim's safety while in England and then following this up with a mission led by Edgar Æðeling when the Scottish king seems to have still demurred. Edgar's persuasion appears to have worked, and Máel Coluim started the journey south with an impressive escort. All of this effort suggests that William Rufus was not planning simply to insult and rebuff the king of Scots and that there was a genuine prospect of a satisfactory conclusion to the diplomatic rift through negotiation. Máel Coluim certainly appears to have been looking for peace and reconciliation, for his southward journey paused at Durham, where he attended the ceremony on 11 August for laying the first foundation stones of the new cathedral, presided over by Bishop William and Prior Turgot, the latter the former chaplain and confessor to Queen Margaret.[77] Only two years previously, the Scots had subjected the city to a six-month siege; now Máel Coluim was an honoured guest in a great religious ceremony there. It may be that the ageing king was seeking to build bridges with the new power in northern England, or was displaying that he had come to terms with the new political realities which anchored Northumbria firmly into the Anglo-Norman realm, or perhaps he was seeking to win friends who could speak on his behalf in what he suspected might be a less-than-friendly meeting with William Rufus.

It took less than a fortnight for Máel Coluim to travel from Durham to Gloucester for 24 August, possibly also making a detour via Wilton Abbey in Wiltshire to visit his daughter Edith there (see p.54).[78] After all the elaborate arrangements and the honour shown to the Scottish king by the escorts sent to accompany him south, William Rufus refused to meet with him or even allow the business to be discussed unless Máel Coluim submitted his claims to William's court. This was, as far as Máel Coluim was concerned, a calculated insult, for to submit to the judgement of the English barons would have reduced him to the level of a vassal of the English crown. He might be prepared to be William Rufus's 'man', but he was not prepared to become his vassal. Máel Coluim's response was to demand that the issue be laid before a joint court of the two kingdoms assembled on the border between them, as was, so he claimed, the tradition in such cases. Receiving no satisfactory answer, Máel Coluim left Gloucester in a fury and returned to Scotland.

Máel Coluim probably arrived back in Scotland towards the end of the first week in September. According to the chronicle accounts, he immediately raised his war-bands and, accompanied by Edward, his eldest son by Margaret, launched raids into northern England, probably towards the end of October.[79] Whether the invading army was inadequate to the task or not,[80] it set about ravaging Northumberland at the onset of winter, bringing the threat of starvation to the peasant communities, whose winter stores were burned, driven or carried off. The *Anglo-Saxon Chronicle* comments that the brutality of the harrying was of no credit to Máel Coluim[81] and, given his recent honoured reception at Durham, must have made him appear to be a faithless hypocrite in the eyes of at least the ecclesiastical elite of northern England. Shortly before mid-November, the Scottish raiding force was heading for home when, on 12 November, it encountered a body of Norman knights, commanded by Robert de Mowbray, at Alnwick, some fourteen miles south of the Norman earl's stronghold at Bamburgh. What ensued is shrouded in myth and propaganda, much of it coloured by subsequent events. According to the *Anglo-Saxon Chronicle* account of the event, the Normans ambushed the king and his party, and Robert's nephew, Arkil Morel, steward of Bamburgh and a 'compater' (a God-relative, gossip or comrade) of Máel Coluim, slew the king.[82] After nearly forty years of opportunist manoeuvring, brinkmanship and violence, the Scottish king's luck had finally run out.

Throughout the narrative of this final raid on England there is a strong tradition of entrapment and betrayal. That tradition, however, focuses on Earl Robert and Arkil Morel, not, as some would have it, on William Rufus.[83] The English king may have acted dishonourably in his insulting behaviour towards Máel Coluim at Gloucester, but he does not appear to have intentionally driven the Scottish king into war. There was no preconceived grand strategy to trick Máel Coluim into an ill-considered attack on Northumberland, where a foregathered army waited to ambush and destroy him. Máel Coluim, however, clearly considered that war was the only recourse open to him after 24 August and, after all, it had generally brought him a satisfactory result when the English kings had moved against him, for in the past they had always preferred to negotiate rather than fight, and he had always succeeded in holding on to the territory which he had recovered in the 1050s and early 1060s in the country between the rivers Tweed and Forth. In 1093, however, it was very different. It was not a royal army that was advancing to meet him, commanded by a king with one eye always looking behind him to the many troublespots and flashpoints around his restless realm, but a local levy commanded by a man who had witnessed the harrying of his own economic resources. Earl Robert may or may not have resorted to treachery in achieving his desired objective, but what he did was an act of revenge for the wasting of his lands, not one of a paid assassin of the English king.

CHAPTER TWO

The Struggle for Scotland 1093–97

M áel Coluim's death outside Alnwick was but the first of a succession of blows to his family that would shake loose its grip from the throne of Scotland. The king had been accompanied on his raid by his eldest son by Queen Margaret, Edward, whom he had already designated as his successor in preference to Donnchad, his surviving son by his first marriage,¹ and apparently also by their fourth son, Edgar. In 1093, Edward was aged about twenty-two and had probably already gained experience of warfare in the course of his father's raids into Northumberland in 1091. Nevertheless, as the king's designated successor, it is probable that he had participated in what was intended principally as a plundering raid in order to gain greater experience of command and to forge personal links with the warriors who would provide the firm foundation of his power in future years. Edward was involved in the thick of the fighting and was carried badly wounded from the field by the fleeing remnants of Máel Coluim's warband. Two days later, on 15 November, he died of his injuries. The crisis of Máel Coluim's death was turned into a disaster by the death also of his designated heir, for while the old king had lived he had been able to impose his decision on the destination of the throne among his family on the Scottish nobilty, and the likelihood that his successor would be an adult and experienced man may have served to strengthen his hand against those who saw his plans for the succession as a dangerous innovation. With Máel Coluim and Edward both dead, the whole question of the succession was once again blown wide open.

For Máel Coluim's children and for the old king's close circle of councillors, supporters and dependents, the crisis quickly worsened. A strong-willed woman such as Queen Margaret might have succeeded in holding her family together and offered effective leadership to the court party who had gathered around her husband. Margaret, however, had been in failing health for some time,[2] and had been largely confined to her bed in the royal fortress at Edinburgh since before the king and her sons had ridden south. The rumour of Máel Coluim and Edward's deaths, confirmed four days after the skirmish by Edgar, proved to be fatal to her. According to her biographer, she rallied for long enough to hear Edgar's report of the events at Alnwick before expiring. In just four days, the three central figures in the leadership of the kingdom and the individuals to whom the rest of the family had looked had been removed. While leadership of the surviving children of Máel Coluim and Margaret would now have devolved upon Edmund, who would have been aged about twenty, the question of who should succeed as king was a less certain matter.

Fourteenth-century tradition claims that Edmund and his siblings almost immediately found themselves besieged in Edinburgh Castle by the supporters of their uncle, Domnall Bán.[3] In accordance with the traditional Gaelic succession practice, Domnall, as eldest male representative of the royal kindred, could have expected to succeed his brother. Máel Coluim, however, had passed over him, and his own sons by Ingibjorg, in favour of Edward. The whereabouts of Domnall in November 1093 are unknown, but he does not seem to have accompanied his brother on the raid into England. It is unlikely, however, that he was in a position to gather his friends and make a bid for the throne so rapidly. Nor is it likely that he would have attacked Edinburgh before having first secured his own inauguration at Scone. The earliest surviving account of Margaret's death and burial, which forms the concluding section of the final chapter of the *Vita Margareti*, states simply that her enshrouded body was taken to Dunfermline and buried by the altar of the church there.[4] Had her corpse and her children been besieged in the castle, it might be assumed that some mention of the fact might have been made by her biographer or his correspondents. John of Fordoun's tale of Margaret's shrouded corpse being smuggled down from a postern at the western end of the castle rock by her children, concealed from the besiegers by a miraculous mist and carried for burial to the church which she and Máel Coluim had built at Dunfermline, should be dismissed therefore as a myth that developed as part of the saintly legend around the queen.

There is broad agreement in our surviving sources over the course of events that followed. According to the *Anglo-Saxon Chronicle*, whose compiler had a keen interest in the fate of the surviving representatives of the West Saxon dynasty, the Scots chose Domnall as their king 'and drove out all the English who were with king Malcolm before.'[5] By 'the Scots', the chronicler presumably meant the leading Gaelic magnates of the kingdom, and 'the English' can be taken to refer to the Anglo-Saxon refugees who had trickled in to Scotland in the years after 1066, and who formed a small but highly visible group clustered around Máel Coluim and Margaret. This was a political rather than a racially motivated act, for the late eleventh-century Scottish kingdom already contained a substantial and long-established English-speaking population in Lothian. Its target was precise: those who had been 'with' Máel Coluim, i.e. those who could have been expected to look to Margaret's children for leadership and who would have formed the core of any group likely to have advanced the candidacy for the throne of the next heir of that line. Domnall's supporters were taking a simple precautionary step to remove a potential source of threat to their chosen king.

If Máel Coluim and Margaret's surviving sons had not already fled with 'the English', their position within Scotland would have become dangerously exposed once Domnall had assumed the kingship. Control of the strategic fortress at Edinburgh could have given them some hope of maintaining a foothold in the kingdom, but it is likely that the nobility of the Gaelic heartlands to the north and west of the River Forth had thrown their backing firmly behind Domnall. The fourteenth-century account of events offered by John of Fordoun claims that the children's uncle, Edgar Æðeling, recognised the danger which his surviving nephews and nieces were in and arranged for them to be escorted to safety in England.[6] There is no corroborating evidence for this story: earlier accounts simply state that Domnall drove his brother's children into exile,[7] and, as has already been suggested, it is possible that Edith had been in her aunt's care in England since as early as 1086 and that both she and her younger sister, Mary, were at Wilton Abbey before 1093.

It was perhaps early in 1094 that David and his elder brothers arrived at the court of William Rufus, probably at Hastings where the king was waiting for favourable weather for his crossing to Normandy. It was a cruel twist of fate that the sons of Máel Coluim should have to come as supplicants for aid to the very man whose actions over the last two years had precipitated the final crisis that had resulted in their father's death. The irony of that situation cannot have been lost on the English king, but he was opportunist enough to make the maximum political capital from this turn of events. The brothers, however, had arrived too late, for William had already recognised the potential in the position in Scotland for him to establish a degree of control over his unpredictable northern neighbour. William would help one of Máel Coluim's sons to win the Scottish throne, but it was not to be one of the Margaretsons.

William already had his own tame Scot to advance as a challenger against Domnall. Donnchad mac Máel Coluim had been among the hostages given to William the Conqueror following the peace negotiations at Abernethy in 1072.[8] He had remained as a hostage at the Anglo-Norman court until 1087, when he was freed by the new king, William Rufus, shortly after his coronation.[9] Donnchad was by upbringing effectively a Norman nobleman, and his identification with Norman aristocratic culture had been completed by William's bestowal of knightly status on him, probably at the time of his release, when the *Anglo-Saxon Chronicle* states that the English king 'honoured [Donnchad] with military arms'. There is no indication that Donnchad chose to return to his homeland and certainly little sign that Máel Coluim was, in turn, interested in the fate of his eldest son other than to make it clear that he did not consider him to be his automatic successor as king. Indeed, Donnchad probably considered it likely that his father had already decided on the destination of his throne and the implication in the *Anglo-Saxon Chronicle* account of the events of 1093–94 is that he had remained close to the English court.[10] If, however, Máel Coluim had not already designated Edward as his *tanaiste* by 1087, then Donnchad's decision to remain in England must surely have quickly settled his father's mind on the matter. Máel Coluim, however, probably understood the strength of a possible future claim by Donnchad, for his decision to designate Edward is as much an unequivocal rejection of the rights of his eldest surviving child as it is a recognition of those of his first son of his second marriage.[11] Clearly, the old king had sought to avoid the weakness and division for his kingdom that a disputed succession would have entailed.

In 1094, Donnchad would have been in his mid-thirties, a warrior at the height of his powers and probably a man of qualities known to William Rufus. In contrast, his eldest surviving half-brother, Edmund, was a youth of about twenty, untried and, more tellingly, a possible rival for the throne of Donnchad's erstwhile patron. It is unlikely that Donnchad had ever met any of his half-brothers before their flight to England, and it is pointless to speculate on what emotions they felt when they first came face to face, but it must have been very clear to the Margaretsons that they held a subordinate place in Donnchad's plans. When Donnchad went to William Rufus, offered him his military service in return for a grant of his father's kingdom, and swore fealty to the English king when he bestowed Scotland on him,[12] Edmund, Æðelred, Edgar, Alexander and David had no choice but to recognise their half-brother's right to the throne. In late spring 1094, when Donnchad marched north, he may have been accompanied by his elder half-brothers, but the younger boys remained behind at the English court, hostages in all but name and living insurance policies for William should his chosen candidate's bid end in failure.

William could not send Donnchad to Scotland backed by a full English army, as he himself was about to embark for Normandy on what was to become a protracted struggle for control of the duchy with his elder brother, Duke Robert. Instead, he permitted his protégé to canvas what support he could among the Norman nobility of England, with whom Donnchad would have been on familiar terms. Probably won over by promises of land and titles in Scotland should they triumph over Domnall, a number of knights joined his expedition. Donnchad also courted saintly aid for his bid for the crown, granting charters, witnessed by his half-brother Edgar, to the monks of St Cuthbert at Durham as he marched north.[13] No detail survives of the campaign which followed, but in May or June 1094, he defeated his uncle, drove him from the heartland of the kingdom, and was proclaimed king in his stead.[14] Donnchad's rule, however, was founded on a military conquest and, despite his ancestry, he appears to have enjoyed no significant support within his new kingdom. Instead, he remained dependent on the 'English and French' who had formed his army. Among these may have been members of that same group of Anglo-Saxons who had been driven from Scotland the previous year, possibly including important members of the exiled Northumbrian House of Bamburgh. As Donnchad's gifts to the monks of Durham indicate, he was keen to secure support from within Northumbria.[15] Earl Cospatric of Northumbria had been a major beneficiary of Máel Coluim's generosity, and his family would have been major losers as a result of the anti-English reaction in 1093. Mutual interest dictated that there should be co-operation between Donnchad and Cospatric's sons, and this is reflected in Donnchad's marriage to Octreda, daughter of Cospatric's younger son, Waltheof.[16] There is no record of when the marriage occurred, but it had taken place long enough before his campaign for the couple to have had more than one child, referred to as *mea infantes* in his charter to Durham.[17] Expedient though such a marriage may have been in securing Donnchad's grip over the southern portion of his kingdom where Northumbrian influence was strong, it did nothing to establish his position within the Gaelic heartland of Alba and may have served rather to sharpen the fears of those who had reacted against English influence six months before.

Donnchad may have over-estimated the scale of his victory in summer 1094 and under-estimated the depth of the hostility of the Scottish nobility to his 'English and French' supporters, who at this time may have included his half-brothers. There are suggestions in the sources that Donnchad may have promised Edmund an appanage, possibly in the country south of the Forth, and this reintroduction of the leading male of the line expelled in favour of Domnall Bán could have been a factor in galvanising the reaction against his rule.[18] Later in the year, the Scots staged a rising which does not seem to have been directed chiefly at deposing Donnchad but at removing his foreign allies.[19] Again, we have no surviving account of precisely what happened, but Donnchad was defeated and the majority of his military backers slain. Following this defeat, the Scots indicated to him that they were prepared to accept him as their king but on the condition that he expel his remaining foreign supporters and seek no more military aid from England.[20] Donnchad had little choice but to accept their terms, but without his knights he had no means of maintaining his position and it appears that he soon faced a rising by supporters of his uncle. While Domnall had been defeated, he had not been broken and appears to have worked through the second half of 1094 to rebuild his position. Late in the year, apparently with Domnall's connivance, Donnchad was killed by Máel Pedair, 'earl' of the Mearns,[21] and his uncle resumed the kingship. William Rufus's first bid to place a dependable vassal on the Scottish throne had ended in disaster.

Donnchad's widow may have escaped from Scotland with her children to the safety of her own family in Cumberland. There, her son William fitz Duncan, probably named in honour of William Rufus who had liberated the hostage prince in 1087 and later advanced him to the Scottish throne, was raised to manhood. In 1094, however, an infant boy was of no use to William Rufus in his plans for the control of Scotland. An alternative had to be found and, as Donnchad's only full brother, Domnall, had died in 1085,[22] the English king was forced to turn to the Margaretsons for a candidate. But the unthinkable had already happened: Edmund, the eldest of Máel Coluim and Margaret's surviving sons, had broken ranks with the rest of his family and made a deal with his uncle. Indeed, both the *Annals of Ulster* and the later twelfth-century English chronicler, William of Malmesbury, state that Edmund conspired with Domnall Bán to kill Donnchad, the latter claiming that in return Edmund gained half of the kingdom.[23] It appears that Edmund had adopted a pragmatic approach to securing his future and had recognised that Donnchad lacked the authority within Scotland to re-establish his half-siblings in the kingdom. We do not know if Domnall Bán had sons, but the Comyn family in the 1290s claimed descent from his daughter, and it is possible that Edmund capitalised on his uncle's lack of a direct male heir to regain his own place in the succession, free from the consequences of his own status as a king that dependence on William Rufus's military aid in gaining his throne would have carried. Edmund was either recognised by Domnall as his *tanaiste*, or was given a share of the kingship, a not altogether unprecedented arrangement in Scotland. The deal, however, alienated Edmund from the rest of his family and also secured the hostility of William Rufus, who was keen to see a subservient vassal, dependent on him for military backing, placed on the Scottish throne. Domnall and Edmund could not have expected William Rufus to react otherwise after the killing of Donnchad, and they quickly took steps to ally themselves with the English king's enemies, who, ironically, were led by Robert de Mowbray, Earl of Northumberland, the man responsible for killing Edmund's father. Early in 1095, Earl Robert had risen in revolt against William Rufus, and it is possible that Domnall Bán, who in effect owed his throne to the earl's successful defence of Northumberland in 1093, and Edmund, who had much to fear from the mercurial English king whose designs he had thwarted, saw in him a means of placing a convenient buffer between William Rufus and themselves. It was a predictable but hardly a wise alliance, for it ensured that the English king would move against them whenever the opportunity arose.

William Rufus was not slow in showing his hand. He had returned from Normandy in January 1095,[24] and seems quickly to have recognised Edmund's second surviving brother, Edgar, as king of Scots, passing over Æðelred, who may have already committed himself to the priesthood. For much of the first half of 1095, however, William Rufus was too preoccupied with restoring stability on his frontier with the Welsh princes and with a protracted dispute with Archbishop Anselm of Canterbury to devote any attention to Scottish affairs. The dispute with Anselm prevented him from settling the frontier crisis satisfactorily and, while both problems were still unresolved, a third crisis – the political relationship between the king and Robert de Mowbray – burst from smouldering hostility into open rebellion. What had started out with a blatant act of piracy by Robert and his men, followed by an ignored instruction from the king to make restitution

to the despoiled merchants, ended in a full-scale rebellion and baronial con-
spiracy encompassing a significant number of Norman landholders
throughout England. The scale and spread of the rebellion suggests that the
earl had not spent the early months of the year idly, but the king was also
prepared in May 1095 to take the conflict straight to Robert's power-base in
the north. Edgar mac Máel Coluim would play an important part in this
northern campaign.

William Rufus spent much of 1095 in the north, broken only by a brief
foray to Wales in September to reinforce Earl Hugh of Shrewsbury. The
centrepiece of his campaign in Northumberland was the siege of Robert in
his chief stronghold at Bamburgh. As part of wider operations probably
aimed at preventing Robert from receiving aid from his Scottish allies or his
slipping away to refuge north of the border, Edgar may have been employed
to secure 'Lothian', the former Northumbrian province between the rivers
Tweed and Forth. The evidence for such action is largely circumstantial, but
a charter in favour of the monks of Durham, issued by Edgar at an assembly
in the churchyard at Norham on the English side of the Tweed, points
strongly in that direction.[25] In this, Edgar was styled as the 'son of Máel
Coluim King of Scots' but only as 'possessing the whole land of Lothian and
the kingship of Scotland by the gift of my lord William, king of the English,
and by paternal heritage'. He is not described as in possession of Scotland
also, although his status as king is implicit in the styling. What can be suggested from this is that William Rufus, having formally recognised Edgar's
rights to the kingship (and ignoring those of Edmund and Æðelred), and
possibly having invested him with a symbol of his kingly status (perhaps a
crown),[26] deployed him against Domnall Bán and Edmund. Among the witnesses to Edgar's act were Alexander and David, almost certainly referring
to his two remaining brothers, and his uncle, Edgar Æðeling.[27] Together, this
group represented the alternative royal lineage in Scotland and would have
provided a powerful focus around which those hostile to Domnall Bán
could rally. The reference to Edgar 'possessing the whole land of Lothian',
and the subject matter of the charter (which deals with property in
Berwickshire), suggests strongly that the expedition had succeeded in gaining control of the predominantly Anglian south-east of the Scottish
kingdom. That, however, was to be the limit of Edgar's success in 1095.

Edgar may have been keen to press on with the offensive against his uncle
and brother to secure the kingdom in which he had been invested by William
Rufus, but the English king had more urgent priorities to deal with elsewhere. The northern campaign was concluded successfully with Earl

Robert's capture at Tynemouth and his wife's subsequent surrender of Bamburgh late in the year, and William Rufus was in the south again for his Christmas court at Windsor. In January 1096, he presided over the courts at which the vanquished rebels were tried and sentenced, then in the spring he entered negotiations with his brother, Duke Robert, who had taken the cross and planned to go on crusade. The near-penniless duke offered his covetous younger brother control of Normandy for three years in return for 10,000 marks of silver to finance his crusading venture. Throughout the summer, William Rufus was preoccupied with raising the cash to clinch the deal and in September sailed for Normandy, where he handed over the silver to Robert at Rouen and received possession of the duchy. As Robert headed south in the late autumn, the king remained in Normandy to secure his grip on his acquisition.[28] Edgar, meanwhile, was kicking his heels in frustration.

He was forced to wait longer yet, for William Rufus did not return from Normandy until early April 1097. Even then, the king had other priorities than Scotland, for the situation on the Welsh marches had remained unstable since the conflicts of 1094 and 1095. Late in the summer of 1097, William granted Edgar the support that he needed to complete the task that he had begun in 1095, and soon after Michaelmas (29 September) the army marched north.[29] The *Anglo-Saxon Chronicle* makes it clear that it was Edgar Æðeling who had command of the English force and that the campaign was no walkover. Apart from the 'hard-fought battle' mentioned in that same account, we have few other details of what occurred. According to the *Anglo-Saxon Chronicle*, Domnall Bán was driven out and, having installed his nephew as the vassal of William Rufus, Edgar Æðeling thereupon withdrew with his army to England. No timescale is offered for this sequence of events, but the consolidation of Edgar's position is unlikely to have taken a short time. The later twelfth-century chronicle of William of Malmesbury, interestingly, claims that Domnall Bán was 'slain by the craftiness' of his youngest nephew, David,[30] whose presence on the campaign is not otherwise recorded. The twelfth-century portion of the *Chronicle of Melrose* follows the basic account of events offered by the *Anglo-Saxon Chronicle*, but an inserted folio refers to the capture of Domnall by Edgar, his condemnation by his nephew and sentence to perpetual imprisonment.[31] A third source, a verse chronicle inserted into the Melrose chronicle, states that Domnall was captured by Edgar, blinded, and died subsequently at Rescobie near Forfar, from where his body was carried for burial on Iona.[32] The fate of Edmund is yet more obscure. William of Malmesbury claims that he was captured and spent the remainder of his life in chains, instructing that at death his body should be buried in those chains as a symbol of his penance for involvement in Donnchad's death.[33] It appears, however, that Edgar Æðeling removed his disgraced nephew from Scotland when he returned from the campaign, for the *Chronicle of the Kings of Scotland* claims that 'Edmund... a most vigorous man and servant of God, and most devout through this present life, rests buried in Montacute',[34] a Cluniac abbey in Somerset. The would-be king had entered religion and died at an unknown date, ignored by his brothers, as a monk, far from his kingdom.

For Edgar and his remaining brothers, Edmund's actions in 1094 had evidently produced an irreconcilable breach. His rejection of William Rufus's lordship, moreover, had added the hostility of the English king to that of his brothers, and once William Rufus's superior wealth and military resources were brought to bear, the reign of Domnall Bán and the aspirations of his eldest surviving nephew to succeed him as king were doomed. In his place, William Rufus had installed a loyal vassal who remained true to his oaths of fealty. While the English king made no onerous demands for service from Edgar, his superiority over him was unquestioned and England gained four decades of stability on its northern border. In Scotland, Edgar was largely left to his own devices and his main concern appears to have been to restore order and stability to his kingdom. One aspect of this can be seen in the treaty which he arranged in 1098 with Magnus Bareleg, king of Norway, whose campaigns in the Hebrides and Irish Sea region had destabilised the whole of the maritime west of the British Isles.[35] Edgar was disengaging himself from a region where Scottish royal power was at best ephemeral. Another facet appears to have been his provision for the future succession. Edgar was unmarried, and it appears that he provided his younger brother, Alexander, with an appanage in Scotland which marked him out as the designated successor.[36] The teenage David, however, despite his possible role in the downfall of Domnall Bán, received no such honour. The last certain evidence for his presence in Scotland is in or shortly after 1097, when he and Alexander were evidently at Abernethy on the south bank of the Tay, where they witnessed a charter of their elder brother, Æðelred, in favour of the Celi Dé of Loch Leven.[37] From then until 1103, there is no concrete evidence for David's location, let alone his activities. For him, the future seemed only to offer a peripheral role as a dependent of his elder brothers, unless he could carve a career for himself outwith Scotland.

CHAPTER THREE

Brother
of the Queen

In 1098, David was a marginal figure on the political landscape. With two
elder brothers, both apparently fit and healthy young adults, the teenage
prince was effectively surplus to the requirements of his family. Aged
between thirteen and fifteen, David was also too young to make a mark for
himself, lacking personal resources with which to attract men into his service or a patron who would promote his interests. Without a patron his
prospects looked bleak, for even a good marriage to an heiress who could
bring land and wealth to a landless and penniless princeling was impossible
to obtain without the support of one of the great magnates who orbited
around the king. There is no indication that William Rufus had any active
interest in furthering David's career; the English king had his vassal king in
Scotland and a seemingly dependable spare in the persons of Edgar and
Alexander. It does appear, however, that David found himself a place on the
margins of William Rufus's household among the younger sons of nobles
and other aspiring youths who hoped to forge a career for themselves and
establish their personal fortunes through service to the crown. To the boy
David in his mid-teens, such good fortune must have seemed almost impossibly beyond his reach.

Fate intervened on David's behalf two years later. For the adolescent
prince, events in the New Forest in Hampshire on 2 August 1100 led to an
unexpected and rapid improvement in his personal fortunes. The death of
William Rufus at the hands of Walter Tirel removed a king at the height of
his power, but also one who lacked a direct heir. Displaying the decisiveness

and hard-headed opportunism that was to serve him well but would also antagonise many of his nobles in future years, William's younger brother, Henry, who had been in the royal hunting party, seized the advantage of his presence in England at this critical moment to secure the royal treasury at Winchester and, with it, the vacant throne for himself. Henry's coup had succeeded and he had been crowned king before his only real potential rival, his eldest brother Duke Robert of Normandy, had time to react. The new king, however, needed to entrench his position as rapidly as possible, for he understood well that his seizure of the throne would inevitably be challenged by his brother. In many ways, Robert was now the more attractive figure; he carried the reputation of a successful crusader and, more importantly, had married recently and seemed likely to produce the heir that would offer stability to the Anglo-Norman political community. Henry, by 1100 probably entering his thirty-third year,[1] despite his already numerous bastard offspring, remained unmarried. The king needed a suitable bride, and rapidly, for a political marriage would help to secure his position in England.

Henry was crowned at Westminster Abbey on 5 August, three days after his brother's death.[2] The first three months of his reign were heavily involved with settling the legacy of political and ecclesiastical disputes which his brother had created, but amidst this all he was also preparing for marriage, and in November 1100, four months into his reign, he married Edith, David's elder sister. Why Henry decided on Edith as his bride is not really open to question; her lineage, if nothing else, made her a sound match for a king seeking to consolidate his hold on a politically divided kingdom. There are suggestions of a long courtship, Hermann of Tournai claiming that Henry had promised Máel Coluim himself that he would marry the girl and would only break that oath should there be a canonical reason to prevent their marriage.[3] It is unlikely, given the events of 1093 and the prince's own status as a virtually landless outsider in the political communities of England and Normandy, that Henry would have been considered a suitable candidate for Edith's hand, given the potential dynastic connotations of such a union. In 1100, however, those same connotations were powerfully compelling to Henry, who was prepared to overcome serious obstacles to secure their marriage. And they were serious, the most difficult to explain away being the roughly fifteen years that his prospective bride had spent in a nunnery and the persistent rumours that she had, in fact, taken the veil.

When David's aunt, Christina, had returned to England in 1086 to become a nun at the rich Benedictine nunnery at Romsey in Hampshire, it is possible that the five-year-old Edith had accompanied her. Romsey had served as a refuge in the aftermath of 1066 into which many aristocratic Anglo-Saxon ladies had retreated to escape the Norman conquerors, but, two decades later, it was attracting the patronage of those same Normans. It was thus into a wealthy, influential and intensely aristocratic sisterhood that Christina and her young charge were accepted. The nunnery, however, was not solely a place of religious seclusion; it also functioned as a schooling place for young noblewomen who had no vocation to enter religion. It is possible that Edith's parents were preparing their daughter for marriage to a Norman aristocrat and were providing for her education in a Normanised cultural milieu. Christina, however, may have had different ideas and probably intended Edith to become a nun also; it was later rumoured that her parents had 'consecrated [her] to the service of God'. The Canterbury monk, Eadmer, recorded in the early 1100s, however, that the princess had herself been implacably opposed to that future.[4] He set out the 'official' version of events which was made public at the time of her betrothal to Henry, citing the authority of Archbishop Anselm, who accepted her argument that her wearing of a nun's veil had been part of a stratagem on the part of her aunt to protect her 'from the raging lust of the Normans.' Edith swore that she had never professed as a nun and had informed the archbishop that Christina had been a harsh overseer, beating her physically and mentally if she tried to set aside the veil. She also claimed that her father had chanced to see her once wearing a nun's veil (probably on his last, fateful visit to William Rufus's court at Gloucester), and that he had been infuriated by the sight and had called down 'God's hatred upon the one who put it upon me'. Edith, although later to develop into a woman of deep personal piety cast in the mould of her mother, was clearly not the material of which submissive novices were made.

Christina's motives were sincere even if her methods were harsh. It is unlikely that Edith overstated her aunt's treatment of her stubbornness, for Christina, who had risen to become abbess of Romsey, clearly had a reputation for severity. She was not, however, simply safeguarding her niece from the 'raging lust of the Normans'; she was also seeking to preserve her as a valuable political pawn. As a daughter of Margaret and niece of Edgar Æðeling, Edith's possible marriage was an issue of tremendous importance. Her husband could inherit through her a legitimate claim to the throne of her Anglo-Saxon ancestors. The Normans could either use her to cement their hold on the throne, or neutralise her claim and those of any of her descendants by marrying her to a loyal nobleman.

In the early 1090s, Edith's marriage had evidently become an issue of great importance and may have featured in her father's last visit to the English court in the late summer of 1093. It has been suggested recently that the agreement which Máel Coluim sought to have William Rufus honour at this time concerned Edith,[5] but most other modern analyses of the crisis of 1093 agree that fulfilment of the 1091 treaty terms between the two kings is more likely to have been the most pressing issue on the Scottish king's mind.[6] Nevertheless, Edith's marriage may have been one of many factors in Anglo-Scottish diplomacy in the period between the 1091 peace treaty and the final failure of negotiations. What actual plans Máel Coluim had for his daughter, however, is far from clear, and to reconstruct a coherent narrative from the hints and conflicting accounts of the early twelfth-century sources on which we are dependent is no easy task.

There are three principal sources that provide some information concerning Edith's pre-1100 career. The nearest to events was Eadmer, who was present at and had subsequent access to the record of Archbishop Anselm's interrogation of the princess in 1100. The second, Orderic Vitalis, although geographically removed from the scene, was extraordinarily well informed about political events in England and Scotland in the 1090s and early 1100s. The third, Hermann of Tournai, although still more remote from the events he recorded, claimed to have discussed the question of Edith's marriage with Anselm during the archbishop's exile from England. None of the three present a complete account and all were writing considerably after the princess's eventual marriage, by which time subsequent events had coloured their view and produced some distortions that can be seen most clearly in Eadmer and especially in Hermann. It is Eadmer who first states that Edith was at Wilton in the 1090s, 'where [she] had been brought up', and this is confirmed by Hermann, who provides what he claims to have been a statement by the abbess of the convent concerning events there in around 1093.[7] It is his account and that of Orderic Vitalis which provide us with some picture of what future for the girl was being planned.

Orderic Vitalis reported that in 1093 Edith had been intended to become the wife of 'Alan Rufus, Count of Brittany'.[8] Edith's own comment, that her father had claimed that 'he would rather have destined [her] to be earl Alan's wife than to consort with nuns',[9] has been taken to indicate that Máel Coluim was the main proponent of the marriage, although, given the earl's reputation, the statement could have been heavily ironic. Alan, as Earl of Richmond, was the most powerful nobleman in northern England and an important figure in the councils of the English king. He would certainly

have made a very valuable ally for Máel Coluim,[10] for his lordship dominated the strategic routes across Stanemore between Cumbria and
Yorkshire, territory which the Scottish king aimed to regain. Alan, an elderly widower, appears to have had a penchant for royal nuns, and abducted
and, for a brief period before his death late in 1093, co-habited with another
former inmate of Wilton nunnery, Gunnhildr, daughter of King Harold
Godwinsson, who then went on to marry the earl's younger brother and
heir, Alan Niger. Yet it is unlikely that Earl Alan's behaviour caused Máel
Coluim to abandon his plans, for, given the dramatic breakdown in Anglo-
Scottish relations after August 1093, William Rufus would have been
unwilling to permit any proposal for Edith's marriage to either of the Alans
being brought to fruition.

A marriage to the head of one of the greatest Anglo-Norman families in
England, whose territorial power could have given Máel Coluim significant
influence in northern England, would have been a major coup. The scenario
offered by Hermann of Tournai, however, takes the possible marriage negotiations onto an altogether more elevated level. According to Hermann, in
1100 the abbess of Wilton, giving evidence before Anselm as to whether
Edith had ever taken vows as a nun, stated that she had not done so and that
the only reason that she had been seen wearing a veil was as a ruse to protect
her from none other than William Rufus. The king, she said, had turned up
unannounced at the convent and demanded admission in order to see Edith
and to pray in the church. Although William's predatory lust for young girls
was not a noted feature of his sexual activity, the abbess claimed that she
feared that 'he, being a young man and a king unrestrained, who would
immediately do anything which occurred to his mind,' would be captivated
by Edith's attractions and attempt to seduce or ravish her. With Edith's agreement, she had placed a nun's veil on the girl's head in the hope that seeing
her so attired would dampen the king's lusts. He, in the meanwhile, had
feigned an interest in the nuns' flower garden in order to gain admission to
the cloister but, on catching sight of the veiled Edith, left immediately, conclusive proof in the abbess's mind that the princess had been the sole reason
for the king's visit. Although William Rufus had departed, Edith continued
to wear the veil and was still dressed that way when her father appeared at
Wilton later the same week. Máel Coluim, according to the abbess, was infuriated to see his daughter dressed as a nun, tore the veil from her head, ripped
it apart and trampled on the pieces before removing Edith from the convent.
This part of the account appears to tally with Eadmer's report of the meeting
between the king and his daughter, and Edith's removal from Wilton is

supported by a letter of Archbishop Anselm to Bishop Osmund of Salisbury concerning her return to the nunnery,[11] but the visit by William Rufus is uncorroborated by any other surviving source. What, if anything, can be extrapolated from these fragments?

In the details provided by Eadmer and Orderic there is a certain consistency that suggests that marriage to Earl Alan was under serious consideration down to August 1093. While such a marriage would have suited Máel Coluim's designs in the north of England eminently well, it would have been distinctly unwelcome to William Rufus, who had just moved to consolidate his borderlands in the north-west. But where does this place William's supposed visit to Wilton in the days before his projected meeting at Gloucester with Máel Coluim? It is possible that his visit to Wilton may have been simply to find evidence that would enable him to veto a marriage between Alan Rufus and Edith on the grounds of her nun's vows, thus freeing him from the foreign and domestic diplomatic fallout from such a decision. Alternatively, it has been suggested that a marriage between Edith and the English king had been proposed as a means of cementing the treaty of 1092 and of securing amity between the kingdoms. Such a marriage would have strengthened both kingdoms and provided William with wider diplomatic ties through Edith's Scottish and West Saxon kin. Coming, too, in the immediate aftermath of William's serious illness, when he clearly believed himself to be dying, it is possible that production of an heir was at the forefront of William's mind, albeit for a very brief period.[12] Finding Edith in a veil would have given him a legitimate excuse for backing out of a match that he no longer regarded as necessary or desirable. Whatever the scenario, it does at least seem clear that the princess's status was bound up in the diplomatic dealings of 1092–93. This last point raises the question of when Edith's father made his appearance at Wilton. It has been suggested that Máel Coluim's visit followed immediately after his humiliation at Gloucester and that when the king returned to Scotland he took his daughter with him.[13] Hermann of Tournai, however, only claims that the king took Edith away with him after his visit to Wilton,[14] not that Máel Coluim travelled the additional fifty miles south from Gloucester to her monastery before racing back north to raise his army. If such a visit did occur, it is more likely to have been before Máel Coluim's failure to secure the audience with William Rufus at which the marriage negotiations may have been intended to feature. The Scottish king, perhaps fearing that he would lose the diplomatic leverage that his daughter provided him with if she were indeed prevailed upon to become a nun, and understanding how William might use his knowledge that she had worn the veil as a weapon against him, would almost certainly have taken his daughter with him both for her safety and also as proof that she was free of any profession. Whatever the circumstances, Edith's removal from the nunnery was only of a few months' duration, for she appears to have returned to Wiltshire early in 1094.

If Edith did return to Scotland with her father in late August 1093, then she was back in the neighbourhood of Wilton before the end of February 1094, less than two and a half months after the deaths of Máel Coluim and Margaret. In March 1094, Archbishop Anselm wrote to Bishop Osmund of Salisbury, the diocesan bishop for the nunnery at Wilton, setting out the business as he understood it.[15] In his letter, the archbishop informed Osmund that although he was aware that Edith had broken her profession and was living in the world, he had taken no action until that point to force her return as he suspected that she had been coerced into her decision, or possibly encouraged to do it by 'the king'; which king, Máel Coluim or William Rufus, is unspecified. Anselm further stated that he had taken the opportunity to ask William Rufus, who was about to sail for Normandy (which places the events into February/March 1094) for his view on the matter. To the archbishop's obvious relief, the king, who around this same time conferred the kingship of the Scots on Donnchad mac Máel Coluim, expressed no real interest in Edith's fate, stating that he had no objections to her returning to the nunnery and that his only personal obligation to the girl was to see to her basic personal maintenance. If William had once had any interest in Edith's marriage, then by early 1094 that interest had entirely disappeared. In light of the king's apparent disinterest in her fate, Anselm instructed Osmund to force her to return to the convent and to report back to him his progress in the matter. While no record survives to confirm or deny that she had returned to Wilton as instructed, the events of 1100 imply strongly that she had indeed re-entered the nunnery.

For the next six years, no evidence survives for the exact whereabouts of either Edith or her younger sister Mary. Despite the probability of her return to Wilton, there seems to have been continued uncertainty over Edith's exact status, for Orderic reports that at some time between 1093 and 1100 William de Warenne, Earl of Surrey, had asked for her marriage.[16] Warenne's proposal, too, failed to become a concrete settlement, and there was clearly no suggestion of a pre-existing betrothal as an impediment to Edith's marriage to Henry in 1100.

From the record of events in late 1100, it is evident that Edith's personal status was the source of serious concern on the part of Henry, who cannot have been unaware of the strong rumour concerning her profession as a nun that was circulating the kingdom.[17] He wanted the marriage and desperately, for a union between an heiress of the House of Wessex, descended from Edmund Ironside and able to trace her lineage back to Alfred the Great – and beyond – and a son of William of Normandy, would have done much to give legitimacy to what was still widely perceived as a conquering, usurping family. That he was prepared to allow a full inquest to be conducted by Anselm and senior ecclesiastical figures into his would-be bride's standing in the world demonstrates both how settled he was on marriage to Edith and also the anxieties which he had to ensure that the marriage was canonical and untainted by any scandal that could affect the legal status of any children which they had. In his father's day, such scandals and irregular liaisons had been no serious bar to the inheritance of the resulting offspring – William the Conqueror himself being a case in point – but the growing power of canon law in respect of marriage and inheritance had changed that. Henry wished to establish a secure and lasting dynasty, not one that would be challenged over its basic legitimacy.

Handing the issue over to the relevant Church authorities was no clever ploy on Henry's part; it was necessity. Anselm, of course, had encountered Edith previously, when in 1094 he had instructed that she be returned to her nunnery. At that time, there had seemed to be no question over her status, although the thirteen-year-old girl may have been quite relieved to re-enter the secure environment of the convent after her recent experiences of the harsh political realities of the world. While William of Malmesbury is at pains to record that Henry was unwilling to proceed with his marriage plans until the question of Edith's possible profession was settled, there is no reference to this earlier event in Eadmer's account of the inquiry, and it seems to have been quietly brushed under the carpet.[18] Edith was as keen as Henry to settle their marriage and she appears to have taken the initiative in securing an audience with Anselm at which she could set out her case. At the end of their interview, even Eadmer's cautious record of events cannot disguise the fact that the archbishop was reluctant to give the marriage his unqualified blessing. Instead, he referred the issue to a council that gathered at Lambeth, which appears to have been diligent in securing as much evidence as it could from witnesses who included the Abbess of Wilton.[19] Although the council eventually decided that, while Edith may have on occasion worn a veil to protect her from unwanted suitors, she had never given her profession as a nun nor had she intended to do so, thus freeing the way for her marriage to Henry, the decision did not entirely remove the question mark over her and

Eadmer, if not Anselm himself, may have continued to harbour doubts after the event. Certainly, there is at least a suggestion, at most a clear statement, by the twelfth-century chroniclers that the fates of Henry and Edith's children and the turmoil into which the kingdom was thrown after 1135 was a sign of God's displeasure. In November 1100, however, Henry had his bride and queen, Matilda of Scotland, as Edith was known after the marriage.

Matilda's marriage to Henry and coronation as queen by Archbishop Anselm at Westminster on Martinmas (11 November) 1100[20] transformed David's status immediately. The prospectless dependant on the fringe of the English court had become the brother of the queen, a style by which he would be referred to in the early 1100s.[21] It did not mean, however, that David was automatically elevated to a position of power and status in the royal household. He was still no more than seventeen years old, probably younger, and his future rested entirely on his relationship with the queen. That status, however, must surely have opened new doors for him at once, and, if he had not previously been a member of the group of noble youths being educated and trained in the royal household, he was quickly admitted to their number. It was probably an electrifying experience for David, being propelled into the company of other ambitious young males – the young bloods of the Anglo-Norman nobility[22] all out to prove their worth and catch the eye of the king, and, even if Henry I's court was an altogether more sober place after the supposed dissolute behaviour that had characterised William Rufus's household, it was far from puritanical and would also have given him a rapid education in worldliness.[23] There are hints, possibly simply employed as conventional topoi to present a picture of the later king's transformation from youthful excess to maturity and godliness, that David entered willingly and wholeheartedly into the lifestyle of his fellows. Ailred of Rievaulx recorded a story, told by David at his own expense, of his youth at the English court. In it, David described how he had been idling in his quarters with his companions, presumably other young men who were being educated and trained in the royal household, and had been summoned by his sister to her apartments. There, he found her washing and kissing the feet of lepers and, when he expressed his horror at her actions, she invited him to join her so that he, too, might find his way to Christ through humility and charity. Clearly, Matilda thought that her younger brother needed to devote as much time to his spiritual wellbeing as he devoted to his other pursuits. Displaying the bravado of youth that covered deep unease at the suggestion, when she started to insist that he join her David laughed at her and returned to his friends.[24]

Whatever the true nature of David's behaviour in his brother-in-law's household after 1100, it has to be recognised that this was the formative period of his later character. Since 1093, it is likely that he had spent very little time in Scotland and the most basic influences on his late childhood and early youth had been very strongly Anglo-Norman. Like his half-brother, Donnchad, before him, David was probably being groomed to be a Norman knight and would have been saturated by Norman-French culture and social mores. William of Malmesbury was later to describe him as 'a youth more courtly than the others, and one who had rubbed off all tarnish of Scottish barbarity through being polished from his boyhood by intercourse and friendship with us'.[25] In language, manners and dress, David would have been assimilated into his peer group. After 1100, however, his education would not simply have been training in arms, 'courtesy' and manners, for it is likely that Henry would have looked to provide for his young brother-in-law and David's later career suggests that he was a young man of talent whom the king would have seen as a potential member of his inner circle of advisors and officials, one of the *curiales*.[26] Indeed, he made his first appearance in a formal adult role at his brother-in-law's court at Windsor on 17 May 1103, when, as 'brother of the queen', he witnessed a royal act.[27] Alongside the conventional training of an aristocratic youth, therefore, David was probably also introduced to the already sophisticated techniques of English royal government, administration and law. It would not just be through his status as Matilda's brother that he would carve his niche in English elite society; any future position would be achieved largely on merit and demonstration of ability.

For David, then, the future being mapped out for him was as one of Henry I's 'new men', the class of new nobility whom Orderic described as being raised from the dust by the king to counterbalance the power of the established Anglo-Norman magnates. Such a career still lay some years in the future for, in medieval terms, David was still *adolescens*, a mere youth who lacked experience and who was not yet considered of an age to bear full responsibility. Although from about the age of fifteen he would have been regarded as 'of age' to witness documents and therefore carry legal credibility as an attestor,[28] he would still have been regarded as a 'youth' until he was twenty-five. In 1107, however, David's already much-disturbed youth would be brought to an abrupt end and responsibility would be dropped unexpectedly in his lap.

CHAPTER FOUR

Prince of the Cumbrian Region

No certain evidence survives to indicate that David had any signifi-cant contact with his elder brothers or paid any visits to Scotland after his appearance as a witness to Edgar's 1095 charter to the monks of Durham, other than William of Malmesbury's reference to his involvement in the overthrowing of Domnall Bán in 1097. It is reasonable to assume that David met with Edgar when the Scottish king came south to carry the cer-emonial sword before William Rufus during his formal crown-wearing ceremony at Westminster on 29 May 1099,[1] but that was Edgar's last visit to the English court. There is no evidence to suggest that either of David's brothers considered it necessary to make any provision for him in the king-dom, particularly since the succession seemed secure. Edgar, although still unmarried at the time of his securing of the throne, was a young man in his very early twenties and had a clearly designated heir in Alexander, who was around two or three years younger than him. It was Alexander for whom provision had been made in the form of an earldom within the heartland of the kingdom north of the River Forth,[2] an arrangement designed clearly to emphasise his status as *tanaiste*. Alexander, moreover, was already establishing a profile as figure of consequence on the Anglo-Scottish scene in the early 1100s, when, for example, he was the only secular individual present at the opening in 1104 of St Cuthbert's tomb in Durham Cathedral.[3] Whether it was ever considered possible that David might step into Alexander's shoes should Edgar – or for that matter Alexander himself die childless is unknown, but the presence in Alexander's court shortly after 1107 of his nephew, William fitz Duncan, the legitimate son of their short-reigned elder half-brother, might indicate that alternative arrangements were not only possible but were already seriously considered.[4] In January 1107, however, David's relationship with his brothers and position within the kingdom was redefined radically by the death of King Edgar.

Edgar's death in Edinburgh on 8 January 1107[5] may not have been entirely unexpected, and provision for the succession had, of course, already been made, but it marked a radical change in direction for David. Down to 1107, he had been merely the youngest of the royal princes and, although he was likely to rise in the service of his brother-in-law, Henry I, was still little more than a hanger-on at the Anglo-Norman court. Here, his status as a young man still to establish a personal position was indicated by his labelling as 'brother of the Queen'. The death of David's elder brother changed that, for it seems that Edgar had bequeathed to David a substantial appanage in southern Scotland. Arrangements for this award may have been made well in advance rather than it being a death-bed bequest, for the gift may have been part of a settlement agreed with Henry which gained his prior approval of Alexander's status as Edgar's successor.[6] If Alexander had been willing to accept this arrangement while Edgar was alive, he was not prepared to fulfil his obligations once he became king and appears to have been reluctant to yield up the territory involved to David.

According to Ailred of Rievaulx in the speech that he put into the mouth of Robert Bruce before the Battle of the Standard in 1138, David only obtained his inheritance from Alexander with the support of his Anglo-Norman friends. 'You yourself, O king', he said, 'when you demanded from your brother Alexander the part of the kingdom which at his death your... brother [Edgar] bequeathed to you, obtained without bloodshed all that you wanted through fear of us'.[7] It is implicit in this statement that David had secured his inheritance, and perhaps more, through the intervention of his powerful friends in England and that Alexander's change of heart had been the result of his being forced to back down in the face of the threat of military intervention. When he did secure control is uncertain, for it is only in 1113, when he established a colony of Tironensian monks at Selkirk, that he can be shown to have been in firm possession of a substantial block of territory in the Southern Uplands of Scotland.

David can be last placed with certainty in England in about May 1108.[8] Thereafter, there is no firm evidence for his actions until his foundation of Selkirk in 1113. Until recently, most historians have simply assumed that he was in his territories in southern Scotland, quietly constructing his infrastructure of administration and setting the groundwork for his later economic, social, political and religious reconstruction of the region.[9] This would require him to have been able to muster aid against Alexander very rapidly during a time when Henry I, his principal patron and likely sponsor, was committed heavily in securing his control of Normandy from his brother, Duke Robert. Although he had defeated and captured Robert at Tinchebrai on 28 September 1106,[10] Henry had still been in Normandy consolidating his grip on the duchy when Edgar died in January 1107. Henry returned to England during Lent 1107 (27 February–13 April) and was occupied for most of the middle of the year in settling religious matters, culminating in a great Church council at Westminster in August.[11] With a new threat to his grip on Normandy unfolding, he returned to the continent in summer 1108. There is, then, a window of autumn 1107 or spring 1108 for Henry to have given his approval for David to make a military challenge for his inheritance in Scotland. However, with Henry himself apparently heavily bound up in early 1108 with the complex administrative reform of his household, aimed at curbing the behaviour that had characterised that of his predecessor recorded by Eadmer,[12] that window narrows considerably. There is some slender evidence to suggest that Henry may have been at least as far north as York in 1109 following his return from Normandy in June of that year, but the evidence for a campaign that resulted in David's securing possession of Edgar's bequest is slender and the possible windows of opportunity too narrow to negotiate.[13] Of course, Henry need only have sanctioned a military operation and need not have participated in person, but several hints combine to provide circumstantial evidence that he did. A garbled early fifteenth-century tradition recorded at Nostell Priory – a community much favoured by David down to 1124 – does involve Henry personally in the campaign, although the date which it offers (1120) is impossibly late, while the alternative date suggested by internal evidence in the story (1105) is impossibly early.[14] The Nostell account does preserve the idea that Henry achieved his business in Scotland 'in peace', a suggestion which accords well with Ailred's manufactured speech for Robert Bruce. For Henry to be active in northern England in support of David, we must push any campaign forward to between at least July 1113, when the king returned from Normandy, and Christmas that year, when Henry underscored his brother-in-law's arrival on the social and political scene with his marriage to Countess Matilda of Northampton and his creation as Earl in her right. It might, therefore, have been nearly six and a half years after Edgar's death before David was able to enter his inheritance.

There is no firm evidence for how David spent this period from about May 1108 (when he last appears as a witness to one of Henry's acts) until Christmas 1113, but the traditional view has been that he was in southern Scotland securing his heritage.[15] While that is a possibility, there are a number of tantalisingly fragmentary hints which survive to suggest that he might have been otherwise occupied elsewhere. As a member of the king's household and, in effect, a trainee knight, it can be assumed reasonably safely that he participated in the military operations that culminated at Tinchebrai in September 1106, and in Henry's continued pacification of Normandy thereafter.[16] Certainly, David gained a familiarity with northern French affairs that suggests personal experience rather than second-hand knowledge. It was during this period that David probably learned of the monastic reform movement centred on Thiron in the Chartrain district, led by St Bernard of Thiron, from which he was to obtain the colony of monks that he planted at Selkirk in 1113. The man whom he later appointed as Bishop of Glasgow, John, who served as David's chaplain down to about 1116 and who spent a period of self-imposed retirement at Thiron, may also have been brought into his service around this time. Indeed, John probably had a close connection with St Bernard's abbey (although, given the nature of Tironensian monasticism it is unlikely that he was a monk there) and is most likely the source from whom David learned about the abbey and its reformed tradition. David also acquired land in Normandy, in the northern part of the Cotentin peninsula, where Robert Bruce, Lord of Brix to the south of Cherbourg, was one of his tenants. David was in possession of this lordship before about 1114, when he confirmed Robert's grant of 'Karkarevil' (modern Querqueville) on the coast west of Cherbourg to the monks of St Mary's Abbey in York.[17] Around the same time, David received possession of Hallamshire (the district centred on Sheffield) in Yorkshire, as part of a series of property redistributions made by Henry I to his support-ers from lands forfeited by nobles who had adhered to Duke Robert down to the time of Tinchebrai.[18] The Norman properties clearly came into David's hands after September 1106 and the Yorkshire lands probably shortly after that. Both should probably be seen as rewards for David's service in Henry's Norman campaigns and also as recognition that the young prince was now emerging as an able and experienced warrior and reliable pair of hands in whom to entrust control of important and, in the case of Hallamshire, strategic lordships. The implication that can be taken from these pieces of evidence is that David was involved heavily in his brother-in-law's conquest and pacification of Normandy from 1106 to 1113 and, therefore, was unlikely to have been in any position to prosecute his claims to the bequest made to him by Edgar.

That position changed in July 1113 when Henry returned to England from Normandy. It has been argued recently that it was only then that the king travelled north to York to set in place, as a reward for loyal service in the preceding years, the operation that would secure his young brother-in-law the inheritance that had been denied him by Alexander. The sequence of major events in David's life that occurred in the latter part of that year – the foundation of Selkirk Abbey, marriage to Matilda of Northampton and his acquisition of the title of earl – all flowed from this point.[19] But what was it that David gained in 1113? What was the bequest left to him by Edgar, and what was its significance?

We know from later documents that the appanage held by David before 1124 comprised the whole of the former kingdom of Strathclyde or Cumbria (extending from the Lennox south to the Solway, but excluding Galloway), excepting the district annexed by William Rufus in 1092 centred on Carlisle and extending south to cover what became Cumberland and Westmorland. In addition, he controlled upper Tweeddale and Teviotdale, the southern portion of the former Northumbrian province of Lothian that stretched from the Forth to the Tweed, which fell within the jurisdiction of the bishops of Strathclyde. As lord of this territory, he was given a number of titles by the clerks who recorded both his own acts and acts that required his consent. He appears as *princeps et dux* of the people of the diocese of Glasgow, under the spiritual authority of which most of David's domain lay. He was also styled *Cumbrensis regionis princeps* (Prince of the Cumbrian Region) and *princeps Cumbrensis* (Prince of the Cumbrians), titles which accord him quasi-regal status over the former kingdom.[20] The clerk who recorded these styles, however, was careful to add that 'he was not in truth lord of the whole Cumbrian region (or kingdom)',[21] alluding to that part of the kingdom that lay in the hands of the English crown. Nor did David have the title of *rex* (king), which emphasises that the kingship of Strathclyde, which had still been a notional reality in the mid-eleventh century, was not revived or granted to him. The style 'prince' suggests inferior status subject to a superior lordship, presumably intended to be the kingship of the Scots, but within his Cumbrian principality there is little sign that David deferred to any superior lordship. But David's domain extended beyond the Cumbrian region into lower Tweeddale, territory that had until the early eleventh century been under Northumbrian lordship. In this zone, he was not *princeps*, for King Alexander's over-riding authority was recognised in various acts relating to property and rights in the whole district extending from the Lammermuir watershed south to the Tweed.[22] The difference in treatment between the two is striking, and it is this which points to a change between what Edgar bequeathed to David in 1107 and what he obtained with Henry's aid in 1113.

A key to understanding what happened lies in the words that Ailred of Rievaulx put into the mouth of Robert Bruce in 1138. 'You yourself, O king', he said, 'when you demanded from your brother Alexander the part of the kingdom which at his death your… brother [Edgar] bequeathed to you, obtained without bloodshed *all that you wanted* through fear of us' (author's italics).[23] There is a tension here between what was 'bequeathed' and what was 'wanted', which could imply that the two were not identical. One suggestion, which has much to commend it, is that what Edgar had bequeathed was Cumbria, and what David obtained was Cumbria *and* lower Tweeddale.[24] Although David would stand in different legal positions in the two portions of his domain – as an autonomous 'prince' in Cumbria and, probably, as a vassal of his elder brother in Tweeddale – it was an arrangement which would have been very satisfactory from Henry I's perspective and which might point to it being Henry's policy. The settlement, which Alexander was clearly unwilling to accept and which required the threat of war to bring into effect, placed control of a territory spanning the whole length of the Anglo-Scottish frontier in the hands of a man on whom Henry could rely. Through this arrangement, Henry was presumably looking to give greater stability to a borderline that, although peaceful since 1097, had experienced protracted disorder and incursion throughout the later eleventh century.

In the late summer and autumn of 1113, it appears that King Alexander was driven by *force majeure* to recognise a settlement that he regarded as detrimental to his dignity and authority as king. Some brinkmanship may have been required to secure his submission and Henry had, if the speech put into Robert Bruce's mouth at Northallerton in 1138 by Ailred carries any truth in it, sanctioned the assembly and advance of an English army to bring Alexander to heel. Probably before the end of the campaigning season, David was in possession of a principality that stretched from the North Sea coast of Berwickshire to the Solway coast of Annandale and Nithsdale and from the northern end of Loch Lomond to the Anglo-Scottish border. His rapid social advancement did not end there, for late in 1113, possibly around the time that Henry was holding his Christmas court at Windsor, the king granted his brother-in-law the marriage of the widowed Matilda de Senlis, Countess of Huntingdon and Northampton. According to the *Vita* of David's younger stepson, Waltheof, later to be

Abbot of Melrose, David, supported strongly by his sister the queen, had asked the king specifically for the marriage, and it is a clear sign of how high David's credit was with Henry at this time that he agreed to what was a very political union.[25] Although Matilda, who was countess in her own right, had sons by her first marriage to Simon de Senlis who would succeed to her titles, this was still a very prestigious marriage that brought more than the title of earl to David. Matilda was the daughter of Judith, the niece of William the Conqueror, and Waltheof, the forfeited and executed Earl of Northumbria, making her a second cousin of the king. Through Matilda, David reinforced his personal connection with the Norman dynasty, underscoring his high standing in Henry I's eyes. On a more material level, the marriage brought him valuable and extensive estates in the eastern Midlands of England from which he could draw a substantial income. Perhaps even more important, however, was Matilda's paternal heritage, which comprised the forfeited earldom of Northumberland centred on the old Northumbrian citadel of Bamburgh and wider claims to the territories of the former earldom of Northumbria in southern Cumbria, Teviotdale, Tweeddale and Lothian. Henry's arrangement of the marriage with Matilda may have been motivated as much by securing the position of a dependable ally in the still disputed frontier zone between the kingdoms as by a wish to reward a loyal servant and brother-in-law.[26]

For Henry, the settlement of his northern frontier may have brought added advantages. Although it is possible that he had sanctioned the designation of Alexander as Edgar's heir before 1107, if the wording of the *Anglo-Saxon Chronicle*'s account of the circumstances of Alexander's accession '...as king Henry granted him' can be read as signifying a previous agreement,[27] there is no evidence that he ever received a formal submission by the new king. Indeed, although Edgar had repeated his formal displays of personal submission to William Rufus as late as 1099, neither he nor Alexander had offered homage to Henry following his coronation in 1100. In 1114, however, Alexander performed military service in Henry's campaign into Gwynedd against Gruffudd ap Cynan,[28] an act which appears very much to have been designed to regain the English king's favour after the crisis of the previous year and in which Alexander both led one of the divisions of the invading army and was credited in the Welsh chronicle account as being responsible for persuading Gruffudd to seek to make peace with Henry. It is possible that Alexander's marriage to Henry's bastard daughter, Sibylla, occurred around this time, the opportunity perhaps being taken while Alexander was in England for the Welsh campaign to forge another bond between the king of Scots and the Norman house.[29] Whether any reconciliation was needed between Alexander and David is unclear, but Ailred in his speech attributed to Robert Bruce at the Battle of the Standard implies that Alexander both hated and persecuted his younger brother for no stated reason.[30] While there is no other source which records any such tension between the brothers, it is entirely plausible that Alexander was never entirely reconciled to the territorial settlement which handed David so large and so economically significant a portion of his kingdom. Certainly, there is contemporary poetic evidence to suggest that David's separate possession of the Southern Upland zone was a position resented by a significant element among the Gaelic elite of Scotland:

> It's bad what Mael Coluim's son has done,
> dividing us from Alexander;
> he causes, like each king's son before,
> the plunder of stable Alba.[31]

It could be argued that the poet's unhappiness at the division of the kingdom that this verse represents was only a reflection of what Alexander himself might have felt. Nevertheless, there is no unambiguous contemporary sign of outright hostility between the brothers and, while David clearly held Cumbria entirely free from his elder brother's superior lordship, it is evident that in lower Tweeddale, which he probably held as a fief of Alexander, the relationship between the two was conducted formally and, apparently, amicably.[32] Beyond their dealings in respect of properties in this region, however, there is no sign that David performed any formal role in his brother's kingdom, appearing as a witness to none of his charters in favour of the churches in the heartland of Scotia. There is also no indication that David was automatically considered to be Alexander's next heir, and Cumbria was clearly not intended to serve as an appanage for the heir apparent but as provision for a younger brother who was destined only to found a cadet house of the elder, ruling line. Unlike his elder brothers, Alexander was married and presumably believed that he would father a son to whom the throne would pass in turn. It is possible that such a prospect had receded by about 1120 when, in Alexander's foundation charter of Scone Priory, an 'Alexander, nepos Regis Alexandri' (Alexander, nephew of King Alexander), probably a scribal error for William, nephew of King Alexander, i.e. William fitz Duncan, is named first among the secular witnesses.[33] It can never be proven conclusively, but it is possible that in the early 1120s Alexander regarded William fitz Duncan as his heir in preference to David.

In 1113–14, however, the question of the succession to the Scottish throne seemed a fairly remote concern and David was presumably far more preoccupied with the need to consolidate his position as ruler in Cumbria. Among his first acts in 1113 had been the fulfilment of what may have been a vow made soon after 1107: the foundation of a monastery to be colonised by Tironensian monks at Selkirk.[34] This act of retrospective piety was followed soon after by the appointment of his personal chaplain and probable former Tironensian monk, John, to the bishopric of Glasgow.[35] Although the re-establishment of the See of Glasgow after what David's later inquest into the properties associated with its church describes as 'a long time' is attributed to the pious motive of rescuing the people of the Cumbrian region from a slide into degeneracy, barbarity and spiritual ignorance,[36] more worldly considerations were also at play. Certainly, as we shall examine later, David's concern for the spiritual welfare of his people was the act of a reform-minded ruler and rests easily with the evidence for his personal religious behaviour and support for reformed monasticism. The proper provision of a diocesan structure to oversee the regularisation of the provincial church would have been at the forefront of his agenda. The appointment of a man very closely associated with David, moreover, suggests that John was also intended to exercise a supervisory role as an agent of the ruler's government who could assist in establishing the prince's authority throughout Cumbria. But the revival of the bishopric raised a series of complex questions concerning the spiritual and political relationships between his bishop, the archbishopric of York, Cumbria generally and the English crown.

David's aim may have been to create a unitary ecclesiastical authority for his principality, matching 'Cumbria' in territorial extent. Such an aim, however, was compromised in lower Tweeddale, which lay within the jurisdiction of the Bishop of St Andrews, in Teviotdale, over which the Bishop of Durham claimed spiritual authority as successor to the old Northumbrian See of Lindisfarne, and in the area around Carlisle, which had evidently formerly fallen under the authority of the 'Cumbrian' bishop but which had been detached from the principality in 1092 and brought under English lordship.[37] These two latter areas of potential conflict were to figure prominently in the long and debilitating struggle to avoid making a formal profession of obedience to the Archbishop of York which engulfed John after 1118. In 1114-16, however, when David was preparing to revive the diocese, such a conflict appears not to have been even remotely considered as a threat. It was only as David's political skills and ambitions grew that the full implications for his authority represented by York's claims were recognised.

There may have been other motives behind David's inquest into the lands of the church of Glasgow concerned with far more secular matters. If, in parallel to his monastic foundation at Selkirk and the revival of the bishopric, David was already beginning to introduce his Anglo-Norman friends as landholders throughout his principality, then it was imperative that the bishop and he should establish as clearly as possible what properties pertained to the 'old but decayed See' to ensure that there was no encroachment on the kirklands.[38] Many of the men who may have received such lands may be listed among the thirteen or fourteen Anglo-Normans who witnessed the inquest. Furthermore, David would surely have provided Countess Matilda with dower lands from what he believed to be his personal domain in the region, and this again would require clarification with regard to ownership rights.[39] Finally, if David intended to employ the bishops of Glasgow as agents of his authority in the western part of his principality, it was essential that he provide them with an adequate landed base from which to project their own temporal authority over their diocese. What the inquest revealed was a series of yawning gaps in the distribution of episcopal properties throughout Strathclyde and Cumbria proper, but even more marked in the broad sweep of country west of Clydesdale from the later Renfrewshire to the northern limits of Galloway. The assertion of royal power over that western district is discussed in a later chapter, but as early as the 1110s and earlier 1120s, David must have been uncomfortably aware of his lack of secure grip over a substantial portion of what was nominally his domain. Bishop John, among his many spiritual duties, would surely have provided his oft-absent prince with a dependable lieutenant within the core of his northern principality.

As Earl of Huntingdon as well as ruler of Cumbria, David clearly led a highly mobile existence that required him to travel between the various portions of his lordship as well as continue to perform his role as a leading magnate in Henry I's administration. He was in southern England certainly in the autumn of 1114, when he witnessed a royal act at Westbourne in Sussex,[40] and it is probably to this period that a group of acts issued by David as earl and all involving Huntingdon properties were drawn up.[41] At least one of these documents was issued by David at Yardley Hastings in Northamptonshire, one of the principal manors of the earldom of Huntingdon.[42] Matilda, in whose name a confirmation of one of David's grants was made,[43] was evidently with her husband in the south, and it appears to have been around this time that she gave birth to their only child, a son, whom David named Henry in honour of the man to whom he owed his good fortune.

Evidence for David's movements from September 1114 until April 1124 is very sketchy, but the fragments which we have indicate that he spent much of the time undertaking what were probably regular tours around his extensive Anglo-Scottish domain. On 28 December 1115, for example, he was at St Albans, a place and date which implies that he had probably spent Christmas at his brother-in-law and sister's court and was heading north towards his Midlands properties before returning to Scotland.[44] David was again absent from his northern principality for an extended period in 1116, and it was probably around this time that he was at Westminster to witness a charter of his sister in favour of the monks of Westminster Abbey.[45] It may have been at this time that David made his second visit to Thiron in an unsuccessful attempt to meet with St Bernard, who died shortly before his arrival, and from where he brought back an abbot and additional monks for his new monastery at Selkirk.[46]

Soon afterwards, one of the major influences on David's early life and career, who had in some ways stood as a surrogate mother-figure to him, was removed with the death at Westminster on 1 May 1118 of his elder sister, Queen Matilda.[47] We do not know if David had been present at court at the time of his sister's death or reached Westminster in time for her burial close to the tomb of their saintly kinsman, Edward the Confessor, but it was probably either at the funeral or shortly afterwards that he set up financial arrangements for the perpetual celebration of mass on the anniversaries of Matilda's and their parents' deaths.[48] David had made no similar arrangements in respect of Edgar, despite his indebtedness to his elder brother for the bequest which transformed him from landless hanger-on to powerful landholder. While it is possible that David's slender resources in 1107 prevented him from making any such ostentatious display, it is equally possible that the provision made in respect of Matilda is more an indication of his closeness to the sister who had effectively looked after his interests from 1097 onwards and who, if the chroniclers are to be believed, used her influence on her husband to advance her youngest brother's career. The personal connection between David and Henry, however, was more firmly grounded than simply on their relationship as brothers-in-law. David was uncle to Henry's children and one of the greatest vassals of the English crown. As a result, there is no evidence that the frequency of David's attendance at court and his witnessing of his brother-in-law's acts diminished after 1118, nor do they appear to have declined in the aftermath of either the death of his teenage nephew William Æðeling in 1120 or Henry's remarriage in 1122. In any case, a lessened frequency of visits to court would not necessarily have been an indication of a cooling in relations between David and Henry, and David continued to spend time in England overseeing the affairs of his estates there. Although he had other concerns, he was still a loyal vassal of the English king and would give him good service yet.

David's close relationship with Henry down into the early 1120s and the clear dependence which he had on the English king during the early years of his reign after 1124 make it difficult to accept that in 1121-22 there may have been a threatened rift between the protégé and the patron. It has been suggested that a series of events and inferences in records of the time point to a crisis that may have threatened to erupt into war between David and Henry. The cause, it has been suggested, was David's unsatisfied ambition with the terms of the 1113 settlement with his brother and Henry.[49] According to Judith Green's interpretation, Bishop Ranulf Flambard's building of a castle at Norham on the Tweed in 1121,[50] and the grant at around the same time of Wark-on-Tweed to Walter Espec, marked a growing concern on the part of Henry over the security of the frontier. These concerns may have been the business which prompted a gathering of northern English magnates at Durham, but we have no record of what was discussed there.[51] About the same date is given in the early fifteenth-century Nostell Priory tradition of Henry advancing towards Scotland with a great army to put down a rebellion, which has recently been suggested to be a conflation and mis-dating of the events of 1107-08 and 1113.[52] The Nostell tradition implies a date of about 1120, but Henry was not in the northern part of his kingdom at that date. In 1122, however, Henry paid the only recorded visit of his reign to Carlisle, where he ordered the strengthening of the defences.[53] The interpretation placed on all these disjointed fragments is that Henry suspected that David was dissatisfied with the earlier settlement and had expected to be given Carlisle after Ranulf le Meschin had yielded it up to Henry in 1120 before being permitted to succeed to the earldom of Chester. It is also possible that he already coveted his wife's lost heritage in Northumberland. If that is so, then it is the only suggestion of tension between David and his brother-in-law. Relations were certainly on a strong footing before 1124 and most of the events of 1121-22 can be interpreted in an altogether more innocent light. Given Ranulf Flambard's general character and his policies for the reorganisation of his temporalities, the building of a castle as the administrative centre of his northern estates of 'Norhamshire' need not be seen as a threatening action towards David. Similarly, the grant of Wark to Walter Espec and of Alnwick to one of David's former court colleagues, Eustace fitz John, hardly constitutes the militarisation of the northern frontier of

England. Indeed, as Judith Green herself states, 'by comparison with the frontier with Wales, or that between Normandy and France in the Vexin, the Anglo-Scottish border does not seem to have been heavily fortified in the twelfth century'.[54] Even the strengthening of Carlisle's defences can be seen as the sensible action of a king who has just recently taken a fortress into his own hands and who, at precisely that time, was seeking to extend his influence into the Irish Sea zone and, beyond that, into Ireland.[55] Given the evidence for David's continued presence at Henry's court through 1121-22,[56] it seems that, if there were any deterioration in Henry's relations with the northern British powers, an alternative cause needs to be identified.

The obvious alternative source of concern for Henry in the north was David's elder brother, Alexander. Important though David already was in Henry's schemes for the wider domination of the British Isles, his significance to the English king grew immensely in the early 1120s, for in July 1122, Alexander's wife, Sibylla, Henry's bastard daughter, died suddenly having failed to produce an heir for the Scottish king.[58] The later twelfth-century English chronicler William of Malmesbury has been responsible for tarnishing the reputation of the queen, claiming that Alexander did not grieve much for her, and describing her as lacking in modesty and refinement.[59] Whatever the truth of those particular accusations, Sibylla appears to have been a pious lady who had been involved closely in her husband's religious reforms. Alexander appears to have begun moves to venerate her memory soon after her death, if any weight can be placed on the fifteenth-century chronicler Walter Bower's claim that the king was planning to found an Augustinian priory at the time of his own death on the 'Island of Loch Tay' at Kenmore where Sibylla is said to have died.[60] Her death transformed the political landscape in Scotland, for, unless Alexander re-married swiftly and produced a legitimate heir, the throne seemed now destined for either William fitz Duncan or for David. Was it this uncertainty over the succession in Scotland that sparked Henry's flurry of activity in the north, and his visit to Carlisle does appear to have occurred in the autumn, after Sibylla's death? Since William does not appear to have challenged his uncle's eventual accession in April 1124, it seems likely that he had not been designated as Alexander's heir or that Alexander reversed any earlier decision and instead nominated his surviving brother. It is purely conjecture, but it is possible that Henry's presence in the north with an army in autumn 1122 was intended to pressure Alexander into acknowledging David and no other as his heir. Rather than being directed against David, the strengthening of English interests on the northern frontier may have been made in association with, and as support for, David. Indeed, two twelfth-century authorities, Orderic Vitalis and Robert, Prior of St Andrews, support the suggestion that Alexander did select David as his heir.[61] For Henry, therefore, pressure in the north must have made it increasingly likely after summer 1122 that his favoured protégé – or his son – would succeed to the Scottish throne.

An increased expectation of his succession to the throne does not appear to have burdened David unduly after 1122. Instead, there is very much an impression of 'business as usual' with David continuing to spend extended periods of time away from Scotland. Of course, there was no suggestion that his brother's health was a cause for concern, or that there were any other reasons for the prince to remain close to Scotland. Indeed, there is even the possibility that David was absent from Britain for an extended period around this time. David appears to have spent much of the summer of 1123 in southern England, where he was present at Winchester on 15 April and at Portsmouth on 3-10 June.[62] His extended presence there was probably a result of the rumours of rebellion which eventually erupted in Normandy in late September 1123 which aimed at securing the duchy for William Clito, the son of Duke Robert.[63] Henry had received warning of the threat as early as April, when he sent his bastard son Robert, earl of Gloucester, and Ranulf le Meschin, earl of Chester, to secure key royal strongholds in Normandy. Henry himself crossed to Normandy in June 1123, the occasion for David's presence at Portsmouth, and it is altogether possible that David, as Earl of Huntingdon, participated in the royal expedition. Indeed, the six weeks between mid-April and early June were perhaps spent in gathering his military resources for the forthcoming campaign. Certainly, we have no idea as to David's whereabouts until the following April, when he had returned to Scotland and, as lord of one of the greatest honours in England and a vassal of Henry's for lordships in the Cotentin, it is inconceivable that he did not receive a summons to perform his service dues in the royal army. It has to be stressed that there is no evidence that would definitely place David in Henry's army at this time, but the likelihood of his non-participation in this major military operation is very low. The absence of any evidence to place David in Scotland or England either at this time could be taken to indicate that he may have remained in Normandy until shortly after the unexpected defeat and capture of the rebel leaders at Rougemontier on 25 March 1124. Towards the end of April 1124, while the English army was still mopping up after the collapse of the Norman rebellion, news was brought to David that would change forever the historical development of Scotland: his brother, the King of Scots, was dead.

CHAPTER FIVE

Stranger in a Strange Land? Succession and Challenge 1124-34

David's exact whereabouts at the time of his brother's death is unknown, but the speed with which events moved in the early summer of 1124 indicate that he was already in the north, perhaps in his castle at Roxburgh. Although it is possible that Alexander had recognised David as his probable heir after Queen Sibylla's death in 1122, it was by no means a clearly acknowledged certainty that David was Alexander's rightful heir, for it was only dynastic accident that had seen the succession within the meic Máel Coluim pass from brother to brother since 1097. Later chroniclers, all churchmen steeped in canon law tradition, for whom legitimate male primogeniture was an established fact, present his succession to the throne as a natural progression. In 1124, however, primogeniture was yet to establish itself as the standard procedure in determining inheritance not just in Scotland. English succession practice was still nominally elective, and the succession from William the Conqueror had passed to his second son, William II Rufus, to the exclusion of his eldest son, Robert Curthose, and from William to the third of the Conqueror's sons, Henry I, while Robert was still alive. Primogeniture, however, was gaining a firm hold as the accepted practice and was one factor used against Henry I in England and Normandy by the supporters of his nephew, William Clito. There were various alternatives for the succession in Scotland, but David had powerful friends ready to support his cause.

The strongest potential challenger to David's succession was his half-nephew, William fitz Duncan, the son of his elder half-brother, King

Donnchad II. Under strict application of the rules of primogeniture, William, who was a mature adult aged over thirty in 1124, represented the senior and legitimate male line descended from Máel Coluim III. He, not David, should have been the successor to Alexander. The fact that he did not succeed and instead enjoyed a close, loyal relationship with his uncle has generally passed without comment by historians. While there was no doubt in eleventh- and early twelfth-century records of the legitimacy of Donnchad mac Máel Coluim, later twelfth- and early thirteenth-century chronicle accounts label him as a bastard and by the fourteenth and fifteenth centuries his illegitimacy in the face of his legitimate younger half-brothers was an accepted fact.[1] This smear was part of an early thirteenth-century chronicle-based propaganda offensive directed against William fitz Duncan's descendants, the meic Uilleim claimants to the Scottish throne, and was designed explicitly to undermine their position.[2] In 1124, there was no imputation of bastardy directed at William's line. Why, then, did he not mount a challenge for the throne?

The answer is probably that David and his supporters bought off William with a bargain that must have appeared to satisfy his ambitions. What that deal was we can only guess, but it may have included an explicit acknowledgement of William's status and possible recognition of him as David's heir. Certainly, under Gaelic inheritance practices, the least William could have expected was to be designated as *tanaiste*, for after David he was the oldest acceptable and legitimate male of the royal house. David's own son, Henry, moreover, was still a child of less than ten years old and, given the fractious state of the kingdom, it was imperative to make provision for a smooth transition of power should David, or indeed Henry, die. If such a deal occurred, it was an astute move on David's part, for it removed the most serious potential challenger to his succession from the equation.

With William's acquiescence bought, David was able to secure his inauguration as king of Scots at Scone. The Scottish king-making ceremony, however, produced unexpected qualms on David's part. In his eulogy of David, which forms part of letter written to the king's great-nephew, Henry of Anjou (soon to be King Henry II of England), Abbot Ailred of Rievaulx claims that the king had not sought the kingship but abhorred it, and had only accepted it because there was no other acceptable alternative. Not only that, but there was something in the ceremony at Scone which offended David's religious principles. Brought up with the sacral nature of Anglo-Norman kingship as his only close personal experience, he may have found the essentially secular ceremony of enthronement and acclamation quite alien. According to Ailred, so strong were David's qualms that the Scottish bishops had grave difficulties in persuading him to undertake the king-making ritual.[3] Nevertheless, David was persuaded to set aside his spiritual doubts and was duly enthroned in the traditional manner. It was the conventional start to what would prove to be a revolutionary reign.

It is possible that the revolution began as early as the festivities which followed David's inauguration in early May.[4] While still at Scone, David issued a charter to Robert de Bruce, granting him the whole of 'Estrahanent' (Ystrad Annan = Annandale) under very vague terms of service.[5] This is the earliest surviving charter issued by a king of Scots to an incoming colonial lord and has generally been taken as indicating that the introduction of Anglo-Norman knights commenced only with David's accession to the kingship.[6] Robert's charter, however, was witnessed by eight Anglo-Norman noblemen, headed by one of Henry I's greatest servants and most prominent 'new men' Eustace fitz John, and including some men who would emerge as powerful lords in David's kingdom, while the ninth witness, the chamberlain Edmund, may have been an English clerk from the new king's Midland's earldom. Not one of the Gaelic magnates was called upon to witness the document and it is only addressed to David's 'French' and 'English' subjects. This peculiarity in the charter's formula and witness-ing is distinctly odd and cannot be dismissed as a product of native Scottish unfamiliarity with new-fangled parchment records, for David's elder sib-lings had all made use of formal diplomas of this type. Nor can it be presented as a product of geography, whereby none of the Gaelic magnates were involved because the subject-matter was far removed from their spheres of interest, for no mention is made of the 'Cumbrenses' who inhabited Annandale and whom David had included carefully in his recent inquest into the lands of the church of Glasgow. Quite simply, the structure of the document reflects very strongly David's personal preferences, cultural inclinations and experience. Although he had ruled over the Southern Uplands since c.1113, he had been absent from Scotland probably since c.1097 and had been raised and educated in the Frankish culture of the Anglo-Norman court, trained as a Norman knight, and schooled in Anglo-Saxon and Norman traditions of government and administration. William of Malmesbury, indeed, referred to David as 'more courtly' than his older brothers, and that he 'had rubbed off all the tarnish of Scottish barbarity through being polished from his boyhood by communication and friend-ship with us (the English)'.[7] Gaelic Scotland was alien to him and, given that it was from the Gaelic regions of the kingdom that the forces which had supported his uncle, Domnall Bán, had come to drive him and his surviving family into exile, and which had killed his eldest half-brother, it is not surprising that David may have looked on his new subjects with suspicion and, perhaps, hostility. Robert and the witnesses to the Annandale charter were former colleagues and friends as well as vassals and servants. They shared a common culture, common values and, in the cases of Robert de Bruce and Eustace fitz John, a similar set of experiences. In his new role as king, surrounded by men whom he barely knew, if at all, this group represented something in which David could place trust.

Given David's need to establish his position within Cumbria after 1113, it seems very unlikely that he had felt constrained to wait until 1124 before granting land in his principality to one of his Anglo-Norman colleagues. His lavish alienations to the Church from his personal estates within the region may have been more easily acceptable to the native elites, but it is highly unlikely that David gave no reward to men who helped him to win his legacy from Alexander. The grant of Annandale to Robert in 1124 may not have been the first award to his Anglo-Norman followers nor, indeed, may it have been the first made to Robert. The grant could represent a reissue of an earlier award done to reflect the changed status of the man whose vassal Robert was, and it has been suggested that he may have received his fief from David as early as *c.*1120 when Ranulf le Meschin gave up his lordship of Carlisle to inherit the earldom of Chester.[8] Indeed, Robert does appear to have been the closest and most important of David's associates from the court of Henry I, and the relationship may have been cemented soon after 1107 when David had acquired his lordship in Normandy.[9] Robert had benefited significantly from his loyal service to Henry during the conquest of Normandy, and had already received extensive estates from the king in northern Yorkshire and Cleveland. His closeness to both David and Henry, therefore, may have marked him out as an acceptable alternative to Ranulf in Carlisle to both men in whom to entrust a highly strategic lordship on the border between both kingdoms. Robert, moreover, may not have been alone in receiving land from David in his principality before 1124, for, as we have seen, the new king had been already surrounding himself with associates from the English court and vassals from Huntingdon in his government of Cumbria after 1113. In 1124, perhaps, the Scots found themselves coming to terms with a new ruler who, although a brother of the late king and Scottish by birth, was a largely unknown quantity, a virtual foreigner who had shown himself a decade earlier to be prepared to bring in the military might of his Anglo-Norman friends to secure him what he wanted, and who had arrived among them backed by the armoured muscle of his foreign companions. David may have been enthroned with such apparent smoothness in April/May 1124 because the Scottish magnates understood fully that the alternative was war, but the hostility that had been expressed towards him as long ago as 1113 among the Gaelic elites had not gone, and his unchallenged inauguration did not equate with unquestioned acceptance.

David's grip on the throne must have seemed to be secure, but the apparent ease with which he had seized the crown proved to be but a deceptive calm before the storm that was about to be unleashed. According to the Normandy-based Anglo-Saxon monk, Orderic Vitalis, the challenge to David came from Máel Coluim, the bastard son of Alexander I.[10] According to Orderic, Máel Coluim fought two battles against his uncle but David's superior experience and resources led to his nephew's defeat. The implication in the brief account of the 1124 rebellion is that it was a challenge that really amounted to nothing, but subsequent events showed that while David may have defeated his rival with comparative ease on this occasion, the young man commanded significant support in the kingdom and would continue to mount a serious threat to his uncle for nearly a decade to come. Victory may have come easily in 1124 for the king, but Máel Coluim had not been captured or killed by David's supporters.

Who Máel Coluim's supporters in his insurrection were is entirely unknown, but it is probable that they numbered among them those who would have sympathised with the sentiments expressed about David in the Gaelic poem which had criticised him some ten years earlier. It is surely significant in this context that there is no evidence that after David's inauguration at Scone in April/May 1124 he set foot in his kingdom north of Fife until possibly as late as 1139-1140,[11] although his personal authority there had been established in the course of the early 1130s. This absence from a region in which his two immediate predecessors had based themselves for so much of their reigns and from where traditionally the kings of Scots had drawn their main support could be read as evidence for a confidence in his powers of control over it, but the political situation which emerges in the early 1130s would indicate otherwise. David, as a legitimate heir of the meic Máel Coluim line, would presumably have enjoyed a degree of almost automatic acceptance among his family's traditional supporters, but there were presumably many others who regarded him as an alien, an outsider about whom they knew little or nothing, and a man whose foreign manners and even more so his foreign friends, were regarded with deep suspicion. For his part, apart from his royal blood, David lacked any attributes that would have enabled him to communicate easily with his new subjects and establish the social connections upon which the unsophisticated Scottish monarchy of his ancestors had depended. Gaelic Scotland north of the Forth was very much a strange land to the foreign-educated king.

There is no sign that David made any serious attempt in the period immediately after his accession and the defeat of his nephew's rebellion to become better known in the Gaelic provinces of his kingdom. No evidence survives of a royal progress north of the Tay, nor any visit to the already traditional hunting-seats of his predecessors at places such as Clunie in Stormont, only a few miles north of Scone and close to his family's former spiritual power base at Dunkeld. While this strange aversion for the Gaelic Alba which he had inherited may in part be explained by poor documentary survival, which renders it difficult to locate David with certainty at almost any given time, it appears that David's interests remained focused firmly on the world with which he was most familiar and where his political connections and ambitions were rooted. Certainly, it was in that region that his main business for much of the next decade lay, the only evidence for any activity north of the Forth being a series of acts in favour of the Benedictine convent at Dunfermline which seems to date from very early in his reign, probably all falling within the period 1124-28.[12] Otherwise, what evidence we have for royal affairs between 1124 and 1130 indicates that the king's principal concerns were with his original power base south of the Forth.

The principal business confronting David in this region at the start of his reign was the continuing problem of diocesan government and the affairs of the sees of Glasgow and St Andrews, which is discussed in detail in chapter nine. This business probably kept David in Scotland in early 1125 when news came of the imminent arrival of a papal legation sent by Pope Honorius and charged with settlement of the long-running dispute involving the claims of the metropolitan see of York to the obedience of the Scottish bishops. Given the sensitive nature of the case, which touched on the status of his kingdom, and David's already robust defence of the independence of Bishop John at Glasgow, David was not going to permit any council in which the fate of his bishops and the possibility of their subjection to York to meet and deliberate outwith his kingdom, nor was David going to allow a settlement of the issues to be made in his absence. As a result, when the legate, John of Crema arrived in Scotland (probably in June or July 1125) David was at Roxburgh, which was establishing itself firmly as his chief seat of government in Scotland, where he was presumably attended by his chief political and religious advisors.[13] This attempt, like those before it, failed and the result was a marked hardening in papal attitudes towards Scotland.

By the middle of 1126, the issue of York's metropolitan jurisdiction over Scotland had reached critical level. At St Andrews, the bishop-elect Robert of Scone remained unconsecrated as a result of his refusal, supported if not instigated by the king, to make any profession of obedience to Archbishop Thurstan, while at Glasgow Bishop John again faced suspension for his failure to comply with the Pope's instructions to him to make his submission to York. All the ecclesiastical parties involved had gravitated towards Rome in early February 1126 in search of a solution, the Scots apparently seeking the establishment of their own national archdiocese which would effectively end all claims from York. The bid failed and word of this decision and the Pope's apparent refusal to deviate from earlier decrees concerning Glasgow would surely have reached Scotland within a few weeks. For David, who saw the reform of the Scottish Church as one of his central duties as king, the continuation of this debilitating and distracting situation was unacceptable and he sought to enlist the support of Henry I in reaching a compromise arrangement that would defer a permanent settlement but still permit his bishops to make progress with their reformist programmes. Church politics and papal diplomacy, therefore, probably lay at the top of the agenda of business which David intended to lay before the English king when he travelled south in the late summer.

David arrived at Henry's court shortly after Michaelmas (29 September) and was to remain in England until the following summer.[14] Henry had much business to discuss with him also, and David would quickly have found that he was in a position to extract concessions from a formerly dominant patron who needed to win as much support as possible for his long-awaited decision concerning the succession to the English throne. After five years of marriage, it had become obvious to Henry I that Adeliza of Louvain was not going to provide him with any child, let alone the son that he so craved. That realisation presented the king with a major problem, for his only remaining legitimate offspring was his daughter, Matilda, a young woman who had been removed from England as a small child to become the wife of the German emperor Henry V and who had returned as a widow in 1125. There were alternatives, his nephews William Clito, the son of his elder brother Duke Robert, and the brothers Theobald, count of Blois, and Stephen, count of Mortain, son of his sister Adela and Stephen of Blois. William Clito, who was compromised by his dependency on the king

of France, was effectively ruled out of the equation, and it is perhaps significant that the chief business which the *Anglo-Saxon Chronicle* reports David
as having advised Henry on was the removal of Duke Robert from the
rather loose custody of Bishop Roger of Salisbury and his confinement in
the castle at Bristol under the watchful eye of Henry's favourite bastard son,
Robert, Earl of Gloucester. The decision, the chronicler adds, was also done
at the urging of the Empress Matilda, which suggests collusion between
uncle and niece in clearing away one rival for her place in the succession. It
is evident, however, that some hard bargaining had been going on behind
the scenes in the closing weeks of 1126.

David was with Henry for his Christmas court at Windsor.[15] It was there
that Archbishop Thurstan, who was about to depart for Rome for the hear-
ing of what was intended to be the final settlement of the dispute with
Bishop John, discovered that the two kings had concluded a political bargain, the price of which for Henry included persuading the archbishop to
soften his stance. The week between Christmas and the Feast of the
Circumcision (1 January) 1127, when Henry had summoned a great assembly of his lay and ecclesiastical magnates to gather at London, witnessed
some complex negotiations involving the kings, the archbishop and the
bishops of Scotland, and the application of considerable pressure on
Thurstan, until he agreed to postpone his journey to Rome. He agreed
instead to send messengers to seek a deferral of the case for a further year
and for a truce to stand for that time during which, with papal permission, a
settlement between the parties would be negotiated.[16] Why Henry had
agreed to support David against Thurstan quickly became clear.

The purpose of the 1 January gathering of the magnates was to secure
from them an oath to agree to support the succession of the Empress
Matilda to the English throne on Henry's death, should the king fail to
father a son by Adeliza before that time.[17] The first of all the laymen to take
the oath was David, presumably in recognition of his status as King of Scots,
Earl of Huntingdon and uncle of the designated successor, but also no
doubt for the strong signal that his willingness to swear his acceptance of
the decision would give to the rest of the assembled earls and barons. It was
for this support that Henry had been prepared to apply pressure to
Archbishop Thurstan over the question of the Scottish Church. There are
signs that David may have struck a deal with his niece, whom he had not
seen for around twenty years, in the suggestion that it was at their joint
prompting that Henry had moved his brother into more secure imprisonment, but this is likely to have been a decision made for purely political

reasons rather than any emotional attachment to a young woman whom he barely knew. Indeed, as we shall explore later, there is little sign of any real affection between the two and David may have been closer to Matilda's cousin and namesake, Matilda of Boulogne, the wife of one of the Empress's most obvious rivals for the crown, her cousin, Stephen, count of Mortain.

The fruits of David's bargaining with Henry became apparent by summer 1127, when David had returned to Roxburgh. Although there is no closely datable evidence to confirm the course of events, it is possible that his northward journey had seen a stop at York for the consecration, without profession of obedience to Archbishop Thurstan, of Robert of Scone as Bishop of St Andrews.[18] If the consecration did not occur there and then, it certainly had taken place before 17 July 1127, when Archbishop Thurstan, Bishop Ranulf Flambard of Durham, Bishop Robert of St Andrews and Bishop John of Glasgow were assembled at the church of St John the Evangelist in the castle at Roxburgh.[19] The chief purpose of this gathering of bishops may have been the consecration of Robert, which would have required two other bishops to support the archbishop in the ceremony,[20] but David's own presence along with what seems to have been a large gathering of his chief councillors in southern Scotland[21] perhaps indicates that the main purpose was a more general council at which the whole question of the submission of the Scottish bishops to York's metropolitan jurisdiction was discussed.

The Roxburgh meeting in July 1127 returns us neatly to the question of the extent of David's sphere of authority within his kingdom. Perhaps one of the clearest signs of the restricted reach of David's kingly power is his continued residence when in Scotland primarily in the country south of the river Forth and especially in Roxburgh. As early as 1114 when he granted property there to his new abbey at Selkirk[22] David had been developing this already ancient settlement as a burgh, an economically and jurisdictionally privileged commercial community of a type which David would develop as the focal market centres for extensive, defined hinterlands, and which would swiftly emerge as the seats of sheriffs in his remodelling of the administrative structures of his kingdom. With the exception of Perth and Dunfermline, which had evidently received burgh status before c.1128, all of David's early grants of burgh status were in respect of communities south of the Forth – Berwick, Edinburgh and Stirling[23] – which again points to a restricted sphere of significant authority. Its key role in David's kingdom can be seen by the relocation in 1128 of the monastery founded in 1113 at Selkirk to a new site in the church of St Mary at

Roxburgh, across Tweed and slightly down-river from his castle and burgh at what became known as Kelso.[24] There are, perhaps, echoes here of the arrangements in London, where a major royal centre and commercial entrepôt all coincided, and it seems likely that David was consciously developing what was for all intents and purposes a 'capital' or chief seat of government for his kingdom. If this were the case, then Roxburgh's location so close to the border with England and great distance from the traditional heartland of Alba north of the Forth signifies an enormous and very abrupt shift in the political centre of gravity in the kingdom. While this shift would appear to be reflected in the character of the men who comprised the king's innermost group of councillors at this time, largely made up of Anglo-Norman knights and clerical servants, many of whom had acquired or were soon to acquire estates in the Southern Uplands, it seems more likely to be a sign of the geographically circumscribed reach of David's authority. Certainly, David appears to have had a strong personal attachment to the Roxburgh area, which would form one of the two points on the axis along which David's expanded kingdom of the post-1138 period would hinge, but it lacked the established royal symbolism of the older centres further north. What Roxburgh did offer, however, was security in the heart of a region over which his authority was strong and where his closest friends and supporters were most thickly clustered.

The temporary cessation of hostilities in the religious controversies with York that had been won in 1127 saw a burst of activity on David's part in respect of the Church. It seems likely that David remained in Scotland through the remainder of 1127 and probably much of 1128, for two projects in which he was closely involved came to fruition that year. The first was the consecration of the new church of the Tironensians whom he had moved from Selkirk to Kelso. This community was still at that time his most favoured and would continue to benefit in future from the patronage of David and his son, and it is very unlikely that he would have failed to attend so significant an event in its development. The second affair was the consecration of Geoffrey, prior of Christchurch Canterbury, as the first abbot of Dunfermline, whose elevation from priory to abbey David had been negotiating since 1126.[25] Like the relocation of Selkirk to Kelso, this event was a hugely symbolic political act which identified David very closely with what his parents had intended to be, and which his brothers had confirmed as, the premier royal monastery north of the Forth. Geoffrey's ordination as abbot by Bishop Robert of St Andrews provided David with the opportunity to very publicly parade himself and his triumphs in the ecclesiastical sphere in

the heart of the kingdom. If the king's general confirmation of the possessions of Dunfermline was issued at this time, then its witness list provides us
with a glimpse of the political community north of the Forth upon whom
any bid to establish and expand his authority would depend.[26] It was a glit-
tering assembly of six of the leading Gaelic magnates of the realm, five
bishops, and a large number of his Anglo-Norman friends and household
servants. The bishops were led by Robert of St Andrews and John of
Glasgow, followed by three probably native Gaelic clerics, Cormac of
Dunkeld, Gregory of Moray, and Macbeth of Rosemarkie. Following them
were earls Áed (probably Earl of Ross[27]), Canstantín of Fife, Máel Íosa of
Strathearn, Ruadrí of Mar, and Maddad of Atholl, plus Gille Mhichel mac
Duibh, kinsman of the Earl of Fife.

In early 1130, David returned to England in a formal capacity for the first
recorded time since April 1127. On this occasion he was to serve as a judge
in Henry's court at Woodstock, presiding over the case of Geoffrey de
Clinton, one of his former colleagues in the service of the English king,
who had been accused of treachery.[28] After the trial David remained in the
south, possibly visiting his Huntingdon estates, before on 4 May he and a
large body of his nobles attended the dedication ceremony of the new
cathedral at Canterbury.[29] From there he may have returned to Scotland, for
around that time Matilda his wife died. Considering how much other
information we have relating to David and his personal life, especially in the
record offered by Ailred of Rievaulx, there is distressingly little of value
relating to Matilda.[30] Even what detail we have provides us with a very one-
dimensional and somewhat shadowy image of the queen. Few documents
survive, however, to show us much of the character of the woman behind
that image beyond a handful of charters recording her religious patronage;
an annual rent of 100 shillings from Hardingstone in Northamptonshire
towards the costs of rebuilding Glasgow cathedral; confirmation of a grant
to Llanthony priory in Gwent by one of her tenants; the witnessing of the
foundation charter of Selkirk; and a grant of 40 shillings in annual rents
from property in Befordshire to the canons of Nostell priory.[31] In contrast
to her sister-in-law and namesake in England, she barely registers on the
historical record and even after her death little appears to have been done to
preserve her memory or build a cult around her. Given her importance in
legitimising Scottish claims to northern England after 1135, this latter point
is most surprising, but there is no indication that there were any moves to
commemorate her in Northumberland. Even her place of burial is decidedly odd, for she was buried in neither a monastery associated with her

paternal inheritance in England, such as Daventry priory or St Andrews at Northampton, nor in the already established mausoleum of her second husband's family at Dunfermline, nor yet in David's own great foundation that had so recently been moved from Selkirk to Kelso. Instead, if we are to trust the report of the fifteenth-century chronicler Walter Bower, she was buried in Scone priory.[32] We should not, however, read too much into this peculiarity, for David and his wife appear to have been genuinely devoted to each other and, unlike his decidedly promiscuous brother-in-law, he never fathered any bastards, even during his wild youth at the English court. Furthermore, after 1130 there is no suggestion that David ever considered remarriage, remaining true to his wife even in death.

In Bower's narrative, the death of Queen Matilda is reported immediately before the reference to one of the defining moments of David's reign, the rebellion and death of the ruler of Moray and the subsequent conquest of his land. If this sequence is not entirely fortuitous, then it is probable that David's absence from Scotland in early 1130, or possibly Queen Matilda's death, was seized as an opportunity by his enemies to mount a fresh challenge for the throne. At the head of the rebellion again stood Máel Coluim, Alexander I's bastard son, but his principal ally was a man who also had a claim to the throne.[33] Óengus of Moray was the grandson of the brief-reigned King Lulach mac Gilla Comgain (1057–8), the stepson of Mac Bethad, both of who had been killed by Máel Coluim III. The suggestion in the chronicle accounts of this event is that Óengus was the senior partner in the attempt, presumably as the legitimate descendant of a recognised king, and that their rebellion was a bid to place him on the throne. What Máel Coluim expected to receive should the attempt have been successful is not recorded, but he must presumably have seen the potential for personal advancement in supporting Óengus. Details of the rising are sparse, but all accounts agree that Óengus and an army from Moray penetrated deep into the heartland of the kingdom before their advance was halted.[34] In command of the defence of David's kingdom was his constable, Edward, son of Siward, who is also described as David's cousin. Very little is known about Edward the Constable, whose father was reported to have been a 'tribune of the Mercians' in the time of King Edward the Confessor (1042–65). He has been identified as the son of Siward, son of Æðelgar, one of the most significant Anglo-Saxon landholders in Mercia to survive the Norman conquest in 1066 and still be in possession of his estates in 1086 when he was recorded in Domesday Book. Siward was descended from the daughter of Eadric Streona, the early eleventh-century earl of Mercia, and Eadgyth the full sister of King Edmund II Ironside, the grandfather of David's mother, Margaret. Siward son of Æðelgar had two sons who appear together in a lawsuit of *c.*1120. The elder was called Ealdred and the younger was Edward. This Edward, son of Siward, therefore, is of the right generation to be an active military leader in 1130 (unlike other contenders for the role, who would have been in their seventies at least by that date) and was also both a true *consobrinus* of David and a Mercian. Siward, son of Æðelgar, moreover was also the patron of the church in which Orderic's father had served and he and his family are frequently mentioned elsewhere in Orderic's history.[35] Beyond brief references to the battle and the death of the Moravian leader, no detail survives of the course of the rebellion or its aftermath. We know from early information incorporated into fourteenth-century chronicle accounts that Óengus and Máel Coluim reached Stracathro near Brechin in Angus, a location which implies that they had come south via the eastern Mounth passes into the Mearns, possibly following the route from Moray through the Cabrach, upper Strathdon and Deeside which crosses the Cairnamount which had seen the battles in which both Mac Bethad and Lulach mac Gilla Comgain were slain. Word of the Moray rising, however, must have travelled quickly, for they had barely penetrated the eastern low-land core of the kingdom before they were intercepted by Edward and his army.[36] The pro-David accounts of the battle which are usually referred to in discussions of the event present it as an overwhelming victory for Edward which saw the slaughter of Óengus and the majority of his warriors, with the victorious commander following up the battle with a campaign into Moray itself, which he proceeded to subdue in David's name.[37] The *Annals of Ulster* record *Bellum itir fhiru Alban [ocus] feru Moreb i torcradar .iiii. mile d'fheraibh Moréb im a righ .i. Oenghus m. ingine Luluigh;* [...] (A battle between the men of Alba and the men of Moray in which four thousand of the men of Moray fell with their king .i. Aengus son of the daughter of Lulach; [...]).[38] Orderic Vitalis reports on Edward the Constable's easy victory and rapid mopping up of the rebels in a punitive raid cum conquest of Moray. By the later twelfth century, some English chroniclers claimed confidently that Moray had been conquered and the 'earldom', a title which creeps into the accounts in an attempt to explain the defeated magnate's status, suppressed in the immediate aftermath of Óengus's death.[39] Yet, even in the 1130 account in the *Annals of Ulster* there are indications that the victory had not been that straightforward, for in an expansion of the entry relating to the battle it is added that 1,000 Scots (later reduced to 100 by a scribe's interlineal gloss) were slain in a counter-attack.[40] Óengus may have been dead but Máel Coluim was very much alive and at large.

The war in Moray and the wider conquest of the North which followed the events of 1130 is discussed in detail in the next chapter, but it is important here to examine the possible sequence of events which followed. Máel Coluim, with Óengus dead, probably took up his late ally's claim to the throne occupied by David. Although illegitimate and, therefore, ineligible to succeed in the eyes of Frankish-inspired and canon lawyers, he was a senior lineal representative of the Scottish royal house and the son of a king. That appears to have been sufficient for him to win widespread support in Scotland and ensure that although Moray may have been knocked out of the contest David would face a severe testing. Máel Coluim would remain at large until 1134, when he was captured and incarcerated for life in David's chief castle at Roxburgh in an echo of the fate of Henry I's main dynastic challenger, Duke Robert.[41] There is little to tell us how the campaign of either protagonist was conducted, but the speech which Ailred of Rievaulx placed in the mouth of Robert de Bruce of Annandale at the battle of the Standard in 1138 may hold some clues:

> Remember when in a previous year you asked for the help of the English against Malcolm, the heir of his father's hatred and persecution, how joyful, how eager, how willing to help, how ready for danger Walter Espec and many other English nobles hastened to meet you at Carlisle, how many ships they prepared, how they waged war, how they built defences, how they terrified all your enemies [until they captured Malcolm himself betrayed; captured, they bound him; bound, they delivered him.] Thus the fear of us, bound his limbs, but bound even more the courage of the Scots, and having quenched all hope of success, removed the audacity to rebel.
> (until they betrayed Malcolm himself; betrayed, they captured him; captured, they bound him; bound, they delivered him.) [42]

The implication in this is that the period 1130-1134 witnessed some hard fighting in which David was dependent very heavily upon his Anglo-Norman friends. Indeed, the suggestion is that David may have had to call upon Henry I for aid and may even have been facing expulsion from the kingdom. It is also implied that the fighting was protracted and involved the building of castles from which territory could be held down and the rebellion gradually contained. It does not, however, suggest that all of this was confined to Moray, which may indeed have been *hors de combat* since

Stracathro and its aftermath. Instead, the references to a muster at Carlisle and a naval campaign involving very many ships indicates that Máel Coluim found at least some of his allies in the Gaelic West and North-West, and David's subsequent ability to grant teinds of his *cáin* from these districts to lowland monasteries could reflect the success of the campaign. These allies evidently included Somairle, King of Argyll, the great west-coast potentate who was to lay the foundations of the power of three of the greatest Gaelic lineages of the west of the twelfth to fifteenth centuries, and who was later to challenge the kings of Mann for control of the Western Isles, or possibly his father, the shadowy Gillebrigte. In 1153, after David's death, the *Chronicle of Holyrood* reported that 'Somerled (Somairle) and his nephews, the sons of Malcolm (Máel Coluim) having allied themselves with a great many men, rebelled…'.[43] Máel Coluim, evidently, had allied himself through marriage to one of the principal warlords of the Gaelic West. Clearly, Máel Coluim was no insignificant challenger and had mustered formidable allies whom David required English help to defeat. The final statement in this section of the speech, however, implies that it was treachery and not fighting which ended the struggle, for it suggests that Máel Coluim was betrayed into his uncle's hands. He never emerged again from his captivity in Roxburgh and nothing more is heard of the 'prisoner of Roxburgh' in David's reign, although his sons were to return to disturb the peace of David's grandsons in the 1150s.

Overall, the first decade of David's reign provides us with no clear picture of how his kingship would develop. Although he had been recognised as king in 1124, apparently without challenge from the most serious potential rival, William fitz Duncan, it emerged rapidly that within the Gaelic heart-land of the kingdom David enjoyed no significant reservoir of support. Nor, of course, may William fitz Duncan have fared much better, for he was the son of a king killed at least partly on account of his anglicising tenden-cies and dependent on English military aid to prop up his regime, and like David had been brought up as Anglo-Norman in culture and tastes. The hostility to David had surfaced early in the person of Máel Coluim mac Alasdair, his bastard nephew, but the initial rising in 1124 appears to have been overcome successfully after some heavy initial fighting. The accounts of the victory in 1124 may be deceptive, however, for there is no sign that David was exercising an effective kingship much beyond the traditional royal centres in Fife and lower Tayside through the 1120s and into the 1130s. Indeed, David can be seen as almost king of Scots in little more than name, for the record of his government indicates that during this time, either by necessity or design, he confined his attention primarily to his former principality in Cumbria and the lands around the Forth and Tay estuaries. Within this circumscribed zone, however, he was practising a new style of kingship modelled closely on Anglo-Norman forms, and was continuing to introduce the innovations in secular and ecclesiastical government, monastic fashions, economic development and land-holding practices that had begun during the period from 1113 to 1124. During this first decade, too, he was to continue his career as an English magnate and one of Henry I's greatest *curiales*, serving as a justice in his former brother-in-law's court. In this, we may see signs of a continuing high level of dependency on his English patron, greatly in excess of the traditional impression of the revolutionary Scottish king, and that dependence, if anything, was heightened at the end of his first ten years as king rather than reduced. It would be going too far to say that 1124–34 saw David engaged in a struggle for survival, for it was a period which did see the foundations of his later power laid in southern Scotland and major advances made in his religious reforms, but it was certainly not a confident start to his reign. Fortune, determination and resourcefulness, however, were already turning the tide by 1134, and in the two following chapters we shall see how David expanded his kingship out of the narrow confines of his southern power base and transformed it into an effective kingship of the Scots.

CHAPTER SIX

The Conquest of the North

For most of the tenth and eleventh centuries the kings of Scots had exercised a fluctuating measure of control over the northern regions of the
mainland beyond the mountain barrier of the Mounth.[1] A series of royal
thanages (estates owned by the crown and administered on the king's behalf by
an appointed official – the thane) extended through what is now Aberdeenshire
to the River Spey, the approximate eastern limit of the province of Moray, and
from there running on as far as Dingwall on the limits of Ross.[2] These indicate
that the crown enjoyed greater influence in this territory than the traditional
historical narratives have allowed. Moray had constituted the original centre of
Mac Bethad mac Findláich's power in the later 1030s and 1040s, but had perhaps been the first part of the kingdom to fall to Máel Coluim on his path
towards his father's throne. Máel Coluim, however, had been unable to entirely
destroy the families of his rivals, kings Mac Bethad and Lulach mac Gilla
Comgáin, who were central to the political structures of Moray. For a while, he
may have been able to contain the North through his relationship with his
stepsons, the joint earls of Orkney and Caithness, but Orkney was a declining
power in the later eleventh century and the earls' participation in King Harald
Hardrádi of Norway's ultimately disastrous bid for the English crown in 1066
may have left the earldom's military strength seriously diminished.[3] Certainly,
the empire assembled by Thorfinn Sigurdsson in the second quarter of the
eleventh century had begun to disintegrate by the 1070s and this may have
been one factor which contributed to the emergence of new challenges to the
authority of the Scottish king in the northern mainland.

Details of what occurred are very sparse, but in 1078 the annals record that Máel Coluim campaigned in the North against 'King' Máel Snechtai, who was later described as the son of King Lulach mac Gilla Comgáin.[4] The war with Máel Snechta, occurring two decades after Máel Coluim killed Lulach, suggests a recent 'coming-of-age' of a son who had been under age in 1058 and who was prepared to make a bid for his father's throne in exactly the same fashion as Máel Coluim himself had returned to reclaim his in the 1050s. The sparse record of events, however, indicates that it was Máel Coluim who invaded Moray, perhaps in a pre-emptive strike against the growing power of a potential rival. According to the *Anglo-Saxon Chronicle*,

> Malcolm captured the mother of Maelslæhta [an Anglo-Saxon scribe's attempt at Máel Snechta]… and all his best men, and all his treasures, and his livestock, and he himself escaped with difficulty…'[5]

It was evidently a significant victory for Máel Coluim but it had failed in one respect; Máel Snechta escaped. The *Annals of Ulster* in 1085 record the 'happy' death of Máel Snechta, a style that usually implies that the dead individual had entered religion before his death.[6] As there is no indication of continuing conflict between Máel Coluim and the men of Moray after 1078, it is possible that entry into the Church had been the price of defeat imposed on Máel Snechta by the Scottish king. For the remainder of Máel Coluim's reign, there were to be no further challenges to his position from members of the Moray dynasty.

There is no evidence for how Moray was controlled under the kings of Scots down into the 1100s, but it is probable that despite the conflict of 1078 a deal had been struck with the family of Máel Snechta. Stability was maintained down to 1130, when Óengus, '*rí*' of Moray, rose in revolt against David only to be defeated and killed (see above p.85–86). Why, after four decades, had the relationship between the family of Máel Snechta and the family of Máel Coluim mac Donnchada broken down so spectacularly? There were probably several factors at work, most notably the still-weak hold which David had over the traditional heartland of his kingdom where Máel Coluim mac Alasdair, the bastard son of Alexander I, appears to have enjoyed his bedrock of support. Máel Coluim, too, was still at large and may have provided Óengus with a vehicle for his personal ambitions; in alliance they would have been immeasurably stronger. The deciding factor, however, was probably Óengus's own pretensions to the kingship of the Scots.

Despite the victory over Óengus won for him by Edward the Constable, and the reports of the wasting of Moray in the aftermath of Stracathro, David was not at first able to capitalise on the position. Indeed, with Máel Coluim still at large until his capture and imprisonment in 1134,[7] there were to be several more years of fighting before the kingdom was again pacified. How that pacification was achieved has been lost to the historical record, but it is unlikely to have been a straightforward task and the disappearance of the Moray dynasty as a political force in the North suggests that it was undertaken with a degree of ruthlessness that saw the elimination of all potential challenge from that family. Furthermore, Moray itself ceased to feature as a source of 'rebellion' for nearly half a century, a position which probably indicates that David's settlement of the province involved the destruction of the cream of its fighting manhood. The tranquillity of Moray for over a generation must surely indicate that pacification was achieved by the sword's edge.

It is widely stated that the defeat of Óengus was followed immediately by the thorough-going conquest and colonisation of Moray by the forces of David I, with the annexation of Moray by the crown representing the most spectacular demonstration of the inexorable march of the new-style 'feudalising' monarchy which David was constructing.[8] Conquest there was, but it was a protracted affair and the colonisation which followed from it an altogether more limited phenomenon than past interpretations have claimed.[9] Indeed, it is possible that the Scots began to make headway in Moray only after the capture of Máel Coluim mac Alasdair in 1134, around which time David began to make property grants from what were probably the lands of Óengus's kin, mainly in favour of the royal abbey at Dunfermline.[10] David's victory in Moray may have been commemorated in around 1135–36 by the foundation of a Benedictine priory at Urquhart near Elgin as a colony of Dunfermline.[11] The symbolism in this act of very public piety has gone largely unrecognised, chiefly because Urquhart has left so little impression in the documentary record and the monastery itself was merged with nearby Pluscarden Priory in 1454 and its buildings dismantled.[12] A few fragments of richly carved late Romanesque stonework in the museum at Elgin are the only physical evidence for the high quality of the church erected by David as a thanks offering for his victory. His action was a declaration of the permanence of his victory: by giving Óengus's ancestral lands to the Church there was no prospect of a return of the disinherited Moray family, for who was going to risk the wrath of God by taking the property back from Urquhart's possession? More importantly, however, David was emulating the behaviour of continental rulers in celebrating their victories, albeit on a much smaller scale than William the Conqueror's Battle Abbey at Hastings or the imperial monasteries founded by the German emperors in their conquests east of the Elbe.[13] Although small in comparison to the rich endowments showered on Battle, David's beneficence towards Dunfermline planted a potent symbol in the midst of newly conquered Moray; a colony drawn from the premier royal monastery of Scotia.

Urquhart's few remaining records support this interpretation of the priory's symbolic role. Its primary function would have been as a victory church, where the monks' masses and prayers would have been offered in eternal thanksgiving for God's favour shown towards David in his triumph over the Moray dynasty and to ensure that God continued to favour the king and his descendants. Urquhart's physical location underscored this commemorative role, for it was sited at the centre of what appears to have been the principal concentration of estates that had belonged to Óengus between the rivers Spey and Findhorn. The priory provided a permanent monument to the new political order in the north of the kingdom founded, quite literally, upon the wreckage of the old. This last point was underlined even further by the nature of the endowments used to support the community. While its landed endowment was never large, certainly in comparison to the substantial gifts made to the new monasteries south of the Forth, such as Holyrood, Kelso or Melrose,[14] David also awarded Urquhart a substantial portfolio of non-landed sources of income. These comprised mainly grants of fishing rights in the rivers Spey and Lossie, plus a portion of the ferme of the new burgh at Elgin,[15] but the largest single award was of a teind of all royal revenues from Argyll of Moray, a huge tract of territory on the Atlantic coast extending from Glenelg to Loch Broom. Now, on one plane this act was simply part of David's policy of extending the mechanism of teinding to support the Church throughout the whole of his kingdom,[16] but it was also a clear demonstration of his belief in the greatly extended reach of his authority into the north-west Highlands and his ability to divert its economic resources to his own uses; David clearly expected to draw revenue from the conquered province – cain, the profits of justice and other income. Certainly, the king believed in the late 1130s that he could enforce payment of this new due from territories over which his immediate predecessors had perhaps exercised little real influence, as the absence of evidence for the existence of royal thanages in Argyll of Moray indicates. The allocation of a teind of this royal income to Urquhart empha-sised the king's close personal interest in the monastery and further reinforced the symbolism of its foundation, for these were the economic resources of the conquered territory being diverted to support the monument to its defeat.

The royal revenues from the heartland of Moray between the Spey and Cromarty Firths were obtained, presumably, from the thanages and other traditional sources which had possibly existed in the region since the later tenth or early eleventh centuries. Apart from the establishment of Urquhart and the planting of royal castles with attendant burghs at old centres of Óengus's defeated estates – Elgin, Forres, Auldearn and, possibly, Inverness – there is little evidence that David took the bulk of the conquered territory into his personal demesne. How, then, was this vast new territory to be governed, for the garrisons of the coastal fringe could not control the extensive hinterland which extended to the south and west? Traditionally, historians have pointed to the introduction of a colonial aristocracy into the region as David's response to the need to secure his conquest, but that development may have been a subsidiary, or even secondary, stage in his plans. The initial scheme may have been altogether more traditional and designed to kill two birds with one stone.

For decades, historians have sought for a means of explaining how the line of pretenders descended from William fitz Duncan who challenged David's successors in the period around 1180–1230 secured such a strong following in Moray and Ross. Furthermore, where did a line so aggressively Gaelic in its culture – they are styled meic Uilleim rather than fitz William – spring from, when William fitz Duncan's one known marriage was to the northern English heiress, Alice de Rumilly?[17] The marriage, moreover, can be dated to around 1137,[18] which leaves little time for an earlier union which produced Domnall mac Uilleim, the first of the meic Uilleim claimants. It would be too easy to dismiss Domnall as an illegitimate son – and William does appear to have had at least one such child (see below p.185) – but, despite the successes of Máel Coluim mac Alasdair in the 1120s and early 1130s, by the time that Domnall was mounting his challenge for the throne in the 1170s bastardy had emerged as an almost insurmountable obstacle in respect of inheritance. No contemporary source, moreover, labels him as illegitimate; the stigmatising of the meic Uilleim comes only after about 1214.[19] The implication, therefore, is that Domnall was the product of a canonical marriage and, given the later strength of support for him and his descendants in Moray, then it is a strong probability that she was a member of Óengus's family.[20] There is evidence for such a marriage, but it is both inferential and late. A thirteenth-century genealogy of the lords of Allerdale and Coupland, lordships possessed by William fitz Duncan in the 1140s by inheritance from his mother, Octreda of Allerdale, and as the husband of Alice de Rumilly, accord William the title 'Earl of Moray'.[21] Then there is the late twelfth-century evidence of William of Newburgh relating to the rising staged by Bishop Wimund in the 1140s, which described the warrior-cleric as 'son of an Earl of Moray'.[22] Wimund's father, as discussed later, was almost certainly William fitz Duncan (see below p.185). Furthermore, the late twelfth-century English royal clerk and chronicler Roger of Howden, who had a detailed and direct personal knowledge of Scottish affairs, referred in the version of his chronicle known under the name of 'Benedict of Peterborough' to Domnall's claim to the throne as being 'by right of his parents',[23] a use of the plural which, if not accidental, implies that his mother's family also carried inherited claims to the Scottish throne. This evidence provides further support for the possibility of William fitz Duncan's marriage to a Moray heiress, for Óengus was Lulach mac Gilla Comgáin's grandson and, through him, inherited a claim to the Scottish throne. William and his possible Moray wife, therefore, would have drawn together the claims descended from Donnchad II and from Lulach.

The purpose behind such a marriage is perhaps more complex than its obvious function as a means of neutralising the threat to David's security posed by the descendants of Lulach. Certainly, by installing one of his most prominent supporters and the senior male representative of the lineage of Máel Coluim mac Donnchada after David himself as ruler of Moray, and further entrenching that man's position through a dynastic union with the defeated rival line, David had scored a signal achievement. But there may have been a more personal political consideration behind the marriage, for the conquest of Moray and the establishment of William fitz Duncan as its 'earl' coincided with the entry into adulthood of David's son, Henry. Down to the mid-1130s, William could have realistically been expected to succeed to the throne should David die leaving only an under-age son. When Henry reached his twenties, however, David, who was pushing strongly for the adoption of primogeniture as the central principle of inheritance, would naturally have looked for him to be acknowledged as his heir. Like David before him, when Edgar and Alexander had effectively removed him from the automatic line of succession in around 1107, the disappointment of being side-stepped in the order of inheritance of the kingship was compensated by the award of a substantial appanage. For David it had been Cumbria, for William, Moray. Rather than being a radical solution to an old problem, this arrangement represented a tried and tested formula but, while it had to a degree worked in the Southern Uplands down to 1124, in Moray it failed.

There are objections to the proposal that William was installed as ruler over Moray. The first is that in no contemporary source does he ever appear so styled. All descriptions of him as 'earl' date from the late twelfth or thirteenth centuries, and where he appears as a witness to David's charters he is simply William fitz Duncan or *nepos regis*. But this non-use of a territorial title cannot be taken as conclusive proof, as titles were not always given by the clerks constructing the charter witness lists. There is also the question of if he was ever actually awarded the title of earl. David, as lord of his huge principality in southern Scotland, was awarded no formal title, his style of 'earl' relating to his English earldom. But Moray was not an earldom in the same sense as Fife or Strathearn, for example, and, although Óengus is accorded the dignity of Earl of Moray by historical convention, that title only occurs in late or non-Scottish sources and probably reflects an attempt to fit his supposed socio-political relationship with David into terms familiar to the readers of that source. Óengus, it is likely, as the Gaelic *Annals of Ulster* described him, considered himself to be *rí*, a provincial 'king' in his own right, but it is equally unlikely that David would have wished Óengus or any of his successors to use a title that could in any way have challenged his own pretensions to the kingship over all Scotland. William, then, may simply have been given lordship over Moray in the way that David had lordship over Cumbria. He was, however, a magnate in David's kingdom, not the ruler of an autonomous principality.

William fitz Duncan and his Moray marriage must have been central to David's plans for the extension of Scottish royal authority into the northern districts of the mainland. William's involvement, however, appears to have been of fairly short duration, for his unnamed first wife was dead before 1137 when he remarried to Alice de Rumilly. From that point until his disappearance from the records in the 1140s, William was a leading figure in David's military operations in northern England, where he himself was involved in a bitter struggle to gain control of portions of both his own and his wife's inheritance. There is no further indication of his involvement with Moray, but it is unlikely that he had simply given up his interest there after the death of his first wife, for he had a young son, Domnall, to whom the province should have passed eventually. While it is possible that he had, in fact, renounced his rights in Moray by around 1137 and been compensated by David who aided him to secure substantial properties in Cumbria and Yorkshire, since these lands were primarily ones to which he had strong legitimate claims, this arrangement does not appear to have been intended to satisfy William for yielding his northern Scottish appanage.[24] William may, in fact, have retained Moray for his lifetime, and it was only following his death in around 1147, at which date Domnall was still a young boy, that David took the 'earldom' into his own hands.

William's apparent neglect of his Moray lordship cannot have been exactly what his uncle had intended, but there is no sign that David was unduly perturbed by the absence from the region of his intended northern policeman, even during the potentially risky period when the Scots were wholly committed to war in England after summer 1136. While central to David's plans, William was not the sole prop of the new Scottish power structure north of the Mounth and west of the Spey. Scottish policy in the region was founded upon a multi-faceted settlement of which William was only one part. Its second major strand appears to have been the forging of a closer political relationship with the rulers of Orkney and Caithness, the one regional power with the resources to dominate the whole of the main-land district north of the Moray Firth.

In the early twelfth century, the earldom of Caithness encompassed at least the whole of the former county of Caithness and eastern Sutherland from the River Oykel and Kyles of Sutherland northwards. Although bitter and bloody internecine feuds within the comital family, who also ruled the Norwegian earldom of Orkney, had resulted in a contraction of the sphere of influence built up by Earl Thorfinn the Mighty in the second quarter of the eleventh century and some political fragmentation around the edges of Caithness where lesser regional nobles had carved out their own local powerbases, the earldom was still a potent force. The further disintegration of Caithness, although perhaps *prima facie* advantageous to a King of Scots bent on extending the effective reach of his authority into the North, was not, however, in David's long-term interests, for it threatened at worst a power vacuum into which other, yet more unwelcome external powers could intrude their influence, and at best a descent into political instability and regional disorder as the lesser regional nobility jockeyed for position. Such instability was fertile recruiting ground for potential challengers to David's authority. Better for him to have a united, strong but politically dependent Caithness-Orkney earldom subservient to him than a decaying fragment over whose remnants aspiring rivals could bicker and from where disorder could spread into his new acquisitions in Moray. The threat to his authority that such a situation could represent was well understood by David, who had confronted similar problems in conjunction with Henry I in imposing strong government in Strathclyde and northern England.[25] There, he had seen that integration of components of the native nobility into the new political structures had given stability and security to those structures. In the North, he most likely recognised that accommodation and integration of the surviving old regional magnates into his new regime was vital for its success. A new understanding with the rulers of Orkney and Caithness, therefore, became vital to his scheme and was rendered even more essential by William fitz Duncan's apparent disengagement from Moray.

At the heart of this strand of David's northern policy was the marriage shortly before 1134 of his kinsman, Maddad, Earl of Atholl, to Margaret, daughter of Håkon Paulsson, Earl of Orkney.[26] It has been pointed out that intermarriage between the key political families of northern and western Scotland 'was fundamental in maintaining and perpetuating an alliance of princes in the northern and western regions of Scotland who opposed the King of Scots',[27] namely dynastic links between Somairle of Argyll, the meic Aeda claimants to Ross, and the earls of Orkney and Caithness, but such bonds were of equal importance in the policies of the kings of Scots designed to counter these hostile alignments. A possible role for Maddad of Atholl in the pacification of Moray after 1130 has been wholly neglected in past analysis of David's – and his successors' – policies in the central and northern Highlands. Traditional accounts of the steady expansion of Scottish royal authority into the central Highlands in the twelfth century have commented on the apparent absence of direct royal intervention in areas such as Badenoch before the end of the reign of William the Lion, but there is some evidence for early crown interest in the region in the form of one recorded thanage at Cromdale.[28] More intensive royal control, it has been argued, in the form of a colonial settlement based upon a series of lordships granted to reliable crown tenants, belonged to the reign of Alexander II (1214–49),[29] but recent research has suggested that the process may have commenced under David I, if not earlier in the eleventh century.[30] David was no less aware than his great-grandson of the central importance that control of Badenoch had for any scheme which aimed at the domination of Moray. Earl Maddad's marriage to Margaret of Orkney, therefore, might imply that in him David saw the agent through whom he could exercise control over the central Highlands and the strategic routeways that radiated from Badenoch.

According to *Orkneyinga Saga*, the initiative for the marriage may have come from Margaret's aunt, Frakkok, a formidable lady of Machiavellian stature who controlled extensive lands in Helmsdale and who occupied an influential role in the councils of her nephew, Earl Harald Hakonsson of Orkney.[31] Frakkok's closeness to Harald, whom the saga presents as having been a vassal of David's for Caithness and Sutherland,[32] had led to her ejection from Orkney following her nephew's suspicious death, for Harald's brother and rival, Paul, suspected that he had been the intended victim of the poison which was believed to have killed Harald and that his aunt was still conspiring against him. Paul was not unjustified in his suspicions, but failed in the old adage about keeping your enemies close, for Frakkok's household in Helmsdale became a veritable court-in-exile for his opponents.[33] There, Harald's son Erlend, a future claimant to the Orkney earldom, and Harald and Paul's sister, Margaret, whose hatred of her surviving brother is a central element in the saga narrative, found shelter and support.[34] In Frakkok's eyes, a marriage to a Scottish nobleman with possible kinship links to the Scottish royal line, at a time when David was extending his authority to within sight across the Moray Firth of her own lands in Helmsdale, offered a potential mechanism through which her great-nephew, Erlend, might succeed to at least his father's Caithness and Sutherland heritage, and might even form a springboard from which a bid for Orkney itself could be launched. For David, it would have developed any (probably nominal) bonds of lordship which had existed between Harald and himself, and would have bound the highly influential Frakkok and her extensive network of powerful relatives in western Caithness into his orbit.[35] The traditional interpretation of the marriage is that its objective was to increase Scottish influence in Caithness and Orkney at the expense of the Norwegian crown, whose influence in the island territories had grown considerably in the late eleventh and twelfth centuries. That, however, was a secondary benefit of the alliance; its primary objective for David was the security of his new prescription for Moray.

From David's perspective, the dynastic strife in Orkney and Caithness took an unwelcome new twist in 1135 when Rognvald Kolsson, a grandson of Earl Erlend Thorfinnsson, to whom the Norwegian king had granted half of the Orkney earldom, arrived in the islands to claim his inheritance. He had received Norwegian confirmation of his rights as early as 1129 and in 1134 this award had been renewed in a fresh grant of half of the earldom by King Harald Gilli.[36] Since the 1120s, various of his family's supporters in Orkney had been working to secure his political interests there and part of their work had seen the development of the cult of Earl Magnus Erlendsson, Rognvald's murdered uncle, who was coming to be venerated as a saint. Rognvald had made a first attempt in 1135 to secure his properties, but was defeated in both Shetland and Caithness. In 1136, however, with backing from supporters of the Erlend family and also from Frakkok and her kinsmen, and probably with the connivance of Earl Maddad of Atholl and his wife, Margaret, Rognvald succeeded in capturing and disposing of Earl Paul. With their mutual enemy gone, however, agreement between the unfortunate Paul's rivals swiftly unravelled, for Frakkok and her family intended that a share in the earldom should be given to Erlend Haraldsson, but Earl Maddad and Margaret saw their young son, Harald Maddadsson, as an alternative candidate.[37] David, who must have considered any further revival of Norwegian influence in Caithness and Orkney by the pro-Norwegian Earl Rognvald as a threat to his newly won authority in northern Scotland, and who saw the Norwegian-appointed sole earl Rognvald Kolsson as that threat personified, presumably supported the Atholl plan. Erlend Haraldsson and his great-aunt Frakkok's kin network could have offered some counterbalance to Rognvald, but their amenability to David's imperial designs probably penetrated little deeper than dynastic expediency dictated. For David, the insertion of the son of one of his own earls into Caithness was infinitely more appealing, still the more so since Harald Maddadsson was an infant and would spend many years of minority under the tutorship of guardians and councillors approved by the king.[38] David could hardly have passed up this opportunity to secure the closer integration of the northern mainland into his kingdom through the appointment of a half-Scottish earl.

David's support for Harald settled the issue in the child's favour. In 1139, aged five, he was admitted to a half-share of the Orkney earldom by Rognvald and given the title of earl.[39] There is no surviving record of any formal grant by David to Harald of the earldom of Caithness, but that award had probably preceded the settlement with Rognvald Kolsson. With the new earl a mere child and unable to offer any personal leadership for many years, it would have been evident to all that this new arrangement was highly vulnerable to challenge from Erlend Haraldsson's supporters, Frakkok in particular. It was recognition of that danger by the Scots which sealed Frakkok's fate, and she was soon afterwards burned to death in her own hall near Helmsdale by a force of men brought north from Atholl by Svein Asleifsson, probably with David's agreement. Frakkok's slaying by Svein was ostensibly a revenge killing for her part in the earlier murder of his father, but Svein Asleifsson was also a notorious political intriguer and violent mercenary who was associated closely with Maddad and Margaret's ambitions. Indeed, *Orkneyinga Saga* presents Svein as their instrument for the removal of Earl Paul in 1136 – the earl was in Svein's hands when he simply disappeared from the records.[40] Family feuding among the Orkney dynasty was clearly being manipulated by David and the Atholl earls in pursuit of wider strategic political interests.

Harald Maddadsson's installation as earl in Orkney and Caithness was a triumph for David. Its main consequence was that through the 1140s Caithness and Sutherland were drawn increasingly into a Scottish orbit while Norwegian influence in Orkney was effectively neutralised. With Scottish power secure in the country north of the River Oykel, and the ruling elite in that area linked directly to the Earl of Atholl to the south, Moray was under effective supervision from all sides. For almost the remainder of David's reign, the region was to present no challenge to the king's authority. That being said, David still had to be on his guard and would continue to take a strong personal interest in the North despite his increasing diversion towards political affairs in the South. Harald was, after all, still a child and Rognvald would enjoy over a decade as the dominant partner in the shared earldom by virtue of a settlement brokered by the Scots.[41] Under his rule, the position of the Erlend party in Orkney was considerably strengthened, not least through his forging of an alliance with the Church. The bishop, William the Old, who been an opponent of the Erlendssons and supporter of Earl Paul, was won over with lavish promises and generous patronage, the most obvious manifestation of which was the establishment of a new cathedral at Kirkwall – in the heart of the Erlend line's main powerbase in east mainland Orkney – and its establishment as the shrine for the developing cult of St Magnus Erlendsson.[42] The political manoeuvring between Rognvald and the supporters of Harald Maddadsson, together with Rognvald's sound working relationships with the other influential agents within the earldom, brought a long period of stability to the islands after the upheavals of the early 1100s. Secure at home, Rognvald believed he could afford to depart on an extended pilgrimage to the Holy Land which carried him through England and the Mediterranean lands, returning via Constantinople, Germany, Denmark and Norway.[43] His absence, however, was quickly to be capitalised on by all his neighbours.

In 1151, King Eystein of Norway, with whom the young Harald Maddadsson had no formal political relationship, arrived in Orkney with a substantial fleet. The teenage Harald, who had been entrusted, at least nominally, with control of both Orkney and Caithness by Rognvald, was at Thurso in Caithness when Eystein arrived unexpectedly and captured him, forcing his submission to Norwegian overlordship as the price for his release.[44] At a stroke, the Scottish domination of the earldom appeared to have been undone and fifteen years of Scottish policy reversed. Having achieved what was his primary objective, Eystein cruised down the eastern coasts of Scotland and England in a demonstration of his power, burning Aberdeen and raiding the coasts of Cleveland, but apparently with no clear purpose other than to win plunder.[45] That same year, possibly in an attempt to counter this unwelcome reverse, David introduced a wild card into the equation by transferring his support to the member of the Orkney dynasty whose ambitions had been frustrated by David's original backing for Harald Maddadsson, Erlend Haraldsson, grandson of Earl Håkon and former protégé of Frakkok. David awarded him half of Caithness, a move intended to re-emphasise the vassalic relationship between the rulers of Orkney and the Scottish crown in respect of their northern mainland earldom. To further complicate matters, King Eystein also granted Erlend Haraldsson Harald Maddadsson's half of Orkney. The result was a three-cornered conflict between Erlend, Harald and Rognvald which lasted beyond David's death in May 1153 and ended only in 1154 with the death of Erlend at Harald Maddadsson's hands.[46] Four years later, the murder of Rognvald – who was later to be venerated as a saint alongside his uncle, Magnus – left Harald in sole possession of the earldoms of Caithness and Orkney. With the undivided resources of the earldoms behind him and with neither the Scots nor the Norwegians in a position to interfere in their government, Harald's ambitions were given free reign.

The career of Harald Maddadsson lies beyond the scope of this book, but it represented a final flourish in the long, turbulent history of the Norse earldom and was bound up deeply in the politics of the early years of David's reign. Dynastic connections saw Harald enmeshed in the tortuous politics of twelfth-century Scotland and his support for the meic Máel Coluim and meic Uilleim claimants to the Scottish throne contributed to the prolonging of the rebellions staged by those families against David's successors Malcolm IV and William the Lion. The importance of Harald in these rebellions cannot be understated, for his second wife, Hvarfloð, is said to have been a daughter of Máel Coluim mac Alasdair, the illegitimate son of David's elder brother, Alexander I. Their eldest son, Thorfinn, was therefore the successor to the meic Máel Coluim claims and, in the eyes of the kings of Scots, an enemy to be neutralised or eliminated. Down to the 1190s, William the Lion undertook a series of campaigns into the far north of Scotland which built on his grandfather's achievements and brought the effective reach of Scottish royal power ever closer to Harald's powerbase in Caithness. The importance placed on Thorfinn can be seen in Scottish demands that he be handed over to them as a hostage for his father's good behaviour in various attempts to secure a settlement after Harald's capture in 1197, although he was neither Harald's eldest son nor his heir.[47] Clearly, the most important objective for William was to eliminate the threat to his position from this rival lineage rather than to control Earl Harald. The unfortunate Thorfinn was handed over as security and, following Harald's renewal of hostilities in 1198, suffered blinding and castration in his prison, dying shortly thereafter.[48] His elimination as a political threat brought down the final curtain on an episode which had started three-quarters of a century earlier in the challenges to David's position at the beginning of his reign.

William fitz Duncan and Harald Maddadsson with his Orkney-Caithness-Atholl axis were the twin props upon which David's settlement of the North depended chiefly through the later 1130s and into the 1140s. That arrangement, however, began to break down in the mid-1140s when William died and was shattered in 1151 when Harald Maddadsson made his submission to King Eystein. It is from this period that evidence of a change in David's policy towards the region can be seen. For some reason, after William's death in around 1147, Moray was not permitted to pass to Domnall mac Uilleim, who appears instead to have received only a portion of his father's lands in Cumberland or Westmorland, nor was William's son, William Puer, admitted to that element of his patrimony.[49] Instead, it appears to have been at this point that Moray was taken into direct royal control and a more radical solution to the problem of management in this huge territory adopted.

Domination of Moray appears to have rested on possession of a limited zone of intensive control which ran through the lowlands of the Laich of Moray and extended westwards along the coast to Inverness and the Beauly Firth. The spine of the new system was provided by the already established royal castles at Elgin, Forres, Auldearn and, probably, Inverness, which David developed not just as military garrison posts from which to dominate the region but as the nuclei for a more deeply rooted system which was intended to speed the integration of Moray into his kingdom. It was probably at this time that David developed the administrative function of these castles, which had become the seats of royal sheriffs before the end of the twelfth century.[50] They also acquired an economic role as the foci for a series of planned colonial communities to which the commercial and jurisdictional privileges of royal burgh status were later awarded. These burghs were, primarily, colonies intended to furnish the king with a reservoir of support embedded in the Moray lowlands, but they were also instruments of economic and jurisdictional domination which functioned in exactly the same manner as the towns founded by Edward I of England in northern Wales in the late thirteenth century. Furthermore, they were the most powerful medium for acculturation, forming the conduits through which most of the ordinary people of Moray were introduced to the new Frankish culture that David was introducing to his kingdom.

Alongside the burgh communities, David was also beginning to implant a colonial aristocracy in the Moray lowlands. These men performed the same military, economic, jurisdictional and cultural role as the burghs. Knights were not simply warriors but were seigneurially empowered controllers of substantial economic resources. The extent of this colonial settlement is unknown, and, if the distribution of motte and bailey fortifications is an indication of its scale, then it cannot be said to have been intensive.[51] Of course, David's monastic foundations also formed part of the colonial process, and the Church was a powerful vehicle for the advance of his political influence in the region. Perhaps significantly in this context, it was only after William fitz Duncan's death that David expanded his ecclesiastical patronage in the North with his foundation of Kinloss Abbey in Moray and his development of the bishoprics of Moray, Ross and Caithness. Overall, therefore, it seems that David adopted a multi-layered approach that provided strength in depth as opposed to the personal authority of individuals upon which his earlier settlement had depended.

If we accept a multiple-layered character for David's new policy of the later 1140s, then the apparent concentration of some of the most intrusive aspects of the colonial settlement in the Laich of Moray becomes less remarkable. Several environmental factors determined aspects of this distribution. The underlying geology of the coastal strip and the micro-climate which exists along the southern shore of the Moray Firth in the lee of the mountainous country to its south and west produced optimum conditions for human settlement and agriculture. This zone represented the primary focus of population and agriculture from the earliest human prehistoric period, and the surviving archaeological monuments of every period from the Neolithic to late Pictish emphasise that it was here that the principal centres of power were located.[52] This same zone seems to have been where Óengus and his family had possessed some of their main estate centres, and it was through this lowland belt that the earlier kings of Scots had their thanages. When David took the lands of the Moray dynasty into his own hands, it was in this coastal district that the bulk of the crown's landed resources were concentrated. It was to secure and administer this valuable economic resource that David developed his chain of fortifications from the Spey to Inverness, probably at former centres of native power. Domination of the principal centres of population and wealth in this zone had provided a significant part of the Moray dynasty's regional power and, we can assume, David intended to dominate Moray in exactly the same way as the dispossessed rulers had done.

While the centres of power upon which David depended for his domination of the region remained essentially the same, the mode of exercise of that power differed profoundly. Unlike Óengus and his predecessors, David could not be a resident lord and was necessarily obliged to delegate power to reliable vassals. Unlike his approach to the control of his former principality in Cumbria, David's new power structure in Moray did not hinge upon the grant of substantial territorial lordships to a group of colonial lords. Instead, the core of his new regime appears to have been founded upon an administrative system from which the later twelfth-century pattern of sheriffdoms emerged. The basis of this system may have been set in place concurrently with the physical establishment of the new castles and burghs. While the king's ministerial agents who were based in these new centres could in no way provide the same form of personal lordship that Óengus and his predecessors had exercised, they gave substance to the bureaucracy which dispensed the fiscal and legal functions of royal government in the province. It was they who were the new power in the land, not the colonial aristocracy whom traditional accounts present as lying at the heart of David's policy.

Belief in the underpinning of David's new regime in Moray by his introduction of aristocrat-colonists lies at the core of most traditional interpretations of the Scottish advance into Moray in the twelfth century. Certainly, in the later twelfth and thirteenth centuries a well-established and numerous nobility, comprised largely of cadets of families already prominent as landholders in the south of the kingdom, can be identified throughout highland and lowland Moray. Evidence for such a nobility in the first half of the twelfth century, however, is almost entirely lacking. The one figure who can be identified is the rather shadowy Freskin, a man of Flemish ancestry whose family's later regional pre-eminence among the settler nobility won them the territorially derived surname of de Moravia or, as they became, Murray. Freskin received from David a grant of the lands of Duffus in the centre of the Laich north of Elgin,[53] which today is one of the principal blocks of arable land in the region. There he erected the great motte and bailey castle which still dominates the landscape of the district.

Its scale and the richness of the land around it have been considered strong evidence for the centrality of Freskin to David's colonial scheme, but appearances are deceptive. While Freskin's lordship of Duffus was extensive, in the twelfth century much of what is now cultivated land was a great expanse of marsh and open water. The district's modern appearance is largely the consequence of schemes of drainage and agricultural improvement dating from the late eighteenth and nineteenth centuries. In the 1140s, the 'good' land in Duffus was much more limited. But it was, perhaps, the nature of the land in the bottom of the Laich that attracted this 'Flemish' colonist. 'Flanders', in the twelfth century, was a term applied loosely to a region of far greater extent than the county of Flanders itself, embracing much of what is now Belgium and the Netherlands. Already in the 1100s, this was a densely populated region where land was at a premium for settlement and where schemes of recovery from coastal marsh and lagoon areas were under way. 'Flemish' settlers were already noted as being prepared to settle on what was considered poorer land by colonists from Normandy and southern England.[54] In Moray, it seems likely that Freskin was enticed in to do what Flemings were already best noted for: drainage and improvement of marginal land. Far from being the key provincial nobleman of David's regime in the North, Freskin was an opportunist speculator who saw the potential wealth to be gained from the Laich's wetlands. He may not have been alone, for vestiges can be glimpsed of a planned settlement of Flemings at the apex of which stands Freskin. Certainly, the Douglas family, part of the Flemish colonisation of upper Clydesdale, and Berowald, who received Innes and Nether Urquhart early in the reign of Malcolm IV and who was a near neighbour of Freskin's original estate at Uphall in West Lothian, may be traces of a colonial venture organised and directed on behalf of David by a *locator* – Freskin – who planted his family at the heart of the network.[55]

David's control of the coastal plain did not rely solely upon secular settlement. A key agent in securing royal interests there in the reign of Malcolm IV was William, Bishop of Moray, whose appointment to the See by 1152 at the latest was certainly controlled by David.[56] William, as bishop, possessed extensive estates scattered throughout Moray from its coastal lowlands to the upper reaches of the Spey. He was not simply a churchman but was also lord of one of the most substantial territorial lordships in northern Scotland.[57] It is probably no coincidence that William's establishment as bishop and the foundation by David of Melrose Abbey's third colony occurred around the same time, and that the new Cistercian outpost was at

Kinloss in Moray.[58] The timing of this foundation – 1150 – within three years of William fitz Duncan's death, might imply that David began to plan it almost immediately Moray came back into his hands. He may have been encouraged in his plans by Bishop William, if he had already been nominated as bishop, who probably began the re-organisation of the diocese in the course of the 1150s to bring its administration and supervision into line with contemporary practice elsewhere in western Christendom.[59] Like his contemporary, Archbishop Malachy at Armagh in Ireland, and the later twelfth-century Anglo-Norman earls of Ulster, David and William placed the Cistercian order at the forefront of the diocesan reconstruction in Moray.[60] The spiritual role of the monks, however, may have been secondary in David's concerns, for the colony at Kinloss was planted in a highly strategic location in the Laich, close to the second of the king's new strongholds at Forres. Supervision and control of the coastal district may have been uppermost in the king's mind.

The establishment of Kinloss provided David with another secure base of dependable vassals planted in the midst of the most densely populated zone of Moray. The significance of the colony can be read on several levels. Firstly, it was a purely pious act on the part of the king, introducing into a spiritually inferior zone of his kingdom monks of an order who had quickly assumed the role of spearhead of reformed monasticism all around the peripheries of Latin Christendom. Secondly, the most common presentation of the foundation is as a supervisory outpost, for the mother house – Melrose – was associated intimately with David, and his younger stepson, Waltheof, was abbot there from 1148.[61] Finally, the community has been presented as part of the pioneering dimension of the Frankish or Anglo-Norman colonial movement into Scotland, for the Cistercians were associated closely with agriculture expansion, land reclamation, and economic development.[62] At all levels, however, the Cistercians at Kinloss were just one additional facet in David's multi-dimensional response to the needs to consolidate royal power in Moray after the death of William fitz Duncan.

There are signs that David may have contemplated a more widespread programme of monastic colonisation in the northern parts of his kingdom from the mid-1140s. In many ways, the clergy provided David with a far more effective mechanism for domination and integration of the remoter provinces than the intrusion of aristocratic colonists. It is surely significant that the first recorded 'Scottish' Bishop of Caithness appears to have been appointed by David in 1145 x 1147,[63] timing that is again coincidental with the death of William fitz Duncan. Down to that time, Caithness had been in effect an extension of the territory of the bishopric of Orkney, a See to which both the English archdiocese of York and, from 1152, the new Norwegian archdiocese of Niðaros or Trondheim had claims of metropolitan jurisdiction. David, having secured at least the temporary suspension of English claims to the metropolitan supremacy of the Scottish Sees had no wish to have the anomalous position in the north of his kingdom re-open that contest. The earldom of Caithness was a Scottish earldom and should not, therefore, be subject to the spiritual authority of a foreign archbishop. It also served to strengthen his influence significantly in the northern mainland by establishing a new diocese with oversight of the whole region, and installing in it a dependable agent. The identity of the new bishop, Andrew, a former monk of Dunfermline, makes it abundantly clear that this appointment was political as well as spiritual. Here was a monk from what was still the premier royal monastery north of the Forth being appointed to the newest and most politically sensitive Sees in the kingdom.

Bishop Andrew in Caithness may have intended to begin the organisation of the new diocese by introducing a monastic colony. As a former Benedictine of Dunfermline, however, it may have been Benedictine rather than Cistercian monks whom he planned to introduce. Traditionally, the seat of Andrew's diocese has been identified as lying at the old Norse earldom centre at Halkirk in Thursodale, but, while later bishops did possess a manor house there, the church at Halkirk was linked closely with the bishops of Orkney and the earls. It has commonly been argued that it was Andrew's thirteenth-century successor, Bishop Gilbert de Moravia, who moved the See to Dornoch following the mutilation of his predecessor, Bishop Adam, in an attack on him at Halkirk,[64] supposedly for the added protection which his kinsmen in southern Sutherland could afford him. Dornoch, however, was an ancient religious centre with a vigorous cult of St Barr, possibly based on a surviving unreformed monastic community.[65] It is more likely to have been there, where recent chance finds of later twelfth-century silver pennies in the old burgh fields around the town, probably carried there in the midden material that had been dumped on the agricultural land, indicate that there was a wealthy and apparently large community on this site, that Bishop Andrew's See was located. Political upheavals in the north of the kingdom in the immediate aftermath of David's death in 1153, however, rendered Andrew's position there nigh untenable as Earl Harald Maddadsson was drawn increasingly into a Norwegian orbit. By the later 1150s, the bishop appears to have become almost permanently resident at the royal court and may never again have ventured north to his nominal

See.[66] It was probably as a consequence of his failure to establish a permanent presence in Caithness diocese that the Benedictine experiment at Dornoch withered away. Too closely identified with the chief royal religious centre of Scotland north of the Forth and with the king of Scots, the monks would probably have found themselves unwelcome in a province that was attempting to roll back the extended authority which David I had established over it.

While the coastal plain represented one form of potential agricultural wealth – principally arable – it would be wrong to regard this as necessarily the most highly prized resource within Moray. The view that arable cultivation, chiefly of cereals, was the culturally superior mode of farming was one facet of the spreading Frankish culture of the twelfth century.[67] It has formed a central strand in Western civilisation for millennia, but its superiority over pastoralism became a key theme in western Christian culture in the Middle Ages and remains at the root of modern perceptions of 'good' and 'bad' land. The comparative lack of 'good' arable land in the straths and valleys that extend south and west from the Moray Firth into the mountainous hinterland should not blind us to the fact that these areas were also populous and economically rich. Recent research has, indeed, demonstrated convincingly that much of the wealth and political power of medieval Moray was located in the hinterland, where a primarily pastoral, cattle-based agricultural regime predominated.[68] This may not have been the most attractive property to the majority of the Anglo-Norman, Breton or Flemish colonists who were being vested with estates in Scotland by David, but it was considered prime land by the Gaelic magnates of the kingdom.

It is a recognised feature of the landed estates of the Gaelic magnates in Scotland throughout the medieval period that the principal concentration of their personal lands was located in more upland districts. This distribution can be seen from Galloway and the western end of the Southern Uplands, into the territory of the earldoms between the Forth-Clyde isthmus and the Moray Firth.[69] In these regions, wealth was not measured in terms of arable production and, through the twelfth and thirteenth centuries, we can see the Gaelic lords of Scotland retaining possession of the grazing while disposing of the arable land to incoming tenants who looked on cultivated land as the basis for their economic support. In the hilly interior of Moray, therefore, where there is no surviving evidence for a settlement of incoming Anglo-Norman colonists in David's reign, a quite different approach to the control of the region was introduced. David well understood that to secure his regime in the Highland zone of the kingdom he needed to establish strong relations with his native magnates. After all, it was on such men that he depended for his political and military support. To set in place a lasting structure of power in the interior of Moray, he needed to win the native magnates' permanent support for his conquest. That was probably achieved by the award to the leading magnates of the kingdom of substantial portions of the dismembered lordship of Moray.

Later in the twelfth century, the leading Gaelic magnates of the kingdom – the earls of Fife and Strathearn – and the earls of Mar, or junior segments of their families, were in possession of substantial estates in the Moray uplands. The Fifes possessed a substantial lordship in Strathbogie and Stratha'an, the Strathearns held Kinveachy and Glencarnie in central Strathspey and Strathdulnain, and the Mars had Abernethy and Aberchirder.[70] It has been assumed traditionally that these properties were acquired by these families as a reward for service to the crown in the course of King William the Lion and King Alexander II's campaigns against the supporters of the meic Uilleim in the central Highlands in the late twelfth and early thirteenth centuries,[71] but recent research has suggested that the carving up of Highland Moray into distinct lordships may have begun much earlier in the twelfth century.[72] To most modern observers, the low-lands of Scotland, especially the arable land, represent the valuable portion of the country. In Moray, the focus is placed firmly on the Laich and its modern acres of rolling barley fields. For incoming Anglo-French colonists also, whose culture was based heavily upon cereal cultivation, such land would have been regarded as the prime property to acquire and develop. Gaelic society, however, viewed things differently. Cattle were the basis of wealth and grazing land prized most highly. Throughout twelfth- and thir-teenth-century Scotland, it is possible to see this distinction at work, with native lords from Galloway to Strathearn and Mar retaining control of the uplands of their domain and disposing of the lowland properties.[73] Although no conclusive documentary evidence survives to confirm the suggestion, it is possible that some of the properties held by the Gaelic magnates in Moray were acquired in David's reign in the aftermath of the destruction of the old ruling dynasty. Certainly, given the close relationship of the Fifes and Strathearns with the king, it seems a strong possibility that they played a key role in the conquest of Moray and took the reward that best suited them – the rich grazing of the Highland straths. Far from being a 'feudal' colonisation, David's settlement of Moray towards the end of his reign may have depended most heavily on the forces of Gaelic tradition.

For David, the settlement of the Moray question represented one of the key achievements of his reign, despite the residual problems which it presented to his successors into the thirteenth century. As a seat of challenge to his lineage's possession of the throne of Scots, it was a threat which had to be faced and overcome, but the struggle for mastery in the north was neither as quick nor as easy as our traditional accounts have implied. The threat from Moray should not be underestimated, for David was subjected to sustained challenge down into the middle of the 1130s, a decade into his reign, and for part of that time may have been confined to a core territory south of the Tay, and possibly even south of the Forth. Victory in 1130, although presented as a glorious triumph followed by a quick and easy conquest of the northern territories, appears instead to have been followed by a hard-fought war of attrition which was only won through David's possession of superior resources in his southern redoubt and through his ability to call on the loyalty of the Gaelic magnates of the core of his ancestral kingdom. While the great Gaelic lords may have been deeply suspicious of the man who would be king, whom they barely knew and who may have regarded them with deep suspicion, David represented continuity of a line which had come to almost monopolise power, which had established most of these native lines in their positions, and which offered security of possession of what they already held and the prospect of further gain. While David may have found it difficult to identify with the culture and society of his Gaelic lords, he was pragmatic enough to recognise that they, rather than his Anglo-Norman friends, represented the key to power in Scotland. David's alliance with his native magnates gave him victory in the north, which in turn provided him with the security to about face and consider a policy of aggressive expansion into northern England, free from threat in the traditional heartland of his kingdom. From being the conflict which almost overthrew his kingship at the outset, the conquest of Moray and the domination of the north proved to be David's first steps on the road to the making of the medieval kingdom of Scotland.

CHAPTER SEVEN

Lord of the West

While the northern part of the kingdom presented a grave challenge to David's power between 1124 and 1134, the west had posed similar problems to him from his first acquisition of power in the Southern Uplands in 1113. The 'west' falls into two distinct blocks: the south-west, an ill-defined zone west of the valleys of the rivers Nith and Clyde; and the west Highland zone, extending from Lennox and Argyll in the south northwards to Argyll of Moray and Argyll of Ross in the north. Beyond them lay a further zone of challenge and threat in the kingdom of Mann and the Isles, a territory over which the Norwegian crown had exercised an active and interventionist overlordship as recently as 1103.[1] The difficulties he encountered and the successes achieved in all of these areas were closely interlinked.

The south-western district appears under the nebulous label of 'Galloway' in the early twelfth century. The name had a more precise political and territorial focus in the kingdom or lordship of Galloway which extended along the northern shore of the Solway Firth from roughly the estuary of the Urr to the North Channel,[2] and which lay outwith the orbit of either the kings of Strathclyde or their Scottish successors. In geographical terms, the country along the northern flank of the Solway is physically isolated from the rest of the Southern Uplands by the hill barrier which extends from Nithsdale westwards to the coast between Wigtownshire and Carrick. As a consequence, it looks naturally to the south and west, to northern England, Man, and to Ireland, and it was with those regions that it had forged its chief cultural, spiritual and political bonds by the beginning of the twelfth century. Lying, moreover, at the pinch point of the North Channel which separates the Irish Sea from the outer Firth of Clyde and the Sea of the Hebrides, it had a strategic importance to rulers in mainland Britain, the Isles and Ireland who wished to control the sea lanes of the maritime west. Relations with the rulers of this highly strategic land would be of critical importance for David in his drive to fix his grip on both his Cumbrian principality and, after 1124, on his throne in Scotland.

Galloway was not just of importance to David and David was not Henry I's only protégé in the north. Some time around 1120, the English king gave another of his brood of bastard daughters to a rising star in the Gaelic world of the maritime west, Fergus, 'King' of Galloway.[3] The date of this marriage and the links which it forged are both highly significant, for in the late 1110s and early 1120s, Henry was seeking to extend his sphere of influence within the Irish Sea zone and into Ireland itself. It is widely recognised that Henry used his numerous illegitimate children to strengthen his influence, either establishing in positions of power his sons, such as Robert, to whom he gave the earldom of Gloucester in 1122, and Reginald, created Earl of Cornwall by the Empress in 1141, or marrying his daughters to important members of the Anglo-Norman aristocracy whose loyalty he wished to bind to the royal house. Although the growing influence of canon law in inheritance practice was placing a great stigma on bastardy, in the early twelfth century any such stigma was more than outweighed by their royal blood. Henry's daughters were married primarily to members of the Norman and French aristocracy, with ties being forged with the ducal house of Brittany, the counts of Perche, and the lords of Beaumont, Breteuil, Montmirail and Montmorenci, all men of strategic importance on the exposed southern and western flanks of the duchy of Normandy. There can be no doubt that Henry had a similar purpose in mind with the marriage of Sibylla to King Alexander I, and far from being a slur on Alexander's worth in the eyes of the English king it is, in fact, a sign of his importance to Henry in that he was deemed worthy of cultivation in this manner. The marriage of another daughter to Fergus of Galloway is a further example of this policy and, for Henry, of equal importance. Through it, Henry forged an alliance with a ruler whose territories occupied a strategic position on the north-western flank of England, and whose naval and military strength made him a key figure in the highly unstable world of the Irish Sea and the Norse-Gaelic west. It was to be the basis of an alliance between the Galwegian and the Norman and Angevin dynasties which endured for over a century.[4]

It is unknown how David viewed Fergus, but Fergus certainly at first saw himself as the equal if not superior of the 'Prince of the Cumbrian Region'. Fergus, in Gaelic tradition, styled himself as *rí* (a king) and clearly considered himself to be free from any subjection to the King of Scots. Men from Galloway had served in Máel Coluim mac Donnchada's armies in the late eleventh century but on what basis is unknown. Given Fergus's own aggressive expansion of his kingdom at the expense of his neighbours to east and west, it is unlikely that any overlordship exercised by David's father over Galloway had survived the upheavals of the decade after 1093. For David, therefore, 'King' Fergus was an unknown quantity who needed to be either won over or neutralised. This uncertainty with regard to Fergus may have been one of several factors which prompted David to strengthen his position around the head of the Solway in the early 1120s. While the establishment of Robert de Bruce in Annandale is generally assigned to 1124 on the basis of the charter in which David, as King of Scots, infefted him with the lordship of that strategic valley,[5] it is now recognised that the original award to Robert may have occurred very soon after Ranulf le Meschin had yielded up Carlisle and Cumberland to Henry I. The grant of Annandale has been presented as part of a wider scheme of co-operation between David and Henry which saw the establishment of Anglo-Norman barons in the three major valleys feeding into the Solway on the 'Scottish' side of the border – Annandale, Eskdale and Liddesdale – possibly before 1120,[6] but all that can be said with certainty is that Robert de Bruce was probably established between 1120 and 1124. While his infeftment in Annandale may have been a response to the removal of Ranulf le Meschin from Carlisle, it is equally possible that it represented either part of a more general building up of David's power in the region at the time of the brief Anglo-Scottish crisis of 1122, or a response to the growing power of Fergus in Galloway.

Fergus, however, quickly proved to be the least of David's worries in the west. His longer term plans for the development of his own power as prince in Cumbria were overtaken rapidly by events in 1124 when his brother died and he succeeded to the throne. As already discussed, David's succession was not universally welcomed by his Scottish subjects and from the outset he had an uphill battle to win acceptance from the Gaelic magnates upon whom the Scottish kings depended for control of the heartland of the kingdom beyond the Forth. His illegitimate nephew, Máel Coluim mac Alasdair, was able to tap into the suspicions of some of the Gaelic lords and mount a serious challenge to David in 1124–25. There is no evidence that

Fergus exploited this situation to his own advantage, possibly because his attentions were already focussed elsewhere but also probably because of the influence exerted over him by Henry I. Other Gaelic powers in the west, however, were not so hesitant and saw in Máel Coluim a heaven-sent opportunity to extend their own personal empires at the expense of the King of Scots. Chief among these men was Gillebrigte, or his son, Somairle mac Gillebrigta, rí of Argyll, who emerged soon after 1124 as the principal supporter of Máel Coluim's bid for the throne.

Gillebrigte or his son, Somairle, was a formidable ally for Máel Coluim mac Alasdair and it is unfortunate that we have no indication of the circumstances which brought them together or exactly when they forged their alliance. David's presence at Irvine twice, once certainly in the period 1124–28, could indicate that it was a connection made very early in the course of Máel Coluim's rising. The alliance between Argyll and Máel Coluim was founded on the pretender's marriage to a sister of Somairle, the date of which is also unknown. Given, however, that Máel Coluim had at least two sons by this marriage before his capture in 1134, who were to join their uncle in an attack on Malcolm IV immediately after David's death in 1153,[7] then the marriage had occurred most probably by 1130 at the latest, and the king's presence at Irvine no later than 1128 points to a date before then.

For the ruler of Argyll, David's extension of his power into the northern and western parts of his Cumbrian principality may have been decidedly unwelcome. Although he was probably regarded as an under-king by the King of Scots (and Edgar's 1098 treaty with Magnus Bareleg of Norway demonstrated the even in the late eleventh century east-coast based kings were still considered to be overlord of their ancestral homeland in Argyll), Somairle was very much a self-made power who had constructed a personal empire at the expense of Manx, Norwegian and Scottish power in the region. To the Scots, the King of Argyll was a vassal lord who, as we shall see, owed tribute to them, but Somairle certainly regarded himself later in his career as effectively a sovereign power free from 'foreign' overlordship. Some historians have presented the conflicts between Argyll and the kings of Scots from the 1120s to the 1160s in terms of Gaelic traditionalists' hostility to the innovative 'feudalising' tendencies of the Scottish crown,[8] but that view entirely misses the point that Somairle or his father were active against David from the mid-1120s, long before his 'feudalising' policies had made any significant impact on Gaelic Scotland. Somairle's probable hostility towards David was driven by no high-minded principles but sprang exclusively from naked ambition and was a collision of two expansionist powers rather than a conflict of cultures. It must be remembered that in the Lennox, David had a territory that marched with Gillebrigte's and Somairle's powerbase in Argyll, while the Clyde estuary represented a zone over which the ruler of Argyll saw himself as the naturally dominant power. The sudden emergence of a new authority on the eastern shores of the firth was something which any ruler of Argyll must have viewed with increasing concern as he established his own lordship in the 1120s. Furthermore, David, Fergus of Galloway, and Óláfr of Man were all firmly within the orbit of Henry I of England, and Somairle may have regarded this extension of English power into regions which he considered his own sphere of influence something which had to be resisted at all costs. On a number of planes, therefore, the King of Argyll and Máel Coluim were natural allies.

No detail survives at all of the fighting which led eventually to the betrayal and surrender of Máel Coluim to his uncle. We can only conjecture from the few brief statements made by Ailred of Rievaulx several decades later that it was protracted and heavy, and involved naval and land expeditions against the centres of power in mainland Argyll and the adjacent islands. It was not, however, a war of conquest. David apparently did not dispossess the King of Argyll once he had secured his objective – the defeat and capture of Máel Coluim – nor did he attempt to intrude his own dependents into Argyll itself. Such colonial expansion in the west was probably far beyond his resources at that point in any case. His aim was submission and acceptance of his overlordship and authority as King of Scots by the ruler of Argyll, and it is clear that he had achieved that design by the middle of the 1130s. Somairle may have remained a reluctant vassal for the remainder of David's reign, but he recognised that David had achieved real lordship in the west.

David's operations against Máel Coluim mac Alasdair and his western allies in the period 1124–34 inevitably led to an extension and tightening of royal authority in the northern part of greater Galloway. The inquest which he had instructed to be carried out into the lands associated with the old Cumbrian church of Glasgow in around 1120–21, while almost certainly not offering anything like a complete picture, reveals an absence of properties in the region later occupied by Ayrshire and Renfrewshire.[9] In the north, this exclusion of Glasgow influence presumably reflects the sphere of influence of the church of Govan, which may have been an older Cumbrian episcopal, or at least monastic, centre. Further south, the position is even hazier, but saint dedications in Carrick, for example, point to religious connections with the Isles rather than with mainland Scottish centres,[10] and a similar picture appears to be the case in Cunninghame. The possible religious affiliations of these western districts do not appear to have reflected the political structures of the later eleventh and earlier twelfth centuries, for clearly the Cumbria bequeathed to David would otherwise not have embraced the whole of what later became the bishopric of Glasgow. That David exercised at least a nominal authority over the lands extending down the eastern shore of the outer Clyde estuary is emphasised by his grant to Selkirk Abbey, recorded in his great foundation charter to the monks of around 1120–24, of the teind of his *cáin* of cheese from 'Galloway'.[11] In his grandson's 1159 charter of confirmation to the monks of Kelso, to where David had moved the Selkirk community in 1128, the detail of the award and its subject matter was greatly expanded to the teind of *cáin* of cattle, pigs and cheese 'from the four *kadrez* of that (part of) Galloway' which had been held by David during the reign of Alexander I.[12] The 1159 charter gives no further information as to where or what these *kadrez* were, but in an earlier charter of around 1136 in which David granted the church of Glasgow the teind of his *cáin* of cattle and pigs 'excepting the years when I come there and consume my *cáin*', four districts – Strathgryfe, Cunninghame, Kyle and Carrick – are named[13] Evidence that these units represented the four *kadrez* of the 1159 charter is purely circumstantial, but the fact that they were included within the See of Glasgow as it emerged in the mid-twelfth century offers strong corroboration.[14] The implication is that David considered those districts to have formed a portion of his Cumbrian inheritance, or that they, like lower Tweeddale, formed an additional territory over which he succeeded in claiming authority.

David's charter to the church of Glasgow reveals that he considered it possible that he would visit his western territories and, as a result, would require his rights to resources there to sustain his household. There is, however, evidence to suggest that David only ever entered the country west of Clydesdale on two occasions in his reign, both probably in the crisis years between 1124 and 1134 when he was fighting to extend his authority out from his political powerbase in the south-east of the country. The first occasion is dated 1124–28, when David issued a command to the vassals of the monks of Dunfermline to perform the services which they owed to the monastery and to assist in the building work there which had probably started soon after 1124. The king's brieve was issued at 'Strathirewin in Galwegia', i.e. Irvine in Cunningham,[15] which would be developed as a burgh later in the twelfth century under its Morville lords. The second occasion is recorded in a charter, also in favour of Dunfermline but after its

elevation to the status of abbey in 1128 and before about 1136, when Earl
Gille Míchel of Fife, one of the witnesses, died. It, too, was issued at
'Strathyrewen in Galwegia'.[16] The issuing of two royal acts on two quite
separate occasions from the same place is not in itself unusual, but given that
these two documents are the only ones to survive that were issued by David
anywhere west of Cadzow and Glasgow implies that Irvine was, at least in
the period before 1136, of particular significance to him.

In the early 1220s, when David's great-grandson Alexander II was undertaking a series of naval and military campaigns in the outer Clyde estuary
and southern Argyll region, Irvine apparently served as the key base from
which sea-borne operations were launched.[17] It seems highly likely, given
the support for Máel Coluim mac Alasdair offered by Somairle mac Gille
Brigta, ruler of Argyll, against whose descendants the 1221–22 campaigns of
Alexander II were launched, that Irvine served in the 1120s and early 1130s
as the springboard for David's offensive against his nephew's allies in the
west. Such activities fit neatly into the speech attributed by Ailred of
Rievaulx to Robert de Bruce of Annandale on the eve of the Battle of the
Standard in 1138, in which reference is made to naval operations from west-
coast bases against Máel Coluim and his associates.[18] Further support for the
possibility that David was based at Irvine in connection with military
actions lies in the subject matter of his second act in favour of Dunfermline,
which freed in perpetuity the abbey's vassals from performance of the
labour service owed to the crown of building fortresses, bridges and other
royal works.[19] In the military crises of this early phase of his reign, David
may have been forced to ignore exemptions from such service dues which
he and his predecessors had granted to the Church, and the need for labour
to build castles returns us neatly to Robert de Bruce's speech, where he
refers to the defences constructed in the course of their operations against
Máel Coluim.

An Argyll alliance with Máel Coluim required David to consolidate his
hold on the western portion of his Cumbrian principality and extend his
direct power all the way to the Clyde estuary proper. Although we have no
surviving charter evidence to support this possibility, it is likely to have been
as a consequence of the threat posed by Somairle's sea-power that David
began to introduce some of his most dependable vassals into this western
district. The most significant awards were to Hugh de Morville, who gained
all of Cunningham with its caput at Irvine, David's western base for the
campaigns against Argyll, and Walter fitz Alan, who received the three districts of Renfrew, Mearns and Strathgryfe and possibly also northern Kyle

by around 1136.[20] It is often forgotten that the Clyde estuary formed one of the most contested internal frontiers of the kingdom in the later twelfth and thirteenth centuries, but David's arrangements for the security of its eastern shores shows acute awareness of the dangerous exposure of this long coast-line to sea-borne assault by Máel Coluim's allies in Argyll and the Isles. Although that direct threat had been neutralised by Máel Coluim's capture and imprisonment in 1134, David remained deeply aware of the threat from the west and chose to extend his authority into that zone whenever the opportunity presented itself.

The events of 1134 probably marked the end for the time being of Somairle's involvement in the challenge of the meic Alasdair for the throne. Certainly, if we can place any faith in the long list of provinces which con-tributed men to the 1138 campaign in England provided by Ailred of Rievaulx, warriors from Lorn and the Hebrides were present at the Battle of the Standard, fighting alongside the men of Lothian, Galloway, Cumbria, Teviotdale, Scotia proper, and Moray.[21] This list of regional contingents alone provides striking evidence for the extended reach of David's author-ity by the later 1130s. It is possible that David's imposition of lordship over Somairle and his Argyll domain, evident by the 1140s in his award of com-ponents of the royal *cáin* from Argyll and Kintyre to the support of the canons of Holyrood Abbey,[22] resulted in David's encouragement of Somairle to expand his own sphere of authority into the island domain of King Óláfr of Man. Certainly, Óláfr appears around the period 1135–40 to have attempted to ring-fence his own position with a series of marriage alliances between his own family and neighbouring powers, among which was a match of one of his illegitimate daughters with Somairle. The precise date of this union is unknown, but is likely to have occurred before about 1140, given the fact that the eldest son of the couple was deemed old enough to exercise kingship by about 1156–57.[23] It would seem, therefore, that a con-certed effort was being made to draw the king of Man into a network of alliances that came together ultimately in David.

Until 1135, Óláfr had, like David, been a protégé of Henry and had enjoyed his protection since soon after 1100. Óláfr, however, also enjoyed strong ties with Stephen, whose lordship of Lancaster made him a near neighbour in the eastern sector of the Irish Sea,[24] and it is possible that he may have aligned with him from the first days of the struggle with Matilda. For David, a weakening of the position of the Manx king may have been a necessary accompaniment to the projection of his own authority into the northern Irish Sea zone. The tying of Óláfr into the Scottish orbit was achieved largely through his marriage, probably shortly before 1140, to Affrica, daughter of Fergus of Galloway.[25] While this match could be presented as an independent action by Fergus designed to strengthen his own influence in the kingdom of Man and the Isles, its probable date suggests strongly that David's hand lay behind it. Certainly, as David consolidated his grip on the north-west of England and, in the summer of 1141 extended his power south through Copeland, Furness and the Honour of Lancaster, he replaced Stephen as the dominant force in the northern Irish Sea zone. That fact and any pressure that was being brought to bear on him by Somairle would have brought Óláfr into David's orbit.

The effectiveness and extent of David's enhanced authority in the west became evident in 1136. The dedication ceremony of the new cathedral at Glasgow occurred in the summer of that year and charters issued around that time indicate the gathering of a significant number of Gaelic and Anglo-Norman magnates in David's company. At Glasgow, David was attended by Fergus of Galloway and his younger son, Uhtred, who was Henry I's grandson, Radulf, son of Dunegal, lord of lower Nithsdale, his brother Domnall, lord of upper Nithsdale, and a number of other native lords from the Lennox and what is now eastern Stirlingshire.[26] A second charter, issued at the royal estate of Cadzow in Clydesdale a short time after the Glasgow gathering, shows that other lords with west-coast interests had been present. These included Hugh de Morville and Walter fitz Alan, both of who probably already held their lands on the Clyde coast by this time.[27] Here, then, we seem to have an assembly of David's key allies and vassals in the south-west, men who would shortly provide him with significant military aid in his invasion of northern England. By 1136, therefore, David had achieved an unprecedented mastery of mainland Scotland. Direct royal authority had been imposed over the whole of the Southern Uplands except for Fergus' domain in Galloway, while north of the Forth royal power was entrenched firmly from the Moray firthlands to Argyll, Fife to Buchan. Outwith that expanded core, the still notionally independent rulers of Galloway, Orkney, Caithness and the Isles had been brought into his orbit, and David's influence extended from Man to the Northern Isles. The reality of that power would be revealed soon afterwards when David shifted from consolidation within his own kingdom to a policy of aggressive expansion.

CHAPTER EIGHT

War in England
1135-39

O n 1 December 1135, Henry I died in Normandy and in the space of three weeks the careful plans which he had constructed to secure the succession to the English throne for his daughter, Matilda, unravelled spectacularly. While the old king's corpse made its slow progress towards burial at Reading, the Empress Matilda remained in Anjou, possibly confident that the oaths sworn by her father's magnates in 1127 would be sufficient to secure her the throne. While she delayed, however, her cousin, Stephen, hurried back to England and, capitalising on anxieties over the instability of the kingdom in the absence of a strong guiding hand, secured the crown for himself.[1] Three weeks after Henry's death, on 22 December, Stephen was crowned king and appears to have gained swift if in some quarters grudging acceptance from the majority of the English and Norman magnates. By the turn of the year, however, the brief calm which his seizure of the throne had brought began to break down.

Among the most serious of the threats faced by Stephen was the invasion of northern England by David and the Scots shortly after Christmas. Some twelfth-century English sources claim that David was acting out of obligation to honour the oath which he had sworn in favour of his niece, the Empress Matilda,[2] but his move occurred too soon after Henry's death and Stephen's coronation to be the result of a co-ordinated scheme planned in conjunction with his niece and her supporters, and appears simply to have been an opportunistic act aimed at winning control of portions of southern Cumbria and Northumbria that William Rufus and Henry I had taken into their hands. Quite simply, David would use the suggestion that he was acting in support of his niece's cause as a fig leaf to cover his naked ambition to gain possession of disputed territory. As has been argued elsewhere, it is probable that David would have invaded England regardless of who succeeded Henry I on the throne, for the perceived weakness of the new ruler after the long and authoritarian rule of the old king would have afforded him an opening upon which he would have been foolish not to capitalise.[3] According to Richard of Hexham, David's initial operation met with considerable success, capturing Carlisle, Wark, Alnwick, Norham and Newcastle, although the symbolic fortress of Bamburgh remained in the possession of Stephen's supporters.[4] Henry of Huntingdon reported that David entered and took Carlisle and Newcastle by guile,[5] which might be a sign that the garrisons of those places had no reason to suspect the Scottish king of any hostile intent, given the two decades of good relations which his presence on the northern side of the border had already brought. Having established effective control over most of the country north of the Tyne, David took oaths and hostages from the regional nobility to secure their allegiance to Matilda, a precaution which could imply that he did not receive an enthusiastic welcome.

There are further indications that the campaign was not a total walkover. David's initial operations in late December 1135 and January 1136, although completed rapidly and with a high degree of success, are described by the normally eulogistic Ailred of Rievaulx as a harrying 'with slaughter and fire'.[6] Although he exculpates David of personal responsibility for the atrocities committed, Ailred implies that elements of the Scottish army – the Galwegians in particular – ravaged their way through Northumberland. While it must be borne in mind that Ailred is consciously and deliberately shifting any responsibility for the brutality of the campaign from his paragon of kingly virtues onto the shoulders of a people who already bore a reputation for almost subhuman barbarity,[7] it is possible that the Galwegians' behaviour may have been one factor which undermined David's efforts to win over the northerners to his side. The Galwegians were useful allies and their ruler, Fergus, had a close personal interest in the outcome of the war for he had been a son-in-law of Henry and his own son, Uhtred, was a cousin of the Empress Matilda. Yet in 1136 and again in 1138 and through the 1140s their unpredictability and Fergus's independent position proved to be a strongly negative factor in David's efforts to win support in northern England.[8] Certainly, the perceived barbarity of the Scots, at least in the eyes of the mainly monastic commentators on the events of 1136–38, proved to be a major stumbling block in securing acceptance of David's rule in northern England.[9]

David's ambitions did not stop with his seizure of Northumberland and southern Cumbria. In early February 1136, David led his army to Durham, intending to capture this key northern fortress and ecclesiastical centre.[10] There, however, he was confronted by Stephen, who had hurried north with his army and arrived at Durham around 5 February. What followed was a stand-off interspersed with protracted negotiations over a period of fifteen days. The result was a treaty between David and Stephen which laid bare the Scottish king's primary goal – territorial gain – for at no point does he appear ever to have sought seriously to advance the Empress's cause, and again used his oath of 1127 as an excuse for his actions in 1135–36.[11] The deal required David to return Newcastle to Stephen but permitted him to retain Carlisle. David did not perform homage to Stephen for this territory, Henry of Huntingdon claiming that this was because of David's role as the first lay oath-taker in 1127. But this was a carefully considered step which left him free from any taint of subservience and able to pursue his ambitions at a later date, still with the ability to claim to be acting in pursuit of the arrangements which he, first before all others, had sworn to uphold a decade earlier. In place of David, however, his son Henry performed homage to Stephen and, technically, it was he rather than his father who held Carlisle and its surrounding region as a fief of the English king. In addition to that, Henry was given the Huntingdon earldom, which had been taken into Stephen's hands following David's invasion the previous December. David had avoided the compromise to his position that any performance of homage to Stephen would have entailed, but Stephen had gained the homage of David's son and heir, albeit solely in respect of his English territories.

Regardless of the various glosses that have been put on the 1136 Treaty of Durham, it is clear that it was neither a total triumph for Stephen nor a craven yielding up of territory by him as the price of peace. Stephen, who was facing a mounting tide of defiance to his rule, had secured what seemed to be peace and stability on his northern frontier at the cost of some remote territories which his predecessors had only recently brought into the orbit of the English crown. Furthermore, although David still clung to the fiction that everything he was doing was done out of his sense of duty to the Empress, Stephen appeared effectively to have detached him from any connection with the Angevin party and compromised his ability to pursue that line in future by receiving the homage of Henry. David, too, cannot be presented as outright winner or loser from the settlement. While he had been obliged to disgorge the most significant portion of his recent gains, he had been confirmed, *de facto*, as being in control of Carlisle. Although Henry had been required to perform homage for the city and for Huntingdon, David was the actual possessor of the former and was free from any personal oath to Stephen which would have limited his future freedom of action. The oath taken by Henry, moreover, was specifically for the English lands. David had successfully eluded any deal and oath-taking which might have compromised the status of his own kingdom.

Whatever can be said about Durham, it was not likely ever to have been a permanent settlement of issues on the Anglo-Scottish frontier. From David's perspective in particular it left huge areas unresolved, especially the question of the earldom of Northumberland, to which Henry had acquired a claim through his mother. Although David had occupied most of the region down to the Tyne in his campaign of 1135–36, he had been forced to surrender his gains to Stephen as part of the price of peace, receiving only in return a promise from Stephen that if he wished to settle Northumberland on any man then Henry's claim to it would first be judged in his court.[12] It was a fudged compromise that satisfied no one. Added to his dissatisfaction with that arrangement was a growing disenchantment with the position regarding the earldom of Huntingdon, which had been settled on Henry under the Durham agreement. There, although Stephen had formally recognised Henry as earl, the king had also acknowledged the claims of Henry's elder half-brother, Simon II de Senlis, and appears to have awarded him much of the Northampton portion of the earldom.[13] It might have been as a consequence of this partial dismemberment of the Huntingdon-Northampton inheritance to satisfy the rival siblings that Stephen had added the highly strategic lordship of Doncaster to the award made to Henry at Durham but, although the new earl came south to his new lord's court in a highly symbolic and very public display of the amity between the Scottish and English royal houses, rumblings of discontent soon made themselves heard.

Within a month of the Treaty of Durham, Earl Henry was in London for Stephen's Easter court. There, according to Richard of Hexham, he was received with honour by the king and seated by him in the place of honour immediately to the right of Stephen. It should, of course, be borne in mind that Stephen's wife, Matilda of Boulogne, was Henry's cousin, the daughter of his aunt, Mary, so there was a close family relationship at work behind the scenes here as well as a need to foster political relationships. The favour shown to Henry, however, appears to have rankled deeply with some of Stephen's leading political supporters, apparently headed by William of Corbeil, the Archbishop of Canterbury, who chose the public forum of the Easter festivities to accuse the young man of treason in Stephen's presence.[14] Joining the archbishop in his denunciation of Henry was Ranulf II, Earl of Chester, who cherished ambitions to regain the lordship of Carlisle that Henry I had forced his father to surrender to the crown prior to his admission to Chester.[15] Ranulf clearly had his own agenda to pursue in the affair and it is likely that there were other men whose territorial ambitions had been thwarted or curtailed by the Anglo-Scottish treaty who used this event as an opportunity to make manifest their deep disgruntlement with Stephen's dealings. It is unclear, however, which other English magnates supported Archbishop William in his accusations, but it is possible that among them was Simon II, whose own patently superior claim to the full Huntingdon-Northampton inheritance had been frustrated by the award of the core of the earldom to his younger half-brother. Regardless of the political imperatives which had produced the treaty, personal animus and baulked ambition quickly derailed the settlement. Although Stephen attempted to smooth over the affair, the damage had been done and David was able to use what he regarded as an insult to his son as an excuse to recall him from England.

Henry's withdrawal from court did not result in an immediate breakdown in the so recently brokered peace treaty, but relations between David and Stephen were clearly very strained. There was a view among some twelfth-century writers that the Empress Matilda and her supporters were lobbying hard with David in an effort to win his full and unequivocal backing for her cause,[16] but there is no firm evidence for any significant diplomacy being undertaken on her part in Scotland. Where we can see David at this time he appears to be preoccupied primarily with domestic affairs, but some of these were certainly coloured by the deteriorating relationship with England. In April 1136, for example, the continuing dispute over the status of the See of Glasgow and Archbishop Thurstan of York's claims to metropolitan jurisdiction took a fresh twist when Pope Innocent II wrote to Thurstan to announce that he had settled in his favour and that a sentence of anathema would be pronounced against Bishop John unless he submitted to the archbishop.[17] Although this was a papal pronouncement, David had previously been able to use his close personal relationship with Henry I to maintain a succession of compromises which had prevented the dispute from escalating into a major crisis. Henry's death

had removed that restraint from the English clergy and exposed David's
ecclesiastical structures to the full force of York's claims. Ecclesiastical politics were to add a further dimension to the mounting tension between the
two kingdoms.

The crisis surrounding Bishop John must have cast a heavy shadow over
proceedings at the consecration of the new cathedral at Glasgow.[18] Around
this time, David was at Glasgow attended by a large concourse of magnates,
possibly for the consecration ceremony. The composition of the group as
revealed by the witness list of a royal charter granting Partick to the church
of Glasgow is very interesting, as it is more than just an assembly of the leading nobles from within the diocese.[19] The secular witnesses comprise largely
native magnates, a composition which might point to a slightly later date
(1137–38?) when David's military intervention in England had strained to
breaking point his relationship with some of his Anglo-Norman colonial
lords, but which also serves to remind us of how shallowly the colonists had
penetrated the western part of Cumbria by that period. The leadership of
the secular group is held by William fitz Duncan, who is not known to have
had any significant property interests within the diocese, followed by Máel
Íosa, Earl of Strathearn, and Donnchad, Earl of Fife, the two greatest secular
magnates in the kingdom, neither of who had any landed interests in the
region. These three men were later to provide much of the military leadership in David's northern English campaigns. Immediately after them, in a
clear indication of his high status, is Fergus of Galloway, again a man with
no properties at that date which fell beneath the spiritual jurisdiction of the
See of Glasgow. The presence of these four men, plus the diverse group of
Gaelic magnates who make up the bulk of the remainder of the list, including several from St Andrews diocese, such as 'Maloden' of Scone, Gille
Brigte of Stirling and 'Dufoter' of Calateria (Callendar near Falkirk), suggest
that this gathering had a primarily political purpose rather than being
related specifically to the ecclesiastical business of the charter, and coincided
with a council at which David may have considered his options for the
future. The same group of magnates, excepting William fitz Duncan and the
earls, appear to have accompanied David from Glasgow up Clydesdale to
the ancient royal centre at Cadzow, where Hugh de Morville and Walter fitz
Alan, two of the most prominent members of the colonial nobility introduced to Scotland by David, join their ranks.[20] That this group remained
together on the move from Glasgow to Cadzow may have been entirely
coincidental as the easiest routes to their lands lay via the Clydesdale passes,
but the timing of the gathering and the identities of the men involved

suggest that important business was being discussed over an extended period. Indeed, it may have been a council of war.

While the Glasgow assembly again betrays no evidence for the presence in Scotland of any of Matilda's agents, there are signs that David's disenchantment with Stephen was made manifest in his increasing amenability to the Matildine party. For example, on the surrender of the castle at Bathampton to Stephen's forces, the leaders of the garrison were exiled as a punishment and found shelter with David in the north.[21] David may simply have been looking to every opportunity possible to provide himself with an excuse to break his treaty with Stephen and, while his motive may simply have been to extend his territorial possessions in northern England, it is probable that he saw his niece's cause as the ideal medium through which to pursue those goals. David had not suddenly awakened to his moral obligations; the opportunist in him saw the potential to capitalise on Stephen's increasing distraction elsewhere to benefit himself.

Early in spring 1137, David broke his peace with Stephen and made his basic objective – the conquest of territory that he considered rightfully his own – abundantly clear. Immediately after Easter, when Stephen was heavily committed to the war against the Angevins in Normandy, David gathered his army with the intention of conquering Northumberland once more. Unsurprisingly, the atrocities committed by elements of his army in 1135–36 had won him few friends in the region and the regional nobility remained overwhelmingly loyal to Stephen. These northern loyalists formed the core of a large army which gathered at Newcastle to oppose David and, presumably forewarned of its presence, David agreed to negotiate rather than fight. A deputation headed by Archbishop Thurstan met with David and Earl Henry at Roxburgh in May 1137 and negotiated a six-month truce that would last until the start of Advent on 28 November, when Stephen was due to return from Normandy.[22] With the truce negotiated, the two armies disbanded and the serious horse-trading began.

David set his cards out clearly on the table at the very outset. Again, there is no mention whatever in the accounts of the negotiations that David had the least concern for the Empress Matilda's rights. Quite simply, territorial aggrandisement was the driving factor behind all of the king's actions.[23] At the end of November, David's messengers arrived at Stephen's court and presented him with an ultimatum: give Henry the earldom of Northumberland or the truce would not be renewed. Stephen, however, was in no mood to yield on this matter and, having won a two-year truce from the Angevins in Normandy, enjoyed greater freedom to focus on the political situation within England. There would be no concessions to Henry. If David wanted Northumberland for his son he would be obliged to conquer it.

It has been said that David's conduct through the whole of this period was 'exceedingly discreditable'.[24] To an extent it is difficult to argue with this view, for, despite the protestations of successive apologists, his operations in England were largely the product of 'ambition and aggression'[25] wrapped up in the more respectable trappings of oath-bound obligation. There is no clearer statement of this apologist line than in the *Gesta Stephani*, where the conflict is presented explicitly in terms of David's sense of moral duty towards his niece arising from his oath to uphold her rights to the English throne ten years earlier.[26] According to this account, the saintly king had been greatly distressed by the accession of Stephen in Matilda's place, an accession which had been advanced by the very men who had sworn with David in 1127 to accept her as their queen. The wording of the narrative is very careful to remove any blame for this turn of events from David, landing it instead squarely on the shoulders of the English baronage, who, the *Gesta's* author states baldly, failed to consult with David. The implication from this presentation of the events of 1135 is that David, if he had received any approach for advice from the English magnates, or any sign of a groundswell of support for his niece, would have acted against Stephen from the outset. Instead, he felt his hands to be tied by the actions of the English barons and he was instead obliged to sit on his hands until events presented him with an opportunity to redress the injustice done in 1135. According to the *Gesta* version of events, it was a letter to David from Matilda which tipped the balance. In it, she set out her case in emotive terms and succeeded in spurring David into taking action on her behalf. As it stands, the scenario put forward in the *Gesta* is wholly fantastic and is designed simply to deflect from David any blame for either his action – or, rather, inaction – on Matilda's behalf in 1135–36 and his wholly self-interested behaviour down to 1138. Its protestations, however, suggest that David himself was well aware of the damage to his reputation which his actions had caused.

It would be wrong to take an overly critical view of David's behaviour in this period, for he was through it all pursuing a clear and sensible policy from a Scottish perspective. What is discreditable to modern eyes is the manner in which he veiled his own ambitions behind claims to be acting in support of his niece. But David was attempting to be all things to all men: seeking to secure territory that he regarded as either lawfully his or the rightful heritage of his son; manoeuvring to avoid censure as an oath-breaker; and striving to win the allegiance of men whose adherence to his

1 BRECHIN CATHEDRAL, ANGUS: already an ancient monastery by the middle of the twelfth century, at Brechin David co-operated with the Gaelic clergy in the setting up of the bishopric there.

2 *Left* ABERDEEN, ST MACHAR'S CATHEDRAL: the establishment of the See of Aberdeen towards the end of David's reign formed part of his scheme for tighter royal control of the northern part of his realm.

3 *Above* CAMBUSKENNETH ABBEY, STIRLING: lying just across the River Forth from the royal castle and burgh at Stirling, the Augustinian canons of Cambuskenneth aided in the ecclesiastical reform of this populous part of the kingdom.

4 DRYBURGH ABBEY, SCOTTISH BORDERS: the founding of monasteries of the reformed orders was not the preserve of the king and his family. Dryburgh, a convent of the austere order of Premonstratensian canons, was founded by David's rich and powerful constable, Hugh de Morville.

5 CARLISLE CATHEDRAL, CUMBRIA: although the See of Carlisle was founded in 1133 by Henry I of England, it was under David's patronage from 1139 that work progressed on the establishment of the cathedral and Augustinian priory in the shadow of his castle.

Clockwise from top left:

6 DUNFERMLINE ABBEY, FIFE: the first monastery of the reformed continental orders founded in Scotland and foremost among the royal monasteries north of the Forth, Benedictine Dunfermline developed as the mausoleum of the Canmore kings. In 1153, David was buried here in front of the high altar.

7 GLASGOW CATHEDRAL, GLASGOW: the remains of Bishop John's cathedral, dedicated in 1136, lie buried beneath its grand thirteenth-century successor. The gathering of nobles for the cathedral's dedication may have seen plans being prepared for the invasion of England.

8 DURHAM CATHEDRAL, CO. DURHAM: the one that got away. From 1136 until his death, David sought to gain control of the influential and powerful northern English see for one of his own clerks, but failed consistently to secure his candidates' appointment.

9 FURNESS ABBEY, CUMBRIA: founded by Stephen while he was Count of Mortain, the abbey grew rapidly in wealth and power. It was here that Wimund, who claimed to be the son of William fitz Duncan, first entered religious life.

10 HEXHAM PRIORY, NORTHUMBERLAND: Richard, the prior of this ancient Northumbrian monastery, and one of his canons, John, are two of our chief chroniclers of the wars waged by David in northern England from 1136. Although their priory benefited greatly from the patronage of David and Earl Henry, Richard and John remained strongly pro-Stephen and critical of David's actions.

Clockwise from above:

11 JEDBURGH ABBEY, SCOTTISH BORDERS: despite his preference for Tironensian monks, Bishop John of Glasgow needed canons to aid in his construction of a reformed hierarchy in his sprawling diocese, and chose to be buried among them on his death in 1147.

12 KELSO ABBEY, SCOTTISH BORDERS: in 1128, David transferred his first monastic foundation, the Tironensian abbey at Selkirk, to a new site at Kelso across the river from his castle and burgh at Roxburgh, a move which underscored its importance in his eyes. It was here that Earl Henry was buried in 1152.

13 KINLOSS ABBEY, MORAY: the third of Melrose's colonies, Kinloss became a symbol of the extension of Scottish power into the heartland of the once rebellious province of Moray, and formed part of David's new power structure for the region following the death of William fitz Duncan.

14 LLANTHONY PRIORY, GWENT: even before his accession to the Scottish throne, David, in association with Matilda, his wife, was a noted patron of many monasteries scattered throughout his brother-in-law's kingdom. Among the beneficiaries of his patronage was the remote Augustinian priory at Llanthony, which received grants of income from his Midlands earldom of Huntingdon.

15 MELROSE ABBEY, SCOTTISH BORDERS: the best-known of all David's religious foundations, Melrose was the first Cistercian abbey in Scotland, colonised in 1136/7 from Rievaulx Abbey in Yorkshire. His stepson, Waltheof, became its second abbot in 1148.

Clockwise from above:

16 ST RULE'S TOWER, ST ANDREWS, FIFE: the lofty
tower of Bishop Robert's cathedral still
dominates the ruins of its bigger later twelfth-
century successor. It was here at the premier
Scottish bishopric that David wished to establish
an archbishopric which would free his kingdom
from the threat of spiritual overlordship by an
English archbishop.

17 RIEVAULX ABBEY, NORTH YORKSHIRE: the
mother-house of most of the Scottish Cistercian
abbeys, Rievaulx enjoyed a close relationship
with David. Abbot Ailred of Rievaulx, a former
steward in David's household, is one of the chief
sources of information relating to the 1138
campaign and wrote an extended eulogy of
David which formed the basis of the king's
saintly reputation.

18 WINCHESTER CATHEDRAL, HAMPSHIRE:
following Stephen's capture at Lincoln in
February 1141, it was the delaying tactics of his
brother, Henry de Blois, Bishop of Winchester,
which staved off the threat of his deposition in
favour of the Empress Matilda.

19 YORK MINSTER, YORK: David cherished ambitions to incorporate England's second city into his realm, and from 1141 until 1149 sought to convert its archbishop into a Scottish metropolitan.

20 BAMBURGH CASTLE, NORTHUMBERLAND: the ancient citadel of Northumbria, David regarded the castle as the rightful heritage of his son, Henry, and fought to secure it for him from 1136, but was consistently denied possession by Stephen in successive treaties until taken by the Scots in 1141.

Clockwise from above:

21 CARLISLE CASTLE, CUMBRIA: although much remodelled in later centuries, the great keep at Carlisle was probably the tower which David is recorded as having built there. One of his most favoured residences, it was the venue for his knighting of Henry of Anjou in 1149 and the scene of the king's death in May 1153.

22 CLITHEROE CASTLE, LANCASHIRE: in 1137–38 and again in 1141, the Scots swept aside the defences of north-west England to establish David's power as far south as the valley of the Ribble. Beneath the walls of Clitheroe castle in 1138, William fitz Duncan routed a force of English knights.

23 DUFFUS CASTLE, MORAY: rising from the level fields of the Laich of Moray, the motte crowned by the remains of a later stone keep was the symbol of the new lordship carved out for Freskin, a Flemish adventurer, as part of the new colonial settlement of the province in the late 1130s or 1140s.

24 EDINBURGH CASTLE, EDINBURGH: already established as the chief fortress of Scottish kings in the reign of David's father, it was within its walls that his mother, Margaret, died in November 1093.

25 HELMSLEY CASTLE, NORTH YORKSHIRE: the stronghold of Walter Espec, one of David's former colleagues in the service of Henry I but a firm opponent in his attempts to secure control of Yorkshire.

26 LUDLOW CASTLE, SHROPSHIRE: held for the Empress Matilda against Stephen, the English king laid siege to the castle in the summer of 1139. In the course of the siege, the king personally rescued Earl Henry, who was being pulled from his horse by a grappling hook thrown from the castle walls.

27 NORHAM CASTLE, NORTHUMBERLAND: first built by Bishop Ranulf Flambard of Durham in 1121, the castle was among David's first targets in 1136, but was secured by him only after a long siege in 1138.

28 CASTLE OF OLD WICK, HIGHLAND: possibly one of the early castles of the earldom of Caithness from which Scottish rule was imposed over this northern province from the 1130s until the end of David's reign.

29 PRUDHOE CASTLE, NORTHUMBERLAND: stronghold of the Umfraville family, lords of Redesdale and Prudhoe, the castle dominated the crossings of the Tyne and the old Roman route between southern Scotland and York. Robert and Gilbert de Umfraville were among the principal supporters of Earl Henry in Northumberland, their loyalty to the prince helping to establish Scottish authority within the earldom.

30 ROXBURGH CASTLE, SCOTTISH BORDERS: the shattered remains of the great royal castle developed by David as the chief seat of his power after 1113. In the great tower of the castle, Máel Coluim mac Alasdair, David's rival for the throne, was shut up for life following his betrayal to his uncle in 1134.

31 WARK CASTLE, NORTHUMBERLAND: the view west from the castle site up the valley of the Tweed towards Roxburgh emphasises the strategic importance of Walter Espec's northern stronghold. David's failure to take the castle in 1136 and spring 1138 was a morale-sapping disaster, but he showed great respect to the defeated garrison when they finally surrendered after an eleven-month siege in November 1138.

32 STRATHMORE AND THE MOUNTH PASSES: a series of key hill routes through the mountain barrier of the Mounth debouch into the lowlands in central Strathmore. In 1130, Óengus of Moray probably led his army through the passes in the centre of this view, to be intercepted and slaughtered by a royal army at Stracathro, on the extreme left.

33 BATTLE OF THE STANDARD MONUMENT, COWTON MOOR, NEAR NORTHALLERTON, NORTH YORKSHIRE: the modern roadside monument commemorates the battle on 22 August 1138. Although often presented as the conflict which turned the tide for Stephen in the north, the defeat was more of a temporary setback for David, who consolidated his position in its aftermath and was able to secure a very advantageous treaty from the English king.

34 INAUGURATION OF A
SCOTTISH KING: the scene
depicted on the fourteenth-
century seal of Scone Abbey
shows the inauguration
ceremony of a Scottish king,
which involved enthronement
and acclamation but neither
coronation nor unction. It
was perhaps the lack of these
sacral aspects of the king-
making ritual which caused
David qualms about
undergoing the process in
1124. [From a nineteenth-
century engraving]

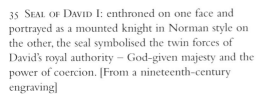

35 SEAL OF DAVID I: enthroned on one face and
portrayed as a mounted knight in Norman style on
the other, the seal symbolised the twin forces of
David's royal authority – God-given majesty and the
power of coercion. [From a nineteenth-century
engraving]

36 SEAL OF ROXBURGH: the thirteenth-century seal of
Roxburgh symbolised the power and authority of one
of the most successful of David's new trading centres.
It was in the towns that the economic momentum to
drive forward the 'Davidian Revolution' was
generated. [From a nineteenth-century engraving]

37 THE CUILLIN MOUNTAINS, SKYE: it was possibly from the Western Isles that Wimund drew much of his support in his bid for power in the late 1140s, and it was on Skye that he probably had the seat of his diocese.

38 ST MARGARET'S CHAPEL, EDINBURGH CASTLE: although the chapel bears his mother's name, it was probably constructed late in David's reign as a private oratory attached to the royal residence on the summit of the Castle Rock.

side would strengthen his hand in northern England against Stephen and, possibly, aid Matilda. The *Gesta*, moreover, suggests that by 1137–38 David was coming under more intense pressure from the Empress and her supporters to take a decisive stand and take the field openly against Stephen. Apart from the supposed letter of appeal from his niece, David was also being lobbied by the son of Robert of Bathampton, who had been among those exiled by Stephen following the fall of Bathampton Castle and, probably with greater effect, by Eustace fitz John, a former associate of David's as a justiciar for Henry I, lord of extensive estates in Yorkshire, centred on the highly strategic castle of Malton and, still more significantly from a Scottish perspective, lord of Alnwick in Northumberland.[27] The adherence of fitz John to David's party by the end of 1137 held out the prospect of a division among the nobility of Northumberland, breaking the unity of opposition to the Scots which had forced David to negotiate in the spring. The defection from Stephen's side of such a man, moreover, would probably have been accompanied by the transfer of allegiance of a significant number of lesser lords who looked to Eustace fitz John for leadership. Indeed, it is possible that in him David saw the means through which he could win control of Northumberland.

The invasion of Northumberland began on 10 January 1138 when William fitz Duncan led a Scottish force down the river Tweed, probably from Roxburgh, to besiege Walter Espec's castle at Wark-on-Tweed, which was held by Walter's nephew Jordan de Bussey.[28] The castle, which controlled a strategic crossing of the river as well as the land routes along the south side of the valley between the river and the northern spur of the Cheviots, was the key to Scottish control of north-west Northumberland. David well understood its strategic importance and was shortly to join with his nephew to place Wark under a close siege, bringing with him engines with which to bombard the stronghold into submission. When after three weeks de Bussey and his knights were still putting up a stout resistance, and had even managed to kill David's personal standard bearer, the king was obliged to leave a force to continue with the siege and march southwards, for there was clearly a risk that he would lose the initiative to Stephen were he to remain longer at Wark. Having sent William fitz Duncan ahead to prepare the way, by 25 January the main Scottish contingent under David's personal leadership arrived at Warden near Hexham.

Contemporary accounts of the ensuing period of military operations by the Scots present what appears, *prima facie*, to be a sustained narrative of brutality, barbarism, atrocity and unchristian behaviour. At the centre of the

criticism lie the account of Richard, Prior of Hexham, a probable eye-
witness to many of the events described, his near contemporary John of
Hexham, and the chronicler Henry of Huntingdon. Despite the protection
and patronage which David offered to Hexham, and the lordship which the
Scots exercised over the monastery down into the 1150s, the accounts of
Richard and John are unrelentingly hostile to the Scots, although attempts
are made to distinguish between the king and the behaviour of elements of
his army. A flavour of the reports can be obtained from the following examples, both in the translations from the Latin by Alan O. Anderson:

> Now the king of Scots, because he had given an oath to king Henry's
> daughter, acted through his followers execrably, as if under the veil of sanctity.
> For they cleft open pregnant women, and took out the unborn babe; they
> tossed children upon spear-points, and beheaded priests upon the altars: they
> cut off the heads of crucifixes and placed them upon the trunks of the slain;
> and placed again the heads of the dead upon the crucifixes. Thus wherever
> the Scots arrived, all was full of horror and full of savagery. There was the
> screaming of women, the wailing of old men; groans of the dying, despair of
> the living.
>
>   (Henry of Huntingdon, *Historia Anglorum*, 260–61)

> So that execrable army, savager than any race of heathen, yielding honour to
> neither God nor man, harried the whole province and slaughtered every-
> where folk of either sex, of every age and condition, destroying, pillaging and
> burning the vills, churches and houses. For they slaughtered by the edge of
> the sword or transfixed with their spears the sick on their pallets, women
> pregnant and in labour; the babes in their cradles, and other innocents at the
> breast or in the bosom of their mothers, with the mothers themselves; and
> worn-out old men and feeble old women, and the others who for any reason
> were disabled, wherever they found them. And the more pitiable a form of
> death they could destroy them by, the more they did rejoice…
>
> It is even reported that in one place they slew many little children gathered
> together, and draining their blood collected it in a stream which they had
> previously dammed up, and thus drank that bloody water, – nay, now for the
> most part blood…
>
>   (Richard of Hexham, *De Gestis Stephani*, 151–52) [29]

We are not required to believe such tales as Richard's of the dammed stream
and drinking of bloody water, which are clearly designed to disgust and

repel the reader and underline the utter inhumanity of this godless horde, but must recognise the implacable hostility towards the Scots which they represent. While Eustace fitz John may have been prepared to deal with the Scots and accept David's lordship, there were many in Northumberland for whom such an acceptance can have been little more than a necessity brought by *force majeure*, and a grudging recognition of unwelcome political realities. Even when we can recognise that the tales of atrocity are stock topoi employed by chroniclers from at least the eighth century onwards to describe the activities of pagan invaders, and understand that the Hexham chroniclers and their fellows saw themselves as the continuators of a tradition begun by Bede which presented the Christian Northumbrians as the bastions of civilisation and faith in the face of the barbarous hordes of the Picts and the Scots, we must also recognise the depths of hostility towards the attackers from the north which lie beneath such accounts.[30]

While we should recognise the hyperbole in the contemporary accounts, we should also acknowledge the evidence which they provide for both the general conduct of the campaign and local resistance to the progress of the Scots. It appears that David had advanced on a broad front down the western side of Northumberland towards the Tyne, avoiding the coastal plain. Richard of Hexham suggests that this was because David planned to ravage the coastal district on his return north at the end of the campaign,[31] but it is more likely to have been a policy designed to avoid the territory of his ally, Eustace fitz John, and to isolate the pro-Stephen fortresses of Bamburgh, Morpeth and Newcastle. Part of the army also crossed the Tyne into 'St Cuthbert's land' (the later County Durham) and devastated its western districts. David was caught between a need to keep his army, comprised largely of Gaelic warriors, active in the field and a desire to establish a more secure grip over Northumberland. These were largely incompatible ends, for his warriors wanted plunder as a reward for their services and his need to give them their head and to keep the support of his native magnates only served to further alienate the very people whom he needed to win to his side. Local deals were struck to safeguard mainly Church property and vassals, such as the protection money paid by the monks of Tynemouth to preserve their land and tenants from plundering, or the arrangements settled by David and Earl Henry with the Prior of Hexham for the security of his monastery and its properties.[32] It is clear that David faced great difficulties in enforcing discipline over his host and in ensuring that the deals brokered with the monasteries were honoured. Richard of Hexham recounts various encroachments on the priory's property plus an attack which led to the devastation of the new Cistercian monastery at Newminster, while John of Hexham records an incident in which it required the intervention of William fitz Duncan to prevent a force of Scots from entering Hexham itself.[33] Finally, around the middle of February, David withdrew his army northwards, apparently falling back in the face of the rapid advance from the south of Stephen with a large force.[34]

Contrary to the traditional depiction of Stephen as a hopeless ditherer, modern assessments of the English king show him to have been decisive and able.[35] His Scottish campaign in February 1138 shows him to have been a skilled strategist and general who sought to inflict as much damage as possible on an elusive enemy. In late February, Stephen arrived at Wark, which the Scots had failed to take, and pressed on from there into Scotland.[36] Richard of Hexham implies that Stephen's objective was Roxburgh, David's principal stronghold and already an important economic centre for the whole of south-east Scotland.[37] The English king's intention was clearly to undertake a punitive raid that would inflict heavy economic damage on David and, perhaps, force him back into negotiations. The Hexham chroniclers both claim that David was planning to trap Stephen at Roxburgh and destroy his army, but Stephen appears to have gained intelligence of David's scheme and, instead of attacking Roxburgh, crossed the river Tweed to devastate the Merse.[38]

Stephen did not remain for long in the north of his kingdom and was back in the south by early April. Almost as soon as Stephen had withdrawn after his punitive raid, David re-crossed the border with his army and launched a second attack through Northumberland. Having systematically plundered the western districts in January/February, the April invasion force worked its way through the districts that had been left untouched in the earlier campaign, crossed the Tyne, and carried out a similar ravaging of St Cuthbert's land.[39] As in the earlier invasion, David had severe difficulties in controlling his ill-disciplined forces, and there is one report that the king himself was threatened when he intervened in a dispute between some warriors over a female prisoner.[40] While Richard of Hexham presents this event as part of a general aura of disorder, uncertainty and poor planning which hung over the campaign, it is evident that David's operations in Northumberland and County Durham were undertaken with clear objectives in mind. For example, he again targeted specific fortifications that controlled strategic routes or river crossings, such as the Bishop of Durham's castle at Norham which dominated the principal crossing of the Tweed between Berwick and Coldstream. It is also clear that the aims of the campaign were on an altogether grander scale than had perhaps been envisaged in January/February, for David also authorised his nephew's harrying of Furness and Craven in what became northern Lancashire. William fitz Duncan had personal claims to both of these areas, the former in right of his mother, the latter as part of the heritage of his second wife, Alice de Rumilly. Both, however, lay substantially to the south of any land to which David had a personal claim, however tenuous. The king, it appears, had decided to extend his authority far beyond Cumberland and Northumberland. How far south his ambitions reached was soon to emerge.

So far, the war in the north of England had been characterised by plundering, marches and counter-marches, and inconclusive sieges. David's two harrying expeditions through Northumberland, however, had failed to bring him any results on the scale of his successes of December 1135–February 1136, and his sieges of Wark and Norham, the two key fortresses on the English side of the river Tweed, had failed to win him the castles. This ill fortune, however, seemed to break in early June, when William fitz Duncan's attack on the lands of Craven brought a morale-boosting success when his army routed a force of English knights at Clitheroe on 10 June.[41] The defeat of Stephen's loyalists in a region where he personally had held extensive estates in the reign of Henry I handed effective control of the north-west of England above Lancaster to the Scots. Their control of the western side of the Pennines, including the main cross-Pennine routes from Carlise southwards, threatened to outflank Stephen's northern outposts in York and Durham.

The victory at Clitheroe brought a major boost to morale in the Scottish army besieging Norham, and the pressure on the castle was increased. According to Richard of Hexham,[42] the garrison consisted of only nine knights and their men, supported by the local peasantry, but they had put up a stern resistance. Despairing of any aid reaching them, the knights negotiated a surrender, for which they were roundly condemned by the pro-Stephen chronicles, for the castle was still well provisioned and its defences were unbroken. David, however, was glad to win the castle without further costly effort and permitted the garrison to pass out of the stronghold and go to Durham to their overlord, Bishop Geoffrey. The king hoped to use his possession of Norham as a bargaining chip with the bishop, whom he hoped to detach from his loyalty to Stephen. Geoffrey, however, refused to break faith with his king and so David ordered that the lands and settlements around the castle be destroyed. Clearly, despite the strength of both his own and his son's legitimist claims to lordship in the region, David was finding it very difficult to win allies in Northumberland and was being forced to use tactics that were unlikely to win over any waverers.

Success at Norham was tempered by failure at Wark, where the garrison sallied out and managed to capture part of David's supply train. The defence of Wark had been especially vigorous, the garrison having earlier managed to capture members of Earl Henry's retinue in forays from their base. David was determined to remove this small but irritating threat to his supply lines, but, despite his bringing siege engines against the castle, he was unable to either storm its defences or force its garrison into surrender. Angered by this failure, for he understood well the need to push on to the south, he ordered the wasting of the townlands of the castle.[43]

David's aim in the summer of 1138 appears to have been to strike a decisive blow against Stephen's position in northern England. That aim, however, was not being served by tying his army down in the sieges of castles, no matter how strategic or symbolic these fortifications were. To break the political support for Stephen north of the Humber, David recognised that he would have to capture one of the key regional centres, Durham or, preferably, York itself. It appears that David had already been preparing for a major offensive in the course of the summer while he was tied down on the Tweed castles, and had sent out summonses to his vassals for an army to mass for a major campaign. Leaving a detachment to keep up the pressure on Wark, he ordered his host to assemble for an invasion of Yorkshire.[44] All contemporary sources agree that it was an impressive army that gathered, comprising his Anglo-Norman vassals and men from Lothian, Galloway, the Western Isles and, it is claimed, even from Orkney, where his influence had been extended significantly as a result of his recent political successes in the North.[45] Despite the scale of the army, however, its quality as a fighting force must have been questionable, for its ill discipline had already made itself manifest in the earlier operations and it was also comprised largely of lightly armed infantrymen whose strength lay in numbers alone. Nevertheless, William fitz Duncan had shown at Clitheroe that such men could confront and defeat Anglo-Norman knights in the field. If David were to be able to consolidate his grip over northern England then that was a victory which he would have to repeat on a grander scale over Stephen's loyal barons.

Recent assessments of Stephen have commented on how he was able to preserve the loyalty of key members of the baronage north of the Humber while David was unable to attract significant numbers to his side. This assessment is, to an extent, true but David did secure the allegiance of several key individuals. The most important of these was Eustace fitz John, who had allied with David before the end of 1137. Fitz John's adherence to the Scots does not seem to have been driven by any particular devotion to the cause of his old master's daughter, but arose from distinctly personal motives. Under Henry I, fitz John had gained several important northern estates, principally Alnwick in Northumberland and Malton in Yorkshire, and, as one of the king's key agents in the region, had been entrusted with the keepership of Bamburgh. Stephen, however, who had been a colleague of his before 1135 and presumably knew him well, had deprived him of that keepership and clearly distrusted him.[46] Fitz John wished to regain his political dominance of the region and saw in David a means by which to achieve that end. When David gathered his army to march south, Eustace fitz John and his men were prominent in its ranks.

Whether at fitz John's prompting or not, the first target of the Scottish army on its southward route was Bamburgh. The castle was the chief place of the forfeited earldom of Northumberland, which had for a while under William the Conqueror been held by Waltheof, the father of David's queen. David regarded both it and the earldom as the rightful inheritance of their son, Earl Henry, and considered it a highly symbolic prize. He had failed to take it in 1135–36 and would again fail on this occasion. The garrison was not unprepared, having constructed a new outer rampart to add to the already formidable defences of the ancient Northumbrian fortress. David may have been deterred from mounting an assault on the stronghold by the strength of the fortifications which faced him and chose instead to bypass Bamburgh and deal with it later. According to John of Hexham, however, a large force of knights from the garrison, emboldened by what appeared to be a Scottish withdrawal, staged a sortie and attacked the enemy columns. The foray quickly turned to disaster as the Scots rounded on their attackers, pursued them back to Bamburgh and burst through the new rampart. Although they failed to break into the citadel, they slaughtered around one hundred of the garrison and proceeded to devastate systematically the fields around the fortress.[47] Bamburgh still held out in Stephen's name, but its chastened defenders appear to have played no further part in this stage of the campaign.

From Bamburgh David marched his army south, burning as they went. In late July the Scots crossed the Tyne into St Cuthbert's lands, where they paused to await the arrival of further fighting units from Cumberland and Galloway. According to Richard of Hexham, the united army numbered some 26,000 strong, an unfeasibly large number for twelfth-century

Scotland but intended clearly to signal that this was a larger force than had ever been seen to come out of the North in the past.[48] At this point, it became clear that David's objective was to win more than simply plunder and that his target lay considerably further to the south. Marching past Durham, whose defences were too strong to be tested without a long siege, the Scots burned their way southwards in a broad sweep through the properties of the bishop and monks before crossing the Tees into Cleveland.

So far, David and his army had encountered only localised resistance from the garrisons of the chief regional fortresses. Unlike in 1136 and 1137, Stephen was in no position to divert his personal attention and increasingly stretched resources from the deteriorating position in the south of his kingdom. There would be no great royal army marching north to counter the Scottish threat. Instead, Stephen was obliged to send north small contingents of men under loyal officers who would lend backbone to the northern resistance. Nominal leadership of the defence of northern England was vested in Archbishop Thurstan of York, but the military leadership was provided by William, Earl of Aumâle, lord of extensive estates in Yorkshire and Lancashire, to whom Stephen had entrusted control of York.[49] Earl William could count on the support of a key group of Yorkshire barons: Walter de Gant, Lord of Bridlington and an important landholder in the East Riding of Yorkshire and in Lincolnshire; Roger de Mowbray, one of the greatest Yorkshire barons; Walter Espec, Lord of Helmsley (and Wark-on-Tweed); Ilbert de Lacy, Lord of Pontefract; William de Percy, lord of extensive estates in the North and West Ridings; Richard de Courcy; William Fossard; Robert de Stuteville, Lord of Thirsk; and Robert de Bruce, David's old associate and Lord of Annandale, who was also Lord of Cleveland.[50] These men represented the baronial leadership of Yorkshire and it is highly significant that they chose to maintain their loyalty to Stephen at a time when the cause of the Empress was beginning to make significant headway in England. Indeed, what is striking is the rareness of defections from their ranks, Eustace fitz John being one of the few who abandoned Stephen. What is equally striking, however, is the narrowness of the group: these were men largely related by marriage and with their estates concentrated in Yorkshire. Outwith that county, Stephen's position in the north of England was in a state of near collapse.

What provided unity to the northern barons was not their loyalty to Stephen and opposition to Matilda but their fear and loathing of the Scottish invaders. Although David was keen to play the legitimist card in respect of his son's rights to Northumberland, he also may have attempted to use his status as a male representative of the old West Saxon royal house to capitalise on any residual antipathy towards the Norman dynasty. By 1138, however, the allure of the Wessex kings was a thing of the past and David found that the hostility towards the Scots bred by nearly a century of violent incursions deep into Northumbria had more than neutralised the possible attraction of his own ancestry. Furthermore, the behaviour of his army since 1135 had served to heighten the antipathy towards the Scots and fear and loathing of those northern barbarians among the northern English was worked upon by influential figures in the Church. Almost every northern English chronicler of the time casts the invading army in the language of Rome against the barbarians, Christian against heathen, presenting David's warriors as the heathen host battering at the gates of civilisation. Stephen's loyal barons were the defenders of the light against the hordes of darkness that threatened to overwhelm the land. It is in this context that Archbishop Thurstan proclaimed that the fight against David was a holy war and ordered priests to accompany the northern barons into the fight carrying processional crosses, holy banners and saints' relics.[51] David, the Christian king, religious reformer and generous patron of the Church, found himself presented in the mould of Antichrist, leading the hordes of the ungodly into a climactic conflict.

Marching under the protection of the banner of St Peter of York, Stephen's barons advanced north from the city to Thirsk. From there, they sent a deputation to David, led by Robert de Bruce, Lord of Annandale, and Bernard de Balliol, Lord of 'Bernard's Castle' (Barnard Castle) in Teesdale, two men with strong personal ties with the Scottish king. According to contemporary accounts, both men pleaded with David to withdraw and in return they and their fellows would prevail upon Stephen to award Northumberland to Earl Henry. David, however, either doubted their ability to deliver on that promise or had already decided that he could secure much more by pressing on, and rejected their pleas. As a consequence, Robert made a formal *diffidatio* – a renunciation of his homage and fealty to David for Annandale, which he yielded up to his former friend – thereby freeing himself of any possible accusation of breaking faith with his sworn lord, while Bernard also renounced his own personal oaths to David.[52] Robert's speech to David on this occasion forms one of the great scenes in Ailred of Rievaulx's extended narrative of the 1138 campaign, *Relatio de Standardo*.[53] The words recorded by Ailred are, unquestionably, pure invention but are constructed by him to articulate the sense of outrage and grievance which many of the northern barons clearly felt towards a man to whom they had been of great service since 1107, and with whom many of them had a close personal relationship. Ailred has Robert list a whole catalogue of instances when David or his brothers had benefited from English support against their enemies, thereby underscoring the charge of ingratitude against him. There is, however, a tension within Ailred's account, for he strove also to exculpate David from personal responsibility for the excesses of his soldiers, and has Robert exonerate the king on that score. He also sought to shift the burden of guilt from the king to his closest advisors, who are presented as pedlars of bad counsel. Ailred, indeed, goes so far as to suggest that David was on the point of agreeing to a truce and a withdrawal only to be dissuaded by the violent intervention of William fitz Duncan, 'a high-spirited man and chief instigator of conflict',[54] who accused Robert of treason. The moment for peace was lost and the two sides prepared for battle.

Archbishop Thurstan and Earl William advanced their army from Thirsk to Cowton Moor a few miles north of Northallerton. At the same time, David crossed the Tees, ordering that his men should burn none of the settlements and fields through which they passed, so that the smoke would not betray their advance to the waiting enemy.[55] On 22 August, the two forces encountered each other on the open ground of the moor. The accounts of the battle which followed – known as the Battle of the Standard after the cart-mounted mast bearing various religious flags around which the English army was massed – continue to make much of the theme of civilisation versus barbarity and Christian against pagan which characterised the narrative of events down to 1138. Henry of Huntingdon and Ailred of Rievaulx report at length speeches by various English leaders, including Bishop Ralph Nowell and Walter Espec, in which the sacrileges committed by the Scots in comparison to the near state of grace enjoyed by the defending army form a central theme.[56] While much of these presentations owes a great deal to traditional Frankish expressions of cultural superiority and contempt for what was perceived to be an alien and inferior culture, there is also running through it a conscious blackening of the reputation of David and his associates. Charges of sacrilege and breaches of faith were devastating weapons to be deployed in a propaganda war and David was vulnerable to both. While Stephen could be accused of breaking his oath of 1127, he had courted the English Church assiduously since 1135 and enjoyed a high reputation for personal piety. David could hardly be depicted as irreligious, for his patronage of the Church in both kingdoms was well known, but his employment of the hordes of barbarians whom he had unleashed on England more than offset the positive dimension of his personal reputation.

The English chroniclers also make much of the barbarity of their enemy in other ways. The Scottish army was numerically strong but it was poorly equipped and ill disciplined for the most part. That ill discipline was to play a decisive part in the battle and, according to Ailred, had undermined the Scots' military strategy even before the fighting began. His account claims that in their council of war immediately before the battle David and his leading earls and captains had agreed that they should place their best men against the English knights and neutralise the English archers with their own. This strategy, however, was opposed by the Galwegians, who claimed the right to form the vanguard of the army. David's lieutenants attempted to resist their claim, arguing that it was foolishness to place the lightly armed Galwegians in the first assault against the heavily armed English and pointing to the danger to morale and discipline should the Galwegians be forced to withdraw. The Galwegians, however, countered this argument, pointing instead to their part in the recent victory at Clitheroe which had been won by lightly armed infantry against armoured English knights. The argument also appears to have revealed deeper tensions in the Scottish army between the Gaelic lords and David's Anglo-Norman knights, with the former, led by Earl Máel Íosa of Strathearn, resentful of the influence enjoyed by the latter in the king's military counsels. Desperate to avoid an open breach between his leading advisors, David agreed to the Galwegians' demands and ordered his army to draw up in battle array.[57]

According to Ailred, the Scots drew up in four lines. The front rank was occupied by the Galwegians, led probably by their king, Fergus. Behind them was the main strength of the Scottish army, comprising the knights, archers and men of Cumbria and Teviotdale under the leadership of Earl Henry and Eustace fitz John. The third rank was made up of warriors from Lothian, Argyll and the Isles, while the fourth, commanded by David himself, consisted of the main body of Scots from north of the Forth, contingents from Moray, and a reserve of knights who formed the king's own bodyguard.[58] Against them, the English drew up in a solid mass around the Standard, the ship's mast topped by a silver pyx containing the consecrated Host and from which flew the banners of St Peter of York, St John of Beverley and St Wilfrid of Ripon. The knights dismounted and took up station in the front rank, supported by archers, while more lightly armed men were placed on the flanks.[59] Despite the contempt which the English chroniclers expressed for the barbaric Scottish army, they agree that the shock of the Galwegians' opening attack almost broke the first rank of the English army and it was only the superior armour and discipline of the knights that prevented the fall-back turning into a rout. Supported by the archers, the English knights rallied the defence and, inflicting heavy casualties on the Galwegians, drove them back into the second line of the Scots.[60] The rout of the Galwegians appears to have been the pivotal moment of the battle, for the fleeing warriors threw the ranks behind them into disorder. Earl Henry and David almost succeeded in reversing the check, but, with casualties among the foot soldiers and their leadership mounting around them, their lieutenants forced them to recognise realities and led them from the field. Against the odds, or so it seemed, Stephen's loyal barons had snatched victory from the jaws of defeat. Surely, exulted the chroniclers, here was the vindication of Stephen's cause; God had smiled on the king, not on the cause of the Empress.[61]

For David, the Battle of the Standard was a heavy blow. The defeat had cost him heavily in terms of both men and prestige, and had succeeded in reinforcing Stephen's crumbling position in the north of England. The scale of the reverse, however, should not be overstated, for like so many 'decisive' battles the Standard did not draw a definitive line under the war in the north. David, Earl Henry, Eustace fitz John and many other leading figures in the war against Stephen had escaped and, while fitz John's castle at Malton was to be besieged and fall to the Stephen loyalists in the aftermath of the battle,[62] his continued adherence to David's party gave the king a still powerful ally in Northumberland. William of Aumâle, moreover, recognised that his victory had at best secured breathing space and his failure to pursue David northwards after the battle, although criticised by later historians, reflected the true weakness of his position. David had been beaten, not crushed, and Earl William understood that he needed to protect Stephen's northern salient in Yorkshire rather than risk a second confrontation which could so easily reverse the result of the first.

That David regarded the Standard as only a temporary setback quickly became clear. He remained in possession of Carlisle, Cumberland and the adjoining districts, and much of Northumberland was still in his hands. Having failed in his drive on York, however, David decided to consolidate his grip on what he had conquered and turned his attention once again to the northern castles which he had failed earlier to take. In early September, he returned to the siege of Wark, which he had left encircled by a detachment of his army two months earlier. But he was no more successful on this occasion than before, losing many men in a succession of failed assaults.[63] While the contemporary northern English chroniclers give the impression that David simply gave up on his attempts to capture Wark following this most recent failure, his personal withdrawal from the castle appears to have been prompted by news of a major mission heading towards Scotland.[64] Quite clearly, David saw that he might gain by negotiation the objectives which he had failed to secure in battle.

The arrival in northern England of Alberic, Cardinal-Bishop of Ostia and legate from Pope Innocent II, was not related directly to the recent conflict. Alberic was charged with settling the various ecclesiastical disputes that had been referred to the papacy, notably concerning the status of Bishop John at Glasgow and Bishop Æðelwulf at Carlisle, but he was to play a key role in arranging a wider political settlement. The legate travelled north from York towards Durham, where he secured the release of David's chancellor, William Comyn, who had been captured by the bishop's men in the flight after the battle at Northallerton.[65] From there he continued northwards along the old Roman road to Hexham, a route which suggests that he had been led to believe that David was at Roxburgh, but from the priory he turned west along Stanegate and on 26 September he arrived at Carlisle. There he found David 'with the bishops, abbots, priors and barons' of Scotland.[66] Clearly, David had been well warned of the cardinal's approach and had assembled his chief spiritual and lay advisors for the expected meeting. The king intended that a far wider agenda than purely ecclesiastical issues should be addressed.

David's meeting with Alberic lasted for three days and a wide range of business was covered. The most straightforward issues appear to have been the cases of bishops John and Æðelwulf, with the former being recalled from his self-imposed exile at Thiron (see p.152) and the latter restored to his bishopric at Carlisle.[67] The more complex matter was the continuing war between David and Stephen, where it quickly became apparent that David was reluctant to cease hostilities. Indeed, Alberic only secured a truce which specifically excluded operations against Wark and which only secured the largely meaningless concession that no Scottish army would invade England for the space of six weeks.[68] As the Scots had already shown preparedness to invade during the winter months, the truce was presumably designed to allow more formal negotiations between David and Stephen to begin. Significantly, and surely a clear indication of what David's aims and objectives had been all along in his invasion of England, there is no sign that David even raised the question of his niece's right to the English throne with Alberic. The legate can have entertained no doubt that David's intervention had been a purely opportunistic bid to win territory. As a sign of his good faith, however, David secured the release of the female captives carried away into slavery by the Galwegians and made restitution to the canons of Hexham for the depredations committed on their property by his men. Satisfied that the truce would hold, Alberic hastened south to meet with Stephen and brief him on the state of negotiations with the Scots.[69]

The truce worked to David's advantage for, while the English were prevented from taking offensive action, the Scots were expressly permitted to prosecute the siege of Wark. The garrison there was in dire straits, reduced to surviving by eating their horses. Keeping true to their lord, Walter Espec, however, they refused to yield up the castle unless commanded to do so by Walter and were prepared to sell their lives dearly in one last sortie. David's blockade of the castle tightened as October progressed but the remaining knights continued to hold out, awaiting word from their lord. Finally, shortly before the expiry of the truce of 11 November, Abbot William of Rievaulx arrived before the castle with a message from Walter Espec, permitting them to deliver their charge into David's hands. After eleven months, David had secured one of his first objectives in the war. Recognising the valour of the pitifully small garrison, David provided them with horses that they might pass in safety south to join with Walter Espec; then he ordered the destruction of the fortification that had cost him so much in lost time, men and effort.[70]

During this time, Alberic was engaged in hard negotiation with Stephen, who, under pressure from his northern barons who had suffered heavy losses to their properties at the hands of the Scots, was at first unwilling to consider any concessions to David. A key role in resolving the impasse is attributed by Richard of Hexham to Stephen's wife, Queen Matilda, who was also David's niece.[71] As has been observed recently, the role of Queen Matilda in influencing her husband's politics and diplomacy has been underestimated consistently,[72] and Richard of Hexham's suggestion that it was her personal affection for her uncle and cousin that moved her should not be dismissed out of hand. She, moreover, was looking to the long-term inheritance in England of her sons, and perhaps took the pragmatic line that it was better to consolidate Stephen's hold over the economic heartland of the kingdom rather than divert resources towards maintaining a grip on remote territories that had only been brought into the English orbit in the course of the previous reign. David, moreover, might perhaps have been more willing to consider proposals in which his niece, the Queen, had been instrumental than any alternatives on offer from his other niece, the Empress, for the husband of the former was in *de facto* control of the crown and able to make meaningful concessions that could be obtained immediately by David, while the Empress's likelihood of securing her father's throne seemed as remote late in 1138 as ever.

Over the winter of 1138–39 negotiations between David and Stephen continued to thrash out terms for a peace treaty, and early in spring 1139 Queen Matilda came north to Durham for a personal meeting with her uncle. On 9 April 1139, the pair settled an agreement which appeared to offer the prospect of a lasting truce between the two kingdoms. The terms of the treaty delivered to David almost everything that the Scots had set out to gain in 1135. Stephen yielded up to Earl Henry the earldom of Northumberland, excepting Bamburgh and Newcastle, in lieu of which he was awarded land of equivalent value in southern England, and the lands of St Cuthbert around Norham and the properties of Hexham. Henry was also restored to Huntingdon and Doncaster, which had been forfeited when war had broken out in 1137, and was confirmed in possession of Carlisle and Cumberland. Stephen also instructed the barons of Northumberland to give their homage to Henry. In return, David and Henry promised to keep the peace and 'be loyal', i.e. to become allies of the English king, and gave a series of important hostages to Stephen, including the sons of Earl Gospatric II of Dunbar, Hugh de Morville, Fergus of Galloway and two other earls.[73] With the settlement concluded, Earl Henry travelled south with his cousin to meet with Stephen at Nottingham, where the treaty was approved and ratified by the king. Throughout the whole process, David made no mention of his other niece's rights; tangible rewards in the present meant far more to him than promises for a vague and possibly unattainable future.

Modern assessments of the second Treaty of Durham have tended to be sharply critical of Stephen's apparent overly and unnecessarily generous concessions to David.[74] The main criticisms are that it failed to offer a lasting solution, for Henry's earldom in Northumberland had been emasculated by Stephen's retention of its two chief fortresses and, sooner or later, David and Henry would seek to gain control of them. The second main objection is that the treaty ran directly counter to the personal ambitions of key members of Stephen's inner circle of supporters, in particular Ranulf, Earl of Chester, who still aspired to regain his father's lost lordship of Carlisle some two decades after Henry I had forced the elder Ranulf to renounce it in order for him to succeed to his cousin's earldom. But these objections do not really stand up to scrutiny of what was yielded by Stephen. R.H.C. Davis believed that the Durham accord handed David all of England north of the rivers Tees and Ribble, but the reality was far more limited. Indeed, the treaty contained the Scots to the district north of the Tyne on the east

and simply confirmed their possession of Cumberland on the west, territory which they already controlled; Stephen was surrendering little more
than what David had already seized. More to the point, the main portion of
the Scots' recent conquests, Northumberland, was settled on Earl Henry,
who gave homage to Stephen for his new earldom. The Scots may have
acquired Northumberland but this act of homage returned it to the lordship of the English crown.[75] Far from being an inexplicably over-generous
award, the treaty was a pragmatic arrangement which recognised both the
weakness of Stephen in the north, despite the scale of his loyal baron's victory at Northallerton, and the reality of David's conquests. It appeared to
end a conflict that had proven to be a dangerous distraction for the English
king and which had placed a severe drain on his already over-stretched
resources. Furthermore, it had brought a restoration of peaceful relations
with his wife's uncle, severed any possible link between David and the
Empress, and bound David's heir to Stephen's cause through his performance of homage. All told, Stephen could look on the Treaty of Durham as a
far from unsatisfactory conclusion to a conflict that had at one time threatened to destroy his position north of the Humber, while David had
succeeded in securing formal recognition of the legitimacy of Scottish
claims to Cumberland and Northumberland.

CHAPTER NINE

The Saintly King

I t is difficult to disentangle the myth of the saintly King David from the reality of the pious but pragmatic ruler who transformed the religious landscape of his kingdom. Much of what was written about David's religious reforms later in the twelfth century self-consciously promotes the image of the holy king, son of a saintly mother, brother of an equally saintly queen, and member of a family of outstanding collective piety. Of his brothers, Æðelred appears to have been designated from early on for a career in the Church; Edgar was a devotee of St Cuthbert and generous patron of the monks of Durham; Alexander promoted the introduction of the Augustinian order into Scotland and began the reform of the chief Scottish diocese at St Andrews; and even the disgraced Edmund ended his days virtuously as a Cluniac monk. His sisters, too, were distinguished by deep personal piety, with Matilda in particular earning a reputation for saintliness and spiritual devotion that almost rivalled that of their mother, and there was clearly the development of a movement to promote her sainthood in the first half of the twelfth century, with the gathering of materials concerning her activities in order to construct a 'Life'.[1] David, too, appears to have been the focus of an embryonic cult and, although there was never any formal process of canonisation, there are indications that he was venerated as a minor saint at Dunfermline in the later Middle Ages, and his name and feast day were added by Archbishop Laud to the 1637 Scottish Prayer Book.[2] David's saintly reputation is examined in Chapter Twelve but in this chapter the focus is on the religious reforms of his reign.

Viewed from the cynicism of the modern age, it is difficult to accept that much of the motivation behind David's support for the Church lay in his intense personal piety and his conviction in the moral responsibility of a ruler to safeguard the spiritual welfare of his subjects. David was the product of an age of spiritual renewal and the root-and-branch reform of the Church. Furthermore, he was also the product of his mother's up-bringing and, while Turgot provides us with a graphic picture of Margaret literally having the fear of God beaten into her children,[3] it is clear that David derived much of his later personal devotion for the Church from his early childhood in the Scottish royal household. Ailred of Rievaulx provides us with a picture, supposedly in David's own words, of an awkward teenager embarrassed by his sister's enthusiastic embracing of the evangelical Christian message and her rather confrontational efforts to persuade her still very worldly youngest brother to renounce his ways and look to his future salvation.[4] This anecdote is not quite the presentation of a youth attempting to kick over the traces of his rather claustrophobic earlier childhood, but it does carry an image of a reassuringly human young man caught between the principles of faith that had been ground into him since infancy and the attractions and pressures of the very worldly atmosphere of the royal household. Of course, the story also serves a purpose as a marker of the Damascene conversion of David from the wildness of youth to the sobriety and piety of adult responsibility, and could itself be a product of the later manufacturing of the king's holy persona. Nevertheless, it serves as a reminder of the spiritual influences that helped to mould the later king.

Among the forces influencing David was the continuing contemporary reform of the English Church that was being carried through by a succession of reformist archbishops and bishops. At Canterbury, the tradition of Lanfranc in the eleventh century, which had been of such inspiration to David's mother, was carried on under Anselm. The archbishop's firm identification with the Gregorian reform movement was to bring him into regular collision with Henry I over issues such as papal 'interference' in English ecclesiastical affairs and the question of lay investiture, but Anselm's reforming zeal and outstanding spiritual credentials transcended his entanglement in secular affairs. At York, a similar but less saintly reputation was enjoyed by Thurstan, although he more than Anselm was active in reconstructing and reforming the structures of spiritual life within his diocese. Thurstan emerged as a particular patron of the Augustinian canons, encouraging the foundation of Augustinian communities within his diocese where they could aid in the process of reform and give practical assistance in ministering to the spiritual needs of the populace. David had already been exposed to the merits of the Augustinians through his sister Queen Matilda's patronage of the order, and well understood their merits and uses in a programme of religious reform. But David also recognised that there were limits to what monks and canons alone could achieve, and while his mother had started with the introduction of Benedictine monks to the kingdom, he would look to bring change at a more fundamental level.

Thorough-going reform of the Scottish Church was not going to be provided by a few Benedictine monks at Dunfermline, although their example would be highly influential on the clergy in general. It was a reformed episcopate that was needed to carry through a programme of reform on continental lines to bring the level of spiritual provision up to the standard expected of Gregorian-influenced clerics. First moves had been made in this direction with the appointment in 1107 of Turgot, the former chaplain and confessor of Queen Margaret and by then Prior of the Benedictine monastery at Durham, to the See of St Andrews by Alexander I.[5] The question of bishop-elect's consecration immediately threw up an issue that was to bedevil Anglo-Scottish Church politics and royal diplomacy into the thirteenth century: the claims of York to metropolitan supremacy over the Scottish sees. Alexander was reluctant to permit the bishop of the chief see of his kingdom to submit to the authority of an English archbishop, presumably because he recognised the potential dangers which such a subjection might pose to his own status as a sovereign ruler. He eventually secured Henry I's aid in securing Turgot's consecration without his making a profession of obedience to the archbishop of York, but only on the understanding that the whole controversy would be settled by a formal process after the consecration.[6] Alexander's relationship with his new bishop, however, quickly soured, and after the quarrels between them in respect of the issue of subjection and Turgot's wish to submit the issue to the arbitration of the Pope had become irreconcilable, in 1115 Turgot resigned his see and returned to Durham.[7] Similar issues plagued Alexander's subsequent efforts to provide himself with a spiritual leader for his reformist efforts. His next choice, Eadmer, was elected in 1120 but had resigned over the issue of his investiture and consecration by early 1121,[8] and his next nomination, Robert, Prior of Scone, remained unconsecrated at the time of Alexander's death on account of the demands for an oath of obedience from him by Thurstan of York.[9] These repeated failures delayed the process of reform generally within the kingdom, but should not be allowed to overshadow the fact that Alexander, immediately upon his succession to the throne, attempted to institute a reformist programme in his national Church, and his patronage of the Augustinian order underscores his efforts to furnish his kingdom with the type of clergy who could undertake the reconstruction which he considered necessary.[10] Although David is often credited with the carrying through of the reformist programme, it was his elder brother who laid the foundations upon which he built.

Alexander's difficulties in finding a bishop and keeping him free from the demands of the Archbishop of York were mirrored in David's own experiences with Glasgow. David in Cumbria was as determined as his brother in Scotland to ensure that his lands were free from spiritual overlordship. He may have owed his position to his brother-in-law's intervention with Alexander, but he was not prepared to compromise his hard-won political freedom by accepting any foreign ecclesiastical jurisdiction over his clergy or people. Here, David was caught between his support for the wider programme of ecclesiastical reform in Europe, which was focused in particular on the question of lay investiture of bishops, and recognition of the fact that any bishop appointed within his principality would be a highly political figure and a key prop to his princely power. While he may have agreed with the principle of ecclesiastical independence, he faced a reality in which he could not risk the consequences of having a bishop installed whose primary oath of obedience was to an archbishop who was himself an agent of a foreign king. He could accept that he himself would not invest the bishop with his office, but he could not accept the submission of the bishop to York, or for that matter to Canterbury.

Soon after he gained control of Cumbria, David appointed his former chaplain and tutor, John, who was either a Tironensian monk himself or deeply influenced by that order, to the vacant bishopric of Glasgow.[11] His appointment occurred at exactly the time that Alexander's quarrels with Turgot were reaching crisis level, but John escaped the demands for subjection to York by the convenient death of Archbishop Thomas II and the resulting five-year vacancy.[12] Instead, David eventually permitted him to go to Rome, where in 1118 he secured consecration at the hands of Pope Paschal II.[13] When the vacancy at York was filled in 1119, however, the new archbishop, Thurstan, was a man determined to rebuild the authority of his see in northern Britain and to roll back Canterbury's claims to primacy over even his archdiocese, and to do so required the submission of all whom he saw as his lawful suffragans. Among these was Bishop John, whose oath of obedience he sought to obtain throughout his pontificate. John, supported by David, was determined not to yield to his demands.

To modern eyes, the wrangling over the obedience of Scottish bishops to an English archbishop might seem a minor issue, but in the twelfth century it was a politically charged question of immense importance. At stake was the potential status of Scotland itself and the nature of its relationship with England. If Scottish bishops were suffragans of an English archbishop, and its ruler the spiritual vassal of the same, what might the implication be for the political relationship between the rulers of Scotland and England? For David, both before and after 1124, it was a situation that could not be contemplated and he was determined to avoid any situation that could possibly compromise his sovereignty.

David found himself in a very difficult position following Thurstan's election to York, for the new archbishop set about with a will to restore the prestige of his see which had fallen to a very low ebb by 1119. In 1118, David had encouraged John to go to Rome to secure consecration at the hands of Pope Paschal II; in 1119 Thurstan went to his successor, Calixtus II, to secure a judgement of his right to John's submission. On 20 November 1119, Calixtus ordered John, and all the other Scottish bishops, to submit to Thurstan as his proper metropolitan.[14] Probably with David's unwavering backing, John refused to yield to this pressure, but in 1122 Thurstan, exasperated by this stance, suspended John from episcopal office. John decided on an appeal at Rome, but the pro-York inclinations of the Pope led to the bishop going on an extended pilgrimage to Jerusalem.[15] In early 1123, Calixtus recalled John from Jerusalem to Rome, and there ordered him to return to his bishopric.[16] For four years, Glasgow had been without its appointed bishop and the programme of reform which David may have been eager to institute in 1113–1114 can barely have progressed. It was possibly only at this juncture that David undertook his so-called inquest into the lands and rights of the See of Glasgow, when John had returned from his extended exile.[17] With or without David's support, however, John still resisted Thurstan's demands for his submission. An impasse had been reached, but the position was to become altogether more complex in 1124 when Alexander I died and David succeeded him on the Scottish throne, thereby bringing together the issue of John and the question of the subjection of the Scottish bishops in general.

In late 1125, following the legation to England and Scotland of John of Crema, during which the legate had met with David at Roxburgh,[18] Bishop John again set out for Rome. John had gone to Rome in the company of William of Corbeil, Archbishop of Canterbury, who was taking his claim to primacy over York to the papal curia. Bishop John, it appears, formed part of a Scottish delegation sent by David in a bid to secure a pallium – the lamb-swool scarf that symbolised archiepiscopal status – for St Andrews.[19] David was clearly as, if not more, determined now to secure his bishops' freedom from foreign metropolitan subjection. When Thurstan arrived to contest William's claim, he encountered John and immediately brought before Pope Honorius II the matter of the bishop's refusal to obey the instruction of the Pope's predecessors, Paschal II and Calixtus II, to submit to York.[20] According to York tradition, moreover, Thurstan refuted the Scottish dele-gation's bid to secure the sought-for pallium by setting out a clear case for the kingdom of Scotland being subject to England.[21] Exactly the argument that Alexander I and David had feared would be used was being articulated by Thurstan. The archbishop may have succeeded in blocking the Scots' efforts to win an archbishopric of their own, but Bishop John was able to dodge the matter of his non-compliance with previous judgements against him by persuading the Pope that he had come to Rome as an envoy on one issue and could not be expected at that time to answer for another. As a result, a date was set early in 1127 for the case to be settled at Rome.[22]

Political events back home in Britain were running ahead of Thurstan and John, and the case was never brought to the curia in 1127. At their meeting at Windsor and London over Christmas 1126, David and Henry had struck a deal whereby, in return for David's support for Henry's plan to settle the suc-cession on Matilda, Henry persuaded Thurstan to seek a postponement of the action at Rome.[23] Evidence of a wider deal, however, can be seen in Thurstan's agreement to consecrate Robert of Scone as Bishop of St Andrews, without profession of obedience, but with the concession that this omission would not establish a precedent and that Thurstan or his successors could pursue their claim in future.[24] In return, David appears to have dropped his efforts to have Robert made an archbishop, and he probably also lifted any Scottish objections to the See of Whithorn acknowledging York's metropolitan supremacy. Given that Whithorn – the See of Galloway – was outwith David's political control in the late 1120s, that was a small concession to make which cost David nothing but gave Thurstan an all-important addi-tional suffragan bishop in his battle to secure his see's independence from Canterbury.[25] For the present, too, nothing more was heard of Thurstan's demands for the submission of John and the other Scottish bishops, perhaps because both sides in the dispute had become acutely aware of the dangers to their common interests posed by recourse to Rome when the Pope had just given a legation to the Archbishop of Canterbury.[26] It was, however, an uneasy truce and the dispute would burst once more into flame in the 1130s.

The issue which triggered the re-opening of the dispute was Henry I's creation in 1133 of a separate See of Carlisle, embracing Cumberland and Westmorland.[27] John, as successor to the bishops of Strathclyde or Cumbria, believed that this territory by rights belonged to his diocese, and in this view he may have been supported by David, who had inherited his family's ambitions to control southern Cumbria. Even although the first bishop of the new diocese was Æðelwulf, Prior of Nostell, an Augustinian monastery with which David had strong personal ties, the king appears to have been strongly opposed to this dismemberment of the old Cumbrian see. The opposition of David and John to the creation of Carlisle, plus David's continuing wider ambitions for the Scottish Church, combined at this time to persuade them to embark on a very dangerous course. In April 1136 Pope Innocent II set out a case accusing John of having 'brought some into the error of schism', which clearly referred to the bishop having supported the Anti-Pope Anacletus II and his having brought David into that same allegiance.[28] Writing to both Thurstan and William of Canterbury, Innocent instructed that John, described as 'pseudo-bishop', should be excommunicated until he had been purged of his errors of schism and had performed his long-demanded submission to York. Why had the Scots given their support to Anacletus when most of the rest of Christendom supported Innocent?

The answer, as Archie Duncan has suggested, probably lies in the concessions that Anacletus was prepared to offer in return for the support of lay rulers that could give substance to his claim to be the true Pope.[29] David could not have been ignorant of the deal struck by Anacletus with Duke Roger of Sicily, whereby in return for Roger's recognition of him as Pope, Anacletus elevated Roger to kingly status and gave him the right of unction and coronation by an archbishop of his choice. These were prizes which David also coveted, for, although there was no question about his kingly status, there was about the nature of the kingship itself, for Scottish monarchs were neither crowned nor anointed. Like the lack of an archbishop, this lack of the full king-making process raised questions over the status of the kings of Scots and their kingdom. If Anacletus had given such favour to Duke Roger, what might he concede to David? It seems likely, therefore, that John had persuaded David to test the water with Anacletus and was sent to negotiate at Rome – occupied by Anacletus and his supporters – and also at Innocent's rival court, on a whole raft of business which probably included his claim to Carlisle as well as David's request for coronation and unction, and, we can assume, a pallium for St Andrews. Innocent, who had already supported Henry I's decision to create the See of Carlisle and who would subsequently urge Stephen to complete the process, could not grant David what he requested without alienating English support, leaving the field open to Anacletus. There is no sign that the anti-pope actually offered anything to David, for, while following Anacletus's death in January 1138 'King' Roger of Sicily was able to secure Innocent's agreement to almost every concession that his old rival had granted to Roger, no such deal was offered to the Scots. Having failed in his efforts and in 1136 threatened with suspension by Innocent, John, perhaps at David's instructions, quit his see and retired into the abbey at Thiron. The whole process appeared to have rebounded disastrously for the Scots.

Matters took a new twist in September 1138 when the papal legate Alberic arrived at Carlisle for discussions with David.[30] By that date, Anacletus was dead and, although the schism did not end finally until early 1139, it was clear that Innocent had triumphed. Already suitably chastened by the defeat of his army at the Battle of the Standard, David was prepared to renounce his former dealings with the now fully discredited anti-pope and accept Innocent without question. The corollary of that was that John would also be expected to accept Innocent's earlier demands. In Alberic's party was Bishop Æðelwulf, whom David agreed to admit to his See in Carlisle, which had been in David's hands and remained in his possession despite his recent defeat by Thurstan.[31] Carlisle was to be established as a separate see despite the hostility of David and his bishop. John, too, was forced to yield, David being required by Alberic to summon him back to his see from Thiron.[32] It is unclear when exactly John returned, but it is unlikely to have been before spring 1139. Thurstan might now have reasonably expected that, after twenty years of wrangling, the recalcitrant bishop might finally profess obedience to him, but when the archbishop died in early 1140 there is no sign that he had received the long-sought-after oath. King and bishop had succeeded in stonewalling their old opponent and the rapidly changing political situation in England offered David some hope that a more satisfactory outcome could yet be achieved.

For three years after Thurstan's death, while England swung between a Matildine ascendancy and a restoration of Stephen's authority in the south, York lacked an effective archbishop. David at once saw the potential in securing the appointment of a sympathetic candidate, and proposed his stepson, the saintly Waltheof, as Thurstan's successor.[33] Stephen, however, was not prepared to allow so politically vital an office to fall into the hands of a man associated so closely with his northern rival, regardless of the treaty relationship which then existed between David and Stephen. Instead, by

January 1141 Stephen had succeeded in engineering the election of one of his nephews, William fitz Herbert, to the archbishopric, despite strong opposition within the diocese. Stephen's capture on 2 February and the manoeuvrings of the episcopate in the following months ensured that William remained unconsecrated, which further delayed the issue of the submission of John or any other Scottish bishop to the Archbishop of York. During this period, David consolidated his relationship with Bishop Æðelwulf at Carlisle and also attempted to install his former chancellor, William Cumin, into the vacant bishopric of Durham. Success there would have placed all of York's nominal suffragans, with the sole exception of Whithorn, within David's sphere of political influence. In 1143, however, fitz Herbert was at last consecrated and David recognised that he had failed to secure Durham, where William de Ste Barbe, Dean of York and one of the electors of fitz Herbert, was chosen over Cumin. The initiative had not slipped entirely away from David, however, for Ste Barbe only secured physical possession of his see with David's active assistance, and before 1143 was out Archbishop William's position in York was being undermined by men who looked to David for assistance.[34]

From 1143 until 1147, Archbishop William found himself fighting a long and ultimately futile defence of his position against accusations of his unsuitability laid before the Pope. This prolonged weakness at York left David to pursue his religious policies in Scotland free from the unwelcome demands of a would-be metropolitan for oaths of obedience from the Scottish bishops. While the Archbishop of York was embroiled in controversy, the Pope was also unlikely to press for fulfilment of the arrangements made in 1126 for a settlement of the dispute before the curia. Such was the disturbance of the See of York that when Bishop John of Glasgow died in 1147, his successor, Herbert, Abbot of Kelso, another Tironensian reformer, was elected and consecrated within months without any demand for his submission being articulated by the archbishop or his officials.[35] David again side-stepped the issue of submission by securing Herbert's consecration by the former Cistercian monk, Pope Eugenius III, at Auxerre in France on 24 August 1147.[36] Eugenius was hostile to Archbishop William and must have been easily persuaded that it was inappropriate for Herbert to have gone to York to be consecrated by a man who was under investigation and who had been deposed only shortly before Herbert set out for the continent. David, clearly, also hoped that maintaining the tradition of papal consecration for successive bishops of Glasgow would serve to undermine future claims by York. Although the Cistercian Abbot of Fountains, Henry Murdac, was elected in fitz Herbert's place in July, he was consecrated at York only in December 1147, by which time Herbert had been consecrated as Bishop of Glasgow. No demand for his oath of obedience appears to have been made by Archbishop Henry.

Events in York seemed now to play even more beneficially into David's hands. Stephen, understandably, was infuriated by the papal intervention in what he considered English domestic affairs, and the king's relations with the Church deteriorated dramatically following his nephew's deposition. Stephen's grip on Church patronage had slipped during the 1130s and many senior ecclesiastical offices were held by reformers who were willing to look regularly to the papacy for direction in the overhaul of practice in England. Even Stephen's Archbishop of Canterbury, Theobald, who was an ardent reformer, defied his king to attend the council summoned by Pope Eugenius at Reims. In punishment, Stephen exiled Theobald and seized the property of the see. By the end of 1148, therefore, Stephen was keeping both of his archbishops out of their sees – he had refused to recognise Henry Murdac and was denying him admission to his temporalities – and the conflict looked set to escalate further when the Pope decided to impose spiritual sanctions on Stephen. It was only Archbishop Theobald's intervention which prevented Stephen from being excommunicated, a suspension which would have freed all of his vassals from their oaths to him, and instead it was England generally that was placed under interdict. Although a compromise was soon worked out between Stephen and Theobald, as 1149 opened, Henry Murdac remained outwith the peace of Stephen and was looking elsewhere for aid to secure his admission to York.[37]

Among those present in David's court at Carlisle in May 1149 was Archbishop Henry. David, it appears, had succeeded in persuading Henry that he was the only man who could secure York for him. David's involvement, however, was hardly driven by altruism or by devotion to the cause of clerical reform, for he could see immense prospects opening up, which included the permanent detachment of York from the kingdom of England. Such a scenario was entirely possible, given the northern archdiocese's steadfast defence of its ecclesiastical independence through the earlier twelfth century.[38] Even Archbishop Thurstan had been prepared to defy his own king and former patron, Henry I, to secure papal confirmation of his see's freedom from the overriding authority of Canterbury. Henry I had seen the risks posed to English political unity by York's insistence on its spiritual independence, and there were historical precedents for a link between ecclesiastical and political independence in the north as recently as the mid-tenth century. For David, control of York was the greatest prize he could gain, for it would have immeasurably strengthened his political hold over northern England and given reality to the 'Scoto-Northumbrian' realm which he had been building since 1136. It would also have removed the inherent dangers posed by the claims of a 'foreign' archbishop, for York would have become a Scottish archdiocese, wholly separate from an England confined to the country south of the Humber. That point, too, must have been very attractive to Henry Murdac, for it would have removed forever from his see the threat to its independence represented by Canterbury and also given him and his successors a real metropolitan authority over northern Britain. When David marched on York in the summer of 1149, then, this was the ultimate aim. It was only Stephen's quick intervention in the north by establishing a garrison in the city that prevented its fall to the Scots. Baulked, David withdrew and the moment was lost, and when Stephen finally admitted Henry Murdac to his see in 1151, the possibility of a Scottish archdiocese with its seat at York was over.

David's scheme for York reveals that the question of a Scottish archbishopric had only been deferred in 1126–27, not abandoned. With Henry Murdac established in York and in the fealty of Stephen, David must have expected the archbishop shortly to re-articulate his see's claims to the metropolitan supremacy of the Scottish Church, the more so since surely this must have been an issue discussed by them in 1149. David's decision to raise the question of a pallium for Bishop Robert of St Andrews in 1151, therefore, was no coincidence and the arrival of the papal legate, John Paparo, at Carlisle on 29 September 1151 must have seemed like a heaven-sent opportunity.[39] Paparo, who was carrying four pallia for the new archbishoprics which had been created in Ireland, was engaged on business clearly very dear to David's heart, and when he returned to Carlisle around Easter 1152 after fulfilling his Irish mission, the king apparently took the opportunity to press the legate to lobby at Rome for the creation of a Scottish archbishopric.[40] The archdiocese envisaged, with St Andrews as its see, would have embraced all of David's Scottish territories and, apparently, Orkney and the Isles also, where David was again seeking to assert Scottish influence over Norwegian.[41] In that aim, however, the legate failed David, for there appears to have been no case made for Scotland at Rome, and in particular on the point of Orkney and the Isles Scottish ambitions were checked by the inclusion of those sees in the new Norwegian archdiocese of Trondheim, which was created in 1152. At the time of David's death a year later, therefore, although the question of subjection had not yet been raised, the spectre of a re-awakening of the controversy of the early 1120s must have seemed to be a likely prospect.

The concentration so far on the affairs of Bishop John of Glasgow and the issue of York's metropolitan supremacy should not distract from the substantial progress made during David's reign in the reorganisation of the Scottish dioceses. No serious historian today would accept the assertion of medieval chroniclers that David found only three or four dioceses when he succeeded to the throne but left nine at the time of his death. Nor can the nineteenth-century view that there may only have been one see for all of Scotland before the twelfth century be taken seriously.[42] There were several dioceses of clearly ancient origin, but whether or not they had had any incumbents on a regular basis through the eleventh century is entirely a different matter. What David, and before him Alexander, were endeavouring to achieve was a regular succession and the appointment of clerics drawn from, or supportive of, the reformist tradition that was by then dominant in the western European Church. Both John at Glasgow and Robert at St Andrews were drawn from different facets of that tradition, John from the monastic Tironensian, Robert from the Augustinian canons, and both were part of the 'colonial' establishment which was emerging in the early twelfth century. It would be wrong, however, to argue that what David was instituting was a 'foreign' takeover of the senior ranks of the Scottish Church. Certainly, 'foreign' clerics were introduced to Scotland, and in significant numbers, but, like his mother before him, David was prepared to work with native Gaelic clergy. What David wanted was modernisation and reform of existing structures, not a root-and-branch reconstruction.

In the majority of Scottish sees, David found Gaelic incumbents, and he clearly had no difficulty in co-operating with them.[43] Had he wished to replace them, the means would have been found to secure their deposition. At Brechin, for example, David either found already in office, or advanced to the bishopric, the native cleric Samson, who appears to have been a member of the family who had come to monopolise the abbacy of the ancient royal monastery at which the see was based.[44] At Aberdeen, the bishop early in David's reign was another man of clearly Gaelic stock, Nechtan.[45] There, David's significant intervention may have been the decision, possibly in the 1130s, to move the seat of the bishop from Mortlach in Banffshire to the politically more secure Aberdeen. It was only in 1147, following Nechtan's death, that David secured the appointment of his former chaplain and chancellor, Edward, to the bishopric.[46] Another Gaelic cleric, Giric or Gregory, had held the see of Moray since the reign of Alexander I, and was still in office in the early 1130s.[47] It has been suggested that Giric was only a 'titular' bishop, i.e. that he was styled 'Bishop of Moray' but never actually exercised any episcopal function within his nominal see,[48] but there is no good grounds to support that view, which appears to be based exclusively on the hypothesis that the Bishop of Moray is identical with the Gregory appointed by David at Dunkeld sometime in the 1130s.[49] Given the political sensitivity of Moray during the reign, it is highly unlikely that David would have missed the opportunity to strengthen crown influence in the province that the establishment of a royalist bishop would have offered, and it is equally unlikely that Moray would have been left vacant from the 1130s until the appointment of the royal chaplain, William, to the see in around 1152.[50] In Ross or Rosemarkie another Gaelic cleric, Mac Bethad, was bishop in the 1120s, and was succeeded by two further bishops who appear to have been drawn from the local monastic tradition.[51] Finally, at Dunkeld, a church connected very closely with David's family, the see had been held since the reign of Alexander I by Cormac, who survived into the early 1130s.[52] Nothing is known of the background of his successor, John, who as a 'bishop from Atholl', undertook a mission to Orkney in the winter of 1138–39,[53] but his successor, Gregory, appears to have been a cleric of native stock.[54] Throughout David's reign, therefore, we can see a marriage of continuity with reformist interests, and it is only in the 1160s that the 'foreign' element among the clergy began to establish a dominant position among the episcopate.

David's readiness to work with the native clergy of his kingdom should serve to caution us against viewing his episcopal policies as driven entirely by political considerations. His concerns with regard to Glasgow and St Andrews do not appear to have extended to the other dioceses of Scotland, but there is also little evidence that either the archbishops of York or the papacy were so concerned with them, other than to enjoin all Scottish bishops to offer their oaths of obedience of Thurstan and his successors. Glasgow and St Andrews, of course, were highly symbolic and most closely associated with royal plans for reform, hence Alexander I and David's anxieties to secure the appointment of reformist clerics to them. St Andrews, however, also had held a special place as the 'chief bishopric' of Scotland through the tenth and eleventh centuries. It was that prominence which marked it out as the preferred candidate for a pallium in the twelfth century and which also lay behind David's determination to ensure that Bishop Robert was free from York's metropolitan supremacy. If the perceived senior Scottish bishopric submitted to York, then what chance was there of resisting York's claims in respect of the other Scottish sees?

A further clear indication of David's acceptance of the traditional structures of the Scottish bishoprics can be seen in the pattern of dioceses which crystallised in the course of his reign. While Glasgow had an obvious coherence and unitary identity as the bishopric for almost the whole of his principality of Cumbria, that unity was artificial and dated only from David's establishment as ruler of the Southern Uplands. Teviotdale and lower Tweeddale, for example, were also claimed by the bishops of Durham as part of their see, having formerly been served by their predecessors, the Northumbrian bishops of Lindisfarne.[55] Here, then, it can be seen that David was attempting to redraw the ecclesiastical map to suit his political agenda. As king after 1124, however, he made no attempt to do likewise with the existing Scottish bishoprics, as can be seen by the untidy fragmentation of their dioceses, which reflected the ancient distribution and acquisition of estates by the monasteries and early sees from which most had evolved. Thus, for example, the See of Dunkeld consisted of a heartland in Atholl and a scattering of detached parishes through southern Perthshire, Angus, Fife and into Lothian. Brechin consisted entirely of properties dispersed through what was otherwise the territory of the See of St Andrews, whose lands were themselves spread from Berwick in the south to within two miles of the seat of the Bishop of Aberdeen in the north. David may have moved the seat of some bishoprics for political reasons, such as the transfer of the See of Mortlach to Aberdeen, but only in one case, Caithness, does he appear to have created an entirely new diocese.[56]

Given that the existence of an effective episcopate was central to David's plans for the reform of the Church generally within his kingdom, what tangible improvements to the provision of spiritual services did the bishops bring? There is very little evidence to show the establishment of a hierarchy of diocesan clergy in place in most of the Scottish sees before the second half of the twelfth century, but it is probably safe to assume that most of David's bishops recognised from the outset that they needed to construct an administration for their see to aid them in the task of reform.[57] Administrations, however, could not be conjured out of nothing and among David's many tasks was that of ensuring that the bishops had access to the resources to support their diocesan officers. Such an aim may have been one of several motives behind David's inquest into the resources of the See of Glasgow, and was also a key factor in his arrangements for payment of teind at parish level.[58] Where Bishop John and, to a lesser extent, Bishop Robert were most active, however, was in encouraging David's establishment of monastic communities whose inmates were able to provide some of the services which the bishops needed to aid them in their tasks. David probably required little encouragement, for his own personal faith convinced him of the need for, and value of, a 'spiritually affluent society'.[59] The cost of establishing monasteries may have been high in material terms but low in material returns, but the return in less tangible benefits was, as David had witnessed in England and on the continent, immense. The monks and canons were exemplars to the rest of society, providing a window for secular men onto a godly world, encouraging them to emulate wherever and whenever possible the lifestyle of the religious. David understood the role played by the monks as 'spiritual leavening'[60] in the process of social and cultural re-engineering, which he embarked upon as soon as he was established in power in southern Scotland.

As a young man at Henry I's court, David would have acquired a close personal experience of royal religious patronage and religious politics in action. While Henry was a noted patron of the religious orders, especially of Cluny, his main acts of patronage date from the 1120s, almost a decade after David had started his remarkable career as a monastic founder. Henry, moreover, was singularly conservative in his patronage while David was notably eclectic in the orders to which he showed favour. Indeed, the very eclecticism of his patronage suggests that Henry's personal example may have played very little part in moulding David's outlook. A far greater influence may have been provided by his sister, Queen Matilda, who was the principal patron of the Augustinian order in the British Isles in the early 1100s, but he may have been more influenced after 1113 by the tight circle of intimates who surrounded him as prince and, later, as king rather than by 'monastic fashion-mongering'.[61] Certainly, it appears to have been purely personal interest, perhaps stimulated by his chaplain, John, rather than emulation of his royal patron that persuaded David to learn more for himself about the reformed Benedictine community at Thiron in the Chartrais founded by St Bernard of Abbeville. The Tironensian order, as it became, did not then enjoy significant patronage outwith the county of Blois and never made any significant impact in England, where they possessed only four small 'alien' priories.[62] David's support for this order more than anything else shows how he was not influenced by the fashions and trends in religious patronage that were circulating at the Anglo-Norman court.

Soon after David gained control of his legacy in southern Scotland he was able to set in motion his planned foundation of a colony of Tironensian monks. The location of the new abbey was Selkirk on the edge of the Forest of Ettrick, the great expanse of hill country in the heart of the Southern

Uplands. There is nowhere in southern Scotland that even in the early twelfth century would have met truly with the reformed orders' preference for solitude and wilderness which they could reshape to suit their own purposes, for this whole region had been subject to human activity for well over four millennia by that time.[63] David's foundation charter, issued to the monks probably shortly after his marriage to Countess Matilda (he is styled *comes* – earl – in the preamble) in late December 1113, gave the new monastery a substantial landed endowment and lists a broad raft of economic rights and privileges from which to support the monks.[64] The main estate centred on Selkirk itself, plus Middleham, Bowden and Eildon to its north and east, Melrose on the Tweed (shortly to be taken from it and used as the chief endowment of a new Cistercian abbey), smaller blocks of land further down the Tweed valley at Sprouston, plus properties in Berwick and in David's new burgh at Roxburgh. It was not just in Scotland that David gave the monks land, for the original grant included a series of valuable Northamptonshire properties gifted from the resources of his English earldom. Why David chose Tironensians to colonise his first foundation rather than, say, Augustinian canons is unknown but should probably be seen as recognition by him of the intense spirituality of the new order. Austere in practice and perceived of as closer to a truly godly lifestyle than the traditional orders of monks, David may have been convinced that they offered the best route to salvation and believed that their purity and simplicity would give them privileged access through their prayers and masses to God himself on his behalf. This, almost certainly, was the belief which lay behind David's subsequent patronage of the Cistercians. But it was more than just David who was considered to benefit from monkly intercession; all of his people received spiritual benefits from the efforts of the monks.

Monks by their very nature, however, could not provide David or his bishops with all of the spiritual services required for the reform of the Scottish Church. Yes, their monasteries offered outstanding examples of how a truly Christian life should be conducted, and also acted as conduits through which European cultural models could be introduced to the kingdom, but their inmates were incapable of fulfilling active missionary roles in the spiritual life of the kingdom. Monks were withdrawn from the world, living and worshipping within the closed precincts of their communities. Spiritual benefits might emanate from within those walls, but the monks themselves did not issue out to preach, pray or conduct services in parish churches. Individual monks might be called out of their cloistered existence to serve again in the world, such as Herbert, Abbot of Kelso, who succeeded

John as Bishop of Glasgow,[65] but the majority remained removed from the world of men. Even bishops such as John, who demonstrated great devotion to the principles of the Tironensian order and who, albeit briefly, entered Thiron itself as a monk, understood that canons, not monks, were what was needed to aid him in the provision of adequate spiritual services.

Although canons were widely perceived as inferior in spiritual status to cloistered monks due to their active involvement in the wider world, their value in the reform process was equally widely recognised by reformist bishops.[66] Basically, the canons were communities of priests living a monastic existence but who could pass beyond the walls of their monasteries to minister in the secular world. Although they became increasingly monastic in the later Middle Ages, by which date a purely secular reformed clergy had assumed all of their functions in the non-monastic Church, in the early twelfth century they could serve as parish priests, preach to lay-folk and minister to the people's physical as well as spiritual needs. It was presumably for those reasons that Bishop John's first monastic foundation was a community of canons at Jedburgh, founded with David's help in 1138–39.[67] It is highly significant that by that date David's personal inclinations had shifted towards the even more austere Cistercian monastic order, but his bishop wanted Augustinians. Their establishment at Jedburgh may also give us some insight on where John perceived the need for reformist clergy to be most acute, for their monastery lay at the heart of the most populous region of his diocese. John needed men who could minister to the people rather than monks whose spiritual value was on an altogether different plane.

In the St Andrews diocese, Augustinians had been established since earlier in the twelfth century, brought to Scone by Alexander I. David's brother had planned further Augustinian communities, at St Andrews, Loch Tay and Inchcolm, but none of these had been established by the time of his death. Bishop Robert, as former Prior of Scone, might have been expected to push ahead with the introduction of canons to his cathedral church, but he and David found themselves confronted by a spirited rearguard action from the secular clergy of St Andrews. Robert has been criticised for failing to do more to bring Augustinians into his see,[68] it only being in 1133 that he secured a canon from Nostell to head a priory attached to his cathedral, but both his own prolonged difficulties in securing consecration and the continuing political disturbances in Scotland north of the Forth surely hindered any plans which he may have cherished on that score. While he may have failed at St Andrews, it cannot be doubted that it was Robert rather than David working on his own initiative who encouraged the foundation in

1128 of an Augustinian abbey at Holyrood just outside Edinburgh.[69] Likewise, in 1142, by which date David had founded two Cistercian abbeys, it was Augustinians who were planted at Cambuskenneth across the River Forth from Stirling.[70] Like the development of Jedburgh in respect of Glasgow diocese, both lay in the major population centre of Robert's diocese along the south side of the Forth valley. Again, the episcopal favouring of canons over monks provides a sharp counterpoint to David's personal preferences.

This dichotomy between preference and need raises the question of what were David's objectives behind his introduction of the monks and canons of the reformed continental orders to his kingdom. Modern studies have tended to focus very heavily on the material benefits to David personally and to his kingdom in general.[71] The monks, especially the Cistercians, have been discussed frequently in their role as agricultural entrepreneurs, who introduced sophisticated management techniques for the more systematic and profitable exploitation of their estates. They provided the model which the Scottish nobility were to ape in their redevelopment of their revenue bases. Cluniac monks and Augustinian canons were noted property speculators, deriving significant income from their burgh-based properties and playing important parts in the whole process of town development. Augustinians, it has been noted, had a reputation also for the quality of the hospitality offered in their monasteries and the inference has been made that the siting of Augustinian abbeys close to major royal residences – Jedburgh, Holyrood at Edinburgh, Cambuskenneth at Stirling, and Scone for both Scone and Perth – had this ulterior motive in mind. But are we to believe that David was more concerned with the quality of the dinner-bed-and-breakfast facilities offered by the canons than the spiritual services which they offered?

Certainly, David, by his Anglo-Norman upbringing and personal witness in England and Normandy, cannot have been ignorant of the very material benefits which the monks and canons brought with them. Monastic estates were generally well organised and, by virtue of the corporate nature of the communities, able to plan future development in a way which lay individuals could not. They were also often part of extensive networks, such as the Cistercian 'filiations', which, while intended primarily for the maintenance of uniformity of discipline and practice within the orders, also gave them access to one of the most highly developed intelligence-gathering systems in the pre-Modern age and brought them into regular communication with the commercial systems of mainland Europe. It was not because he had nothing better to give that David granted the monks of Thiron the right to have one of their trading ships put in anywhere in his domain and be free of payment of *cáin*.[72] This was a valuable privilege to a monastery and an order which was active in the commercial traffic of the North Sea world. Nor were the monks of Thiron alone in securing this privilege, indicating that the monasteries of David's Scotland were significant players in the burgeoning trading life of his kingdom: they had surpluses to sell and commodities which they could not produce in Scotland, such as wine, to buy. Quite clearly, therefore, the monasteries were fully integrated with David's wider ambitions for the economic development of his kingdom and were important players in the switch to a market economy which David was encouraging through his policies of burgh plantation and the introduction of coinage.

The image of the monk as a pioneer in the 'wilderness', winning new land for cultivation from the 'waste' of moor, marsh and forest, features repeatedly in most accounts – medieval and modern – of the spread of the new orders across Europe in the course of the twelfth century. The Cistercians in particular gained a reputation for such pioneering activity all around the margins of Latin Christendom from the Slav lands east of the Elbe to Ireland, central Iberia to northern Scotland and Scandinavia.[73] The Cistercian monasteries established by David I and Earl Henry have been traditionally presented in this manner: Melrose supposedly importing innovative techniques in arable cultivation and stock management to central Tweeddale; Newbattle making profits from the wastes of the Lammermuir and Moorfoot hills; Holmcultram winning new land from the saltmarshes of the Solway coast; and Kinloss clearing woodland and draining marshes in the Laich of Moray. The evidence seems plain enough, but is it accurate? From the outset, for example, Melrose breached one of the fundamental principles of the Cistercian rule in that its location could hardly be classed as a desert remote from the distractions of the world of men.[74] The site of the abbey was in the heart of a concentration of important royal estates in one of the most densely populated and intensively exploited zones of the Southern Uplands. Indeed, none of the locations chosen by David for his Cistercian foundations matched the monastic ideal of a desert fastness lying in the midst of an uncultivated wilderness. There were few areas in Scotland where such ideals could in any case be met, for the whole of the Scottish landscape had already been subject to over 10,000 years of systematic exploitation by its inhabitants, and even what might be presented as 'wilderness' or 'waste' had possessors who were already in some way exploiting its resources. Of course, the cultural mentality of the Cistercians and other Continental churchmen did not recognise such traditional forms of exploitation as true cultivation. Native practices were, in the eyes of the predominantly Anglo-Norman monastic colonists, primitive, culturally inferior and represented a typically barbarous waste of God's gifts to humanity. Their introduction of what they deemed to be proper, civilised modes of agriculture could be presented as pioneering reclamation from waste. But there were also other factors at work, and the Cistercian traditions of God's frontiersmen labouring at the limits of civilisation should be seen as less of an expression of reality and more as a homilistic icon which represented the physical achievement of Cistercian spirituality.

Clear parallels for the Scottish experience in David's time can be drawn from the Cistercian penetration of eastern Europe, where the pioneering image can be seen unequivocally as a work of propaganda.[75] There, the Cistercians were but one instrument in the wider triumph of militant Christianity in a pagan land. But the monks also presented themselves as the champions of a superior spirituality armed with a superior technology, together placing them on an altogether higher plane of civilisation from which they would impose their standards on peoples whom they regarded as inferior in almost every way, but especially in terms of religion, culture and economy. When seen in that light, the monks were even more central to David's colonial establishment in Scotland, for they constituted another dimension of the cultural tradition in which he had been raised and which he regarded as the civilised norm. The Cistercians, Tironensians and Augustinians brought into Scotland by David after 1113 were as much a part of his cultural revolution as the Anglo-Norman knights and townsmen whom he settled in the kingdom. That role for the clergy has been fairly widely accepted for some time, for historians have long recognised the service given to David and his successors by the Church in bolstering their position in the face of domestic dynastic challenge and in aiding in drawing remoter parts of the kingdom into the political fold, but the attendant cultural elitism of the colonial Church, and especially of the Cistercians, is not so widely recognised in Scotland. Yet, from the first exposure of the Scottish Church to the discerning gaze of the reformed Benedictine clergy, the incomers subjected the native tradition to sustained and often sneering criticism. The Scots, sniffed Turgot in his *Vita Margareti*, 'were wont to celebrate mass contrary to the custom of the whole church; with I know not what barbarous rite'.[76] While the projection of Anglo-French culture as a dynamic force in the process of conquest is a familiar enough concept and the dominance it achieved through royal patronage recognised,[77] the scathing contempt of Cistercian monasticism in Scotland for what it perceived as an inferior society is not. Ailred of Rievaulx and his biographer, Walter Daniel, cannot conceal their contempt when describing the 'plantation' of Dundrennan Abbey in the 'savagery' of twelfth-century Galloway; their words carry all the arrogance of Cistercian chroniclers of the colonisation of Poland and Silesia, and carry sentiments readily familiar from the European colonisation of Africa and south Asia.[78]

This expression of Cistercian superiority, which carries a strong racialist message, brings us full circle to the question of David's aims in introducing the foreign clerics to his kingdom. He was an ardent religious reformer, a king who took absolutely seriously his responsibility before God to advance and secure the spiritual welfare of his people. We must cast aside modern cynicism and recognise that sense of duty as David's primary motivation, bound inextricably to his own conscious desire to safeguard his soul and ensure its future salvation. But David was also a revolutionary, politically, socially and culturally, bent on the transformation of his inheritance into a modern, European-style monarchy. Knights and burgesses were indispensable elements in the process of transformation, but monks and canons were no less central to the cultural revolution underway in the twelfth-century kingdom. Alongside the spiritual leavening which the clergy brought to the melting pot of Scottish culture, they provided the 'indispensible tasks of civilising and refining' the kingdom at large.[79]

CHAPTER TEN

The 'Scoto-Northumbrian' Realm
1139-49

The second treaty of Durham marked the opening of an altogether new phase in Anglo-Scottish relations. It had been hoped in 1139 that those relations would be amicable and peaceful, and the prospects for such a future seemed excellent. Stephen well understood the need to ensure that the treaty worked and aimed to integrate Earl Henry firmly into the loyalist political community in England. There was to be no repeat of the treatment of the prince at his court which had led to David recalling his son in 1137 and which had handed the Scots a legitimate grievance to use against the English king. Instead, Henry was treated with great honour and accompanied the king on his campaign in the West Country of England in the second half of 1139 where, according to Henry of Huntingdon, Stephen personally rescued him from capture at the siege of Ludlow.[2] This active participation on Henry's part in the campaigns against the rebel barons was hugely significant for Stephen, for not only did it demonstrate the prince's sincerity in his adherence to the treaty terms and the oaths which he had sworn to the king for his English earldoms, but it also served to underscore how the King of Scots and his heir accepted the legitimacy of Stephen's position as king. There could be no more unequivocal a statement of Scottish rejection of the claims of the Empress to their loyalty. Before the end of the year it appeared that the Scottish heir had become an accepted member of the inner circle of Stephen's political-military elite when the king arranged his marriage – no doubt much to the satisfaction of David – to Ada de Warenne, sister of William II, Earl of Warenne, and half-sister of the Beaumont twins, Robert, Earl of Leicester, and Waleran, Count of Meulan[3] These bonds, however, worked two ways, for while they tied Henry to Stephen's cause, they also secured Henry the support of one of the most well-connected families in Stephen's party in preserving Henry's interests in England against encroachment by potential rivals, such as his elder half-brother, Simon de St Liz, the alternative claimant to Huntingdon-Northampton. At the end of 1139, David had good cause to feel satisfied with the outcome of the Durham accord.

David also had personal reasons to be more than satisfied with the treaty. Although the northern English territories were, in theory, held by Henry as fiefs of the English crown, David effectively occupied Cumberland as though it were an integral part of his own realm. Soon after the conclusion of the treaty, and certainly by the mid-1140s, David may have begun work at Carlisle which transformed the old stronghold into a new fortress with a castle, erected in the most up-to-date fashion, and a strong circuit of walls.[4] His aim was to tighten his grip on Cumberland and provide himself with a bastion from which to dominate the region. Over time, Carlisle emerged as a more southerly counterpart to Roxburgh and an alternative claimant to the title of David's most favoured residence. His interest in Cumberland, however, was not limited to purely military concerns, for its economic value to him was immense. Control of Cumberland also gave him control of the valuable silver mines at Alston on the South Tyne in the east of the shire. Soon after this acquisition, David started to issue his own silver coinage in Scotland, the first 'native' money produced in his kingdom.[5] The bullion which flowed from the Cumberland mines was to more than replace the revenues of the earldom of Huntingdon as the liquid on which the 'Davidian Revolution' in Scotland was to be floated.

No one in 1139 could have predicted the dramatic collapse in Stephen's political fortunes in England, nor could they have foreseen his capture at Lincoln on 2 February 1141. His seizure by the Empress's supporters transformed the situation in England overnight, although it presented his captors with a dilemma. Now they had captured Stephen, what did they do with him? As an anointed and crowned king, he could not simply be disposed of like a common criminal, although the Empress and some of her closest partisans may have wished to do just that. Matilda's decision was to have herself likewise crowned and anointed, placing her on parity with her cousin and removing from Stephen the unique basis for his authority in England. This sudden change in the English conflict presented David with new and intriguing possibilities, but as well as being 'too good an opportunity to miss'[6] it also presented him with a serious threat. The treaty which had handed northern England to Earl Henry and David had been a treaty with Stephen, not the Empress Matilda. She had no reason to honour it, all the more certainly since her uncle had already proven himself to be perjured by his failure to honour his own oath to support her claims to the English throne. Furthermore, the victory at Lincoln had been largely a consequence of the defection from Stephen's side of Ranulf, Earl of Chester, who had once again articulated his inherited claims to Carlisle and Cumberland.[7] What price might Ranulf extract from Matilda for his service to her?

David showed at once that he was not prepared to sit and await developments to unfold. He had no reason to believe that his niece's capture of Stephen did not draw a line under the conflict that had riven England since 1135/36 and was determined to secure his place in the new regime. His opportunism may have been breathtaking in its sheer gall, but it was also a masterly display of political pragmatism and realism. He had gained much and was determined to capitalise even more on the changed political circumstances. In the early months of 1141, therefore, David casually disregarded his treaty with Stephen and set about extending his power into northern Lancashire and north-west Yorkshire, where William fitz Duncan had both inherited claims to land of his own, plus claims in right of his wife to the important lordships of Skipton and Craven which he had pursued so vigorously in 1137–38. David also saw clear potential to intrude his power into St Cuthbert's land, where Bishop Geoffrey of Durham died shortly after Easter 1141. If David could secure control of the See of Durham, the immense regional political influence of the bishop (plus the extensive episcopal estate) would hand him the regional dominance of the country north of the river Tees. The stakes were high and David was prepared to gamble everything that he had gained so far on securing even more.

David's first step was to secure Durham. Soon after 28 May, according to John of Hexham, the king made a diversion on his journey south to join the Empress and was admitted into the city. There, in a clear bid to conciliate the influential clergy of a city with which he and his family had had a long and ambivalent relationship for well over a century, he instructed that there should be no decision on a successor for Bishop Geofrey until Matilda had been consulted. David, however, could not conceal his ambitions for the see, for he also installed his chancellor, William Cumin or Comyn, to administer the affairs of diocese until a decision as to successor was made.[8] The assiduous courting of Durham, which had been a characteristic of the period since the settling of the second treaty with Stephen, continued, with Earl Henry, who had accompanied his father, issuing two charters in favour of the monks of Durham and their priory cell at Coldingham.[9] David had made a display of adhering to procedure in respect of episcopal appointments, but he was clearly aiming to add Durham to the portfolio of northern English centres which he had in his grasp.

Around the end of May or beginning of June 1141, David, accompanied by a large party of his nobles and household officials, set out southwards from Durham to meet with his niece, who was still preparing for her coronation.[10] Given that the Empress's supporters had captured Stephen at the beginning of February, the fact that she remained uncrowned nearly four months later should perhaps have sent warning signals to David. Stephen's winning of the throne in 1135 had been based on rapid and decisive action; Matilda's dilatory approach was simply allowing Stephen's core of supporters to rally behind the redoubtable figure of David's other niece, Matilda of Boulogne. It has to be said, however, that the Empress had needed to overcome major objections from among the clergy to her simply taking the crown while Stephen was still alive. In the first place she had to win over the papal legate to England, Stephen's younger brother Henry of Blois, Bishop of Winchester. After four weeks of tortuous negotiations in which the Empress made far-reaching concessions to Bishop Henry which gave him immense political power in her planned new regime, she received the reluctant blessing of the English Church in a ceremony at Winchester early in March. Instead of using that breakthrough to secure a quick coronation at Winchester, Matilda was determined to be crowned at Westminister, but needed first to secure her military domination of the lower Thames valley and London. Another month was wasted at Oxford as her supporters prepared the ground for her triumphant entry into the chief city of her kingdom, but in the ecclesiastical council at Winchester that gathered in April to formally approve the Empress's election to the throne, the Londoners defied calls for the deposition of Stephen and her elevation, demanding instead that the king should be freed and restored to his full authority.[11] Despite that setback, she was determined to proceed with her plans and, following the murder of her cousin's chamberlain in London in mid-May, for once moved rapidly and entered the hostile city.

David was with his niece for the one turbulent week in which she held court in London in early June. His aim was clearly to win himself a key place in the queen-to-be's close circle of advisors, among whom the spoils of victory would surely be shared, but it is equally clear that he was still seeking to operate purely within the framework of the kingdom of England in respect of all that he hoped to gain from the new regime. The favours which he sought, especially the approval of his nomination of William Cumin to the vacant See of Durham, demonstrate clearly that he recognised that the gift of the bishopric lay in the hands of the English monarch. Without the approval of the English ruler, no bishop could hope to secure possession of the northern diocese. Most chroniclers dwell on David's attempts to secure Cumin Matilda's approval for his elevation, but, given her concession of authority to Henry of Blois in the question of ecclesiastical appointments, it is likely that he courted the legate rather than the Empress.[12] He cannot but have been dismayed at the limited support which Matilda so clearly commanded, with most of her baronial backers being drawn from a very circumscribed area in south-western England. Admittedly, all the English bishops attended on her in preparation for her enthronement, but their presence could not conceal the fact that the larger part of the kingdom remained at best uncommitted and at worst openly hostile to her. Furthermore, the majority of the Londoners remained implacably opposed to her and their opposition stiffened while she failed to offer them any kind of concession to woo them to her side. There are suggestions that David was horrified at his niece's patent inability to be magnanimous, pragmatic, or to take counsel, and her personal arrogance, haughtiness and vanity served only to alienate potential waverers rather than impress a sense of her inate majesty upon them.[13] He offered her advice on how to proceed, but his counsel was ignored.[14] It may have taken David very little time to realise that he had backed the wrong horse in the race for control of England.

After only a week in control of London, Matilda and her party were forced to abandon the city in the face of the mounting hostility of the Londoners. Despite the deteriorating position of her party, David remained in the south with her and accompanied her and her supporters on the return march to Oxford, from where she could still attempt to dominate central southern England and the routes into the Midlands. While there was still the possibility of her coronation, for Stephen was still her prisoner, David was unwilling simply to abandon her and return to the north. His reluctance may have been based on simple recognition that, in her desperation to win over barons and secure the shaky loyalties of some who had switched their allegiance so recently, even his Midlands earldoms were not secure from encroachment.

The six weeks spent at Oxford revealed the Empress's weakness and indecision that her arrogance and bluster in London had concealed.[15] It was only at the end of July that decisive action was taken and then it was probably David and Matilda's half-brother, Robert, Earl of Gloucester, who pushed the policy. Instead of returning to London, Matilda's army marched on Winchester, where Bishop Henry had abandoned his probably duplicitous support for the Empress, realigned himself with Queen Matilda, and was again working for a restoration of his brother to his kingship. The Empress's army burst into the city and seized several of its chief buildings and strongpoints, but Bishop Henry was secure in his strongly fortified palace, Wolvesey Castle, which stood on the edge of the city, and other places within the walls also held out against the attackers.[16] The result was a bizarre series of mini-sieges within Winchester, which quickly became even more complicated when an army of Londoners and Stephen's loyalists arrived outside the city and set up a counter-siege. The Empress now found herself encircled by her enemies and in danger of capture herself. What followed was a confused series of skirmishes in and around the city on 14 September to which the name 'Rout of Winchester' has been given by later generations. This was not quite for Matilda what Lincoln was for Stephen, for the Empress escaped in the confusion to the security of her western strongholds, but it was a major disaster for her party. David, too, escaped from the field, but Robert of Gloucester, the lynchpin of the Empress's party in England, was taken captive.[17] As David fled north to the security of his own territory, he cannot have had any clear idea of the scale of the defeat that lay behind him. He had gambled and failed; it remained to be seen what the consequences would be for his position in northern England.

From Winchester, David managed to make his way through largely hostile territory to Durham, where he was joined on 29 September by his chancellor, William Cumin, who had also managed to escape from the rout.[18] While David's hopes of securing an even better settlement from his niece, including a royal award of the vacant See of Durham to Cumin, had been shattered by the recent events in the south, he had at least de facto control of the city and, as a consequence, sought to secure his chancellor's election in the face of local opposition from the monks of the cathedral-priory. It is difficult to disentangle from the extremely hostile Durham accounts of Cumin's tenure of the bishopric as its administrator exactly what occurred in the period 1141–44, and caution must be exercised in using the fiercely partisan record available to us. According to one Durham account, on the death of Bishop Geoffrey, Cumin had the prelate's corpse preserved in salt to conceal his death from the Durham monks while he hurried to David's court to present a case for his candidature to succeed

Geoffrey. The same account suggests that Cumin had the support of a powerful group of nobles at David's court, including Eustace fitz John, Robert de Bruce II of Annandale, Hugh de Morville, and the already powerful Teesdale and Northumberland lord, Bernard de Balliol,[19] who had evidently transferred his loyalties to the Scottish king or Earl Henry after 1138, and all of whom are accused by the chronicler of looking to benefit financially from aiding Cumin to power. In late May 1141, it is reported that David entrusted Cumin with the direction of the affairs of the see until such time as the Empress decided on a successor to Bishop Geoffrey.[20] This arrangement, to the Durham monks, looked too much like an attempted *fait accompli*, and they had sent a delegate south in David's company to lobby against Cumin, but he learned of their mission and accompanied the king instead.[21] What arrangements were made in Cumin's absence for the running of the diocese *sede vacante* are unclear, particularly since Durham's metropolitan see, the Archdiocese of York, which would have had responsibility for ensuring the installation of a suitable administrator, had been vacant since the death of Archbishop Thurstan in 1140. What does appear clear, however, is that the Durham clergy at least recognised the reality of David's power over them, probably understanding well that he was the only man in the north of England with the authority to protect their interests during this period of hiatus. Cumin may temporarily have quit his prospective diocese to plead his case in person at Matilda's court, but the city remained firmly in David's orbit and, by also making an approach to the Empress, the clergy had indicated that they recognised the apparent reality of her authority.

It is evident that the legate, Henry of Blois, to whom the case was presented at Winchester, was playing a careful game in respect of Durham. Since the capture of his brother, he had shown outward signs of a readiness to reach an accommodation with the Empress and her party and had secured many concessions from her in respect of his authority over religious matters. Bishop Henry, however, was playing a double game and was actively lobbying at Rome to secure a decision on the kingship of England that would favour his captive brother. So, while he probably did not wish to see one of David's closest advisors appointed to the powerful northern bishopric, he could not openly oppose the move. Instead, he indicated that due ecclesiastical process would have to be followed and, should Cumin ignore that decision, he would face excommunication.[22] This decree appeared to hand victory to the Durham monks, for they would never accede to the election of Cumin, but David succeeded in extracting a letter from his niece which gave Cumin her unqualified endorsement. In effect, the monks were being instructed by the Empress to elect him and no other. This was the situation to which David and Cumin returned in late September 1141.

David, in his perhaps chastened post-Winchester mood, understood that he could not force Cumin upon the monks without wholly alienating this highly influential community. In late 1141, the king was working hard to entrench his position in the north of England and salvage as much as possible from the disastrous failure of the Matildine party to capitalise on its possession of Stephen. It was probably more in hope than expectation that David withdrew from the city, leaving Cumin with a garrison in possession of the bishop's castle, glowering across the hill-top at the prior of Durham and his monks. Fearing the worst, perhaps, the monks secured the king's agreement that he would stand surety between garrison and convent against any injuries inflicted by the one upon the other.[23] Through this whole period after September 1141, however, David continued to stress that his current possession of Durham and Cumin's appointment as administrator was done entirely within the context of Matilda's overriding authority as Queen of England. Like Cumberland and Northumberland, the see was acknowledged to be part of the kingdom of England, although it was in Scottish hands.

The king may have hoped that by removing the immediate heat from the situation at Durham, which his presence may have intensified, Cumin could gradually win the monks over. Indeed, the Durham records note that Cumin attempted to ingratiate himself in every way to his potential electors, but at the same time he was continuing to build up support among the lay elite of the diocese.[24] His attempt, however, failed, for on 1 November 1141 Stephen had been released in exchange for Earl Robert of Gloucester and, although the king was never subsequently to exercise his authority in the north of England as effectively as he had done before February 1141, the monks could with confidence look to him for 'moral authority', if nothing more tangible, in their conflict with Cumin. After this point, there are signs that David may have washed his hands of active involvement in the struggle for control of the diocese and he appears to have played no direct part in the election of William of Ste Barbe, Dean of York, to the see in 1143.[25] Through 1142 and 1143, the Durham accounts present Cumin as an increasingly predatory figure who, acting like a robber-baron, plundered the lands of the diocese and its lay vassals, who had tried to mediate in the continuing dispute. Among these, apparently, was Bernard de Balliol, who was an important vassal of Earl Henry in Northumberland as well as being a

Durham tenant in Teesdale.[26] Such men had evidently remained in their loyalty to David after November 1141 and, although both David and Earl Henry are accused of double-dealing and continuing pro-Cumin sentiment in their attempts to reach an amicable settlement with Bishop William after 1143,[27] it is unlikely that they would have willingly supported actions that threatened to undermine their political influence in the country between the Tyne and the Tees. Even before Cumin finally gave up his bid to secure the bishopric and surrendered the castle at Durham to William of Ste Barbe on 18 October, David had been moving towards an accommodation with the new bishop. Indeed, the active support which David offered Ste Barbe and the haven which he provided for him on Scottish-controlled Lindisfarne may have served to quickly blunt the hostility which Cumin's actions had honed.[28] Durham itself may have remained obstinately outwith David's homage and an outpost of pro-Stephen interests in the north, but its bishop was not as implacably opposed to the Scottish king as might have been expected after the bitterness of the disputed election.

Failure to secure Cumin's election at Durham has been interpreted as a sign of David's general inability to fix a firm grasp on the political community of northern England and the continuing strength of Stephen's authority in the remoter reaches of the kingdom.[29] There can be no denying that the election of William of Ste Barbe was a blow to David's ambitions, for, as Dean of York, the new bishop came from a church that had already demonstrated pro-Stephen inclinations through its election of the king's cousin, William fitz Herbert, to the archbishopric in the same year. Yet, it is equally clear that Stephen had no direct role in the Durham election: William of Ste Barbe's elevation came after two years of struggle, and the new bishop only secured entry to his see and, more importantly, its lands and castles, with the agreement of David and Earl Henry and at the price of concessions to his defeated rival, William Cumin. Certainly, David had failed to get his man into Durham, but, if Ste Barbe was Stephen's candidate, there is little sign that David's influence in the country south of the Tyne was much affected or that Stephen's effective authority there was re-established. Durham tradition does accord Bishop William II an unhappy pontificate of nine years, during which he endured the 'unjust exactions of the King of Scotland',[30] and continuing depredations on his estates by neighbouring barons. If the Bishop of Durham was Stephen's 'man in the north', then David quite effectively isolated and neutralised him.

It would be wrong to take the impression from this extended discussion of the Durham contest that control of the see was David's overriding

concern in the four years 1141–44. The same period saw both David and his
son set about converting their shallowly bedded tenure of Northumberland
and Cumberland into firm possession. One obvious consequence of David's
abandonment of the second treaty of Durham and open alignment with the
Empress in 1141 would have been the forfeiture of Earl Henry for his part in
his father's betrayal. Northumberland and Cumberland were far beyond
Stephen's reach, but Huntingdon was taken into Stephen's hands, certainly
after 1 November 1141, and awarded instead to Simon II de St Liz, Henry's
elder half-brother. David and Henry's lordship over the Midlands earldom
could hardly be classed as shallowly rooted, given the nearly three decades
during which it had been in their possession, and David in particular had
forged close bonds with the both the leading vassals of the earldom and
lesser families, many of whom had provided colonists for his settlement of
southern Scotland.[31] The loss of the honour of Huntingdon led instead to
an intensification of efforts to cultivate the same kind of bonds for Henry in
Northumberland as had underpinned David's lordship in the Midlands.
While Northumberland had been held explicitly from Stephen as a fief
under the 1139 accord and had continued to be regarded as part of the kingdom of England, from 1141 it was for all intents and purposes detached from
England and ruled as an extension of the Scottish kingdom.[32] Much has
been made by some historians of the evident hostility towards Scottish rule
displayed in the work of some of the monastic chroniclers in the region,
such as John of Hexham.[33] This hostility was still evident in the 1150s after
David, Earl Henry and Stephen were all dead, but attempts to present this
tradition as symptomatic of wider dissent fails to recognise the overall effectiveness of that Scottish rule, which another of those chroniclers, William of
Newburgh, saw as providing peace and stability as far south as the Tees, in
sharp contrast to the disturbed condition of the rest of England.[34]

In his earldom of Northumberland, Earl Henry successfully built up a
strong group of important vassals around him immediately after the settlement of 1139. At first the leading figure in the group, unsurprisingly, was
Eustace fitz John, who appeared regularly in the earl's company and
occurred frequently as a witness to his acts.[35] Eustace was also a significant
beneficiary of Henry's patronage, having received from him in probably
1139 or 1140 confirmation of all his lands in Northumberland that he had
held from the English crown under Henry I and Stephen, plus additional
properties in Huntingdon.[36] Of greater long-term significance to Henry,
however, was the Umfraville family in the persons of Robert de Umfraville,
Lord of Redesdale and of Prudhoe on the south side of the Tyne between

Corbridge and Newcastle, and his son, Gilbert.[37] Robert had been one of Henry I's new lords in the north and was one of the greatest landholders in the earldom, whose properties commanded the main route between David's power centre at Roxburgh and Durham, and straddled the east-west routes between Newcastle and Carlisle. The adherence of this family to their allegiance to David and his son was of far greater significance to the Scots than the grudging acceptance offered by the Prior of Hexham and his convent, but even the often acerbically critical Prior Richard attended court in Scotland and witnessed David and Henry's charters.[38] Gilbert de Umfraville developed a very close relationship of service to Earl Henry, functioning as his constable and probably also serving as his justiciar within the earldom of Northumberland.[39] Gilbert benefited greatly from his service to Henry, receiving estates at Kinnaird and Dunipace in Stirlingshire, and Keith in Midlothian, and his family eventually acquired the earldom of Angus in the thirteenth century.[40] Clearly, he and his father were central to the new regime in control of the earldom after 1139 and functioned as key members of Henry's *curia* in Northumberland. They rarely, however, appear to have been part of his travelling retinue outwith the earldom, attending court at Carlisle but rarely crossing into Scotland proper beyond the Tweed. It has to be stressed, however, that contrary to the argument that the Scots failed to attract support from the wider baronial group in the northern shires, it was not just on an elite such as Eustace fitz John or the Umfravilles that Henry's power in Northumberland was based. All the leading members of the regional nobility, such as the Balliols, the Bertrams, the Bolebecs and the Merlays, holders of key lordships throughout the earldom, were active in Earl Henry's service.[41]

Scottish control of Northumberland was not a military occupation founded on garrisons based in the main fortresses of the earldom from which a restive, if not openly hostile, populace could be policed. Certainly, Earl Henry held both Newcastle and Bamburgh, the key strongholds on which Norman power in the region had been founded down to 1136, but his control of Northumberland was much more deeply founded on bonds of lordship and service forged between the regional nobility and himself. It is not just in the service of these nobles, however, that the reality of Scottish control over Northumberland can be seen, but in the wider evidence for the apparatus of governance established by Henry. Beneath him, we can see a functioning administration of his lands; a judicial and administrative hierarchy with justiciar and sheriffs; a quasi-regal military organisation; and a sophisticated fiscal machine which included a mint at Corbridge where he had coins struck in his own name using the silver from the mines of Alston.[42] The basis for Henry's authority may have lain in the concession of the earldom to him extracted by David from Stephen first in 1136 and subsequently in 1139, and probably confirmed again on David's insistence by Matilda in 1141, which emphasised that Northumberland was still a province held of the English crown by a tenant-in-chief, but after September 1141 there can have been few people naïve enough to believe that David and his son recognised any overriding authority to their own. The award of Northumberland to Henry by both of the individuals who claimed the crown of England, one of whom was surely the legitimate monarch, may have offered some of the regional nobility a fig-leaf behind which to hide their exposed principles, but in reality the Scottish king and his son offered the stability, security and good lordship that both Stephen and Matilda had failed to provide, and from which even the partisan canons of Hexham had benfited.

In Cumberland, a significantly different policy was adopted by David who, although the region had formed part of Stephen's award to Earl Henry, effectively operated within it as if it were an integral part of his own realm. While Bamburgh and Newcastle formed the chief centres of Henry's power, Carlisle became with Roxburgh and Edinburgh a vital focus for David's authority. Part of the negotiations with the papal legate Alberic in September 1138, which had led to the treaty with Stephen early the next year, had been David's agreement to re-admit Bishop Æðelwulf of Carlisle to his see, from which the king had expelled him.[43] Æðelwulf had been living in southern England probably since David first occupied Carlisle in 1136 and was a regular witness of Stephen's charters from then until 1140. Around that time, he, like so many other leading northerners, recognised the changed political realities of the time and entered David's peace.[44] Æðelwulf and David appear to have quickly established a good working relationship, and the bishop accompanied the king on his journey south in 1141 for Matilda's expected coronation. For the remainder of the reign, he was associated with David's government in the north and occurred regularly as a witness to charters of the king and Earl Henry.[45] By forging a close alliance between Church and Crown in the See of Carlisle, David provided himself with the firm underpinning to his government that had contributed to his successful assertion of his authority within his original principality of Cumbria.

Too close a focus on the failure of David and the Matildine party in southern England in the late summer and autumn of 1141 runs the risk of ignoring or down-playing the significance of the Scottish conquests in the north-west of the kingdom. As had been made very evident in the campaigns of 1136–38, David and the Scots had ambitions to extend their controls south from the Vale of Eden around Carlisle through Westmorland and the Lake District towards Lancaster. There were private claims to some of this territory, William fitz Duncan in particular having interests in his maternal heritage in Allerdale and in his second wife Alice de Rumilly's heritage in Copeland in the western part of the Lake District and Craven in western Yorkshire. William's raid as far as Clitheroe in 1138 had been driven as much by ambition to gain his wife's inheritance as by the strategic needs of his uncle. The southern part of the region also represented something of a threat to the Scottish domination of Cumbria, for here, in around 1120, Henry I had given his nephew Stephen, at that time the Count of Mortain, the lordships of Furness, Cartmel, Lonsdale, Amounderness and the great block of country represented by Lancashire south of the river Ribble.[46] Before 1141 was over, David had extended his authority across almost the whole of this great swathe of territory and considered himself to be sufficiently in control of the region to issue charters of protection to the monks of Shrewsbury Abbey in respect of their properties in the Honour of Lancaster.[47] The charters were issued at 'the new castle of Tulketh', which had probably been built by Stephen in the 1120s to command a crossing of the Ribble east of Preston,[48] or had perhaps been thrown up on David's own instructions in 1141.[49] The western side of England to a line parallel with the Humber estuary was firmly in Scottish hands and, to emphasise how David viewed his possession of this land, he issued the charters in respect of it in his capacity as King of Scots with no reference to any overriding authority of the English crown. David's lingering deference to the authority once exercised by his great patron had finally been broken by the debacles at London and Winchester, and there was a new awareness that neither Stephen nor Matilda possessed the capability to assert their mastery over the whole of England or the resources to fight each other and roll back the Scottish advance.

One key factor behind the rapidity and effectiveness of the Scottish takeover in the region was the manner in which David intruded his lordship into the territory at the expense of Stephen's. While Stephen's personal estates were taken over by David, some to be granted away subsequently as the price for stabilising this extended salient of Scottish power, elsewhere in the north-west English provinces he simply inserted a new layer of lordship between himself and the existing tenants.[50] Instead of dispossessing the families in place in 1141, he gave them security of tenure in return for pledges of loyalty to himself,[51] and placed in superior lordship over them a number of his key supporters. William fitz Duncan gained both Allerdale and Copeland, and, given Scottish control of Amounderness and Lancaster, probably also Craven. His son, William, was certainly in possession of Craven and Skipton by 1149–52.[52] A second major beneficiary was Hugh de Morville, whose career in David's service had taken off meteorically in the later 1130s and who had already acquired the substantial Scottish lordships of Lauderdale and Cunningham and a scattered series of other properties in Lothian.[53] To him, David granted the lordship of North Westmorland, centred on the castle of Appleby which controlled the northern end of the Stanemoor route into Teesdale, and possibly also South Westmorland with its castle of Kendal.[54] Together, these territories rendered him one of the greatest of David's vassals in the extended south of his kingdom. Hugh had already secured the office of constable by 1140 [55] and the award of these highly strategic lordships to the crown's chief military officer is surely no coincidence. Over the next decade, the extended Morville family was to put down extensive roots in the region which would give their Scottish descendants claims to Westmorland lordships well into the thirteenth century.[56]

Apart from the insertion of such key men as William fitz Duncan and Hugh de Morville into the great lordships of the north-west of England, David did little to disturb the existing pattern of lordship and settlement in the region. The same policy of careful cultivation of the regional barons as was employed in Northumberland was also used in the western territories, with the established baronage being gradually enmeshed by and integrated into David's political and administrative regimes. As in Durham and Teesdale, certain members of the regional nobility were reluctant to break their faith with Stephen at first, but David had the advantage on his side that few of the second rank of greater landholders west of the Pennines held property elsewhere in England that still lay within Stephen's effective sphere of authority.[57] David was not forcing the barons to make a choice between loyalty to him and the loss of lands in southern England or support for Stephen and expulsion from the north. For most, although the decision may have caused some pangs of conscience, there was no prolonged anguishing over divided loyalties. David's regime in English Cumbria and Northumberland, therefore, was founded on a secure base, largely free from the undermining effect of individual waverers. It was a problem, however, that would significantly weaken his efforts to extend his power through Yorkshire to the Humber.

Traditional accounts of David's wars in northern England imply that his greatest objective was Durham. It is clear, however, that his sights were set on a far greater prize: York. The city had been his objective in 1138 when he had been baulked at Cowton Moor and was to remain the object of his ambitions for over a decade yet. The reasons for David's attraction to York are not difficult to see. Not only would control of the city give David possession of the whole of the former kingdom of Northumbria and secure his domination of England north of the Humber, but in the twelfth century York was still, after London, one of the greatest commercial centres in the British Isles. To hold York would give David access to resources vastly in excess of what he could draw from his existing kingdom. Perhaps of greater significance to David, however, was the neat solution which it would offer to the dispute over the claimed metropolitan supremacy of the archbishops of York over the Scottish Church. If York were a Scottish archdiocese, then the secular political edge to the issue would be removed. Furthermore, the archbishops were still among the most influential secular political figures in England north of the Humber, where they possessed extensive lands and rights. Were David to secure the appointment of at least a not unfriendly archbishop, then his designs for wider control in the region would have received a significant boost.

Among the many factors that had influenced David in his decision to break faith with Stephen in 1141 was the death of Archbishop Thurstan. The archbishop had been a key figure in organising the northern English resistance to David in 1136–38, both as a diplomat and war-leader, and throughout his pontificate had been a pillar of the English crown's authority in the north. Although he had started his career as a household clerk and, apparently, personal friend of Henry I,[58] after his appointment to York by the king in 1114 he had become a zealous defender of the rights of his archdiocese as well as a vigorous promoter of his patron's interests. As a consequence, he involved himself in aggressive defence of his status as a metropolitan, seeking to exclude Canterbury's primacy from his own see and assert his own rights over the Scottish bishoprics. This latter stance had resulted in a bitter conflict involving Alexander I and David in Scotland, which only the Scottish king's personal relationship with Henry I and Henry's need to secure David's aid in the question of the succession to the English throne had brought to an uneasy truce. Personal friendship with Henry I or no, Thurstan could not offer his allegiance to Matilda in 1135 and he swiftly emerged as a central figure in Stephen's regime in the north of England. His long-expected death tore an enormous hole in the pro-Stephen establishment in Yorkshire.

The stability which had been brought to the north with the second treaty of Durham meant that Thurstan's death in February 1140 did not seem to represent an immediate crisis. Stephen, indeed, was at the height of his power during this period and David had no wish to break the treaty and exploit, if possible, the removal of such a strong supporter of English royal authority. Stephen, therefore took time over the appointment of a successor, benefiting from the traditional right of the crown to draw the temporal revenues of vacant sees during the interval between the death of an incumbent and the investiture of his successor. It was only in January 1141 that he secured the election of his nephew, William fitz Herbert, to the vacant see. Stephen's capture at Lincoln only a month later was to undermine Archbishop William's position in the longer term, for the new archbishop was exposed immediately to accusations of his unsuitability and charged with having gained his position through the corrupt intervention of his uncle. Despite this mounting hostility to him from certain segments of the clergy of his diocese, most notably from the reformist abbots of the Cistercian and Augustinian houses, fitz Herbert was consecrated as archbishop in 1143 and gained possession of York itself. Stephen, slowly rebuilding his political position after his release by the Empress in November 1141, had apparently succeeded in placing his man into the vitally strategic northern archbishopric. That, however, proved to be only the start of a sustained campaign by the Cistercians to have him deposed and a 'suitable' candidate installed in his place. David was certainly well apprised of the situation in York and capitalised on his close connections with the Cistercians to establish links with Henry Murdac, the Cistercians' preferred candidate to replace fitz Herbert. Although Murdac was not openly in David's allegiance in 1147 when his friends succeeded in securing the deposition of fitz Herbert and his own election, David must have considered this change a positive development for his own wider ambitions. Before he could move to capitalise on the ecclesiastical coup, however, other events intervened to distract his attention from York.

The death of William fitz Duncan in around 1147, rather than finally resolving the still awkward question of the royal succession, triggered a wholly unexpected crisis for David.[59] Shortly after his nephew's death a claimant emerged to a share in William's titles and rights in the person of Wimund, a bishop in the Isles. Details of this extraordinary episode are scanty in the extreme, and it has often been dismissed as an overblown or even fantastical myth, largely on account of difficulties in reconciling the limited evidence with traditional accounts of David's reign. The identities and relationships of the key figures in the affair, moreover, have been consistently misinterpreted, and the objectives behind the rebellion misunderstood. Contemporary evidence is limited, the best account coming from William of Newburgh, a northern English cleric and chronicler active after 1170 who had access to information about Wimund's later years in enforced retirement in William's home monastery, Byland Abbey in Yorkshire.[60] William's account starts by describing Wimund as having been 'born in the most obscure spot in England', which might not appear to support his claims to rights in Scotland. He records how after a basic education, the young Wimund professed as a monk in the Savigniac convent at Furness, which had been founded in 1127 by Count Stephen of Mortain (the future King Stephen), and after rising to prominence there was one of a group of monks sent to the Isle of Man. He probably arrived in Man in 1134 as one of the colonising brethren of the daughter-house of Furness at Rushen founded by Óláfr I Godredsson, King of Man, in that year. Possibly at the same time as his foundation of Rushen Abbey, King Óláfr awarded Furness the right to elect a bishop for his kingdom,[61] and shortly afterwards he confirmed the monks' nomination of one of their own number to the bishopric.[62] The bishop-elect appears to have been Wimund, for a profession of obedience to an Archbishop of York – erroneously identified as Archbishop Thomas II (1109–14) in a late twelfth-century source,[63] but almost certainly to have been Archbishop Thurstan (1119–40) – by a bishop of that name is recorded in York tradition. In his profession, Wimund styled himself bishop of the *sancta ecclesia de Schith* (the holy Church of Skye), one of the many locations which served as the seat of the bishops of the Isles before its eventual establishment at Peel on Man. His cathedral may have been the church at Snizort which again served as the seat of the Scottish See of the Isles for a period in the later Middle Ages after the final loss of Man to English control. For Wimund, this base in the Western Isles of Scotland would prove vital for his secular political ambitions in the late 1140s.

According to William of Newburgh, Wimund established a high reputation and great personal popularity among the Islesmen and these factors stoked distinctly unreligious ambitions. Acting more like a warlord than a bishop, he gathered around him a warband of 'needy and daring' men, proclaimed that he was the son of an unnamed Earl of Moray, and that he had been 'despoiled by the King of Scots of the patrimony of his fathers'. His stated intention, in William's account, was not only to secure recognition of his rights, but also to take revenge for undefined wrongs which had been perpetrated against him, and with that aim he launched an invasion of

David's territories. William's account gives no indication of the date at which the conflict started or its duration, but his implication is that it was neither a short nor a localised affair, for Wimund successfully eluded an army sent against him by David by retreating into the mountains or withdrawing to his ships whenever David's men drew near. While nowhere is it explicit in the account, the implication is that the rebellion was directed at western mainland Scotland, possibly adjacent to Skye, and that Wimund for some time held the initiative. Even the defeat of his army by a force commanded by an un-named Scottish bishop, from whom Wimund had demanded tribute, failed to end his inroads and David was eventually forced into negotiations. The result of these was that the king ceded him the rule of a province which included his old abbey at Furness. William's narrative ends with an account of Wimund's arrogant and oppressive behaviour as ruler of his province, which finally resulted in his seizure by a force of locals who blinded and castrated him, after which he was confined in the monastery at Byland until his death many years later.

It is a lurid and sensationalised account which raises many more questions than it answers, but it also contains sufficient detail for it to be considered as a serious record of an actual event. There are three central questions to be resolved: who was Wimund; what was his relationship with the 'Earl of Moray'; and who was that earl? In the past, most historians assumed that the earldom of Moray had been suppressed by David in the immediate aftermath of the death of Óengus, Earl of Moray, at the battle of Stracathro in 1130. On that basis, they have identified the man claimed by Wimund as his father with Óengus and, consequently, have been prepared to place Wimund's rebellion as starting possibly as early as 1134–42.[64] The largely circumstantial evidence for the direction of Wimund's main attacks, moreover, has been taken by some to suggest a prolonged campaign to regain control of the lost earldom itself, where a son of Óengus could be assumed to have enjoyed substantial support. There is, however, a strong alternative interpretation.

William of Newburgh, who was in a position at Byland Abbey to have obtained detailed information relating to his subject, is emphatic that Wimund was born in England. When this is considered alongside his profession as a monk at Furness and his later award of lordship by David over a territory which included or lay near that abbey, then it is probable that Wimund had had strong personal links with that area since his childhood. It has been suggested that the most likely province near to Furness is Copeland, a district with a significant Norse-Gaelic element in the population and which had formerly strong political and cultural links with the kingdom of the Isles.[65] Probably more significant than this Isles link, however, is the fact that down to around 1147 the Lord of Copeland was none other than William fitz Duncan, who held the lordship in the right of his second wife, Alice de Rumilly. Now although William invariably appears in Scottish royal acts as 'the king's nephew' or 'my nephew' there is, as discussed earlier, one thirteenth-century genealogy dealing with the descent of the lords of Copeland and Allerdale which refers to him as Earl of Moray.[66] While this genealogy remains unsupported, there is no obvious reason for the claim to be invented, and William's status as a member of the Scottish royal house has probably masked any other titles or lordships that he held in Scotland, despite his clear position as a man of the first rank in the kingdom. If Wimund's claim was based on his being the son of William fitz Duncan, then his invasion of Scottish controlled territory must surely be dated to after the death of his 'father'.

William fitz Duncan had very strong Cumberland connections. After the killing of his father in 1094, it is most probable that the young William had been brought by his mother, Octreda, to live with her kinsmen in Allerdale, and he probably remained there until his appearance at Alexander I's court in the early 1120s. The chronology of Wimund's ecclesiastical career indicates that he must have been born before 1110 for him to have been a fully professed monk by the time that Rushen was founded in 1134. Such a date would certainly tally with William's time in Allerdale, when he would have been in his late teens. There is, then, strong circumstantial evidence to suggest that Wimund was an illegitimate son of the young William, fathered before William returned to Scotland to pursue his career at the courts of his uncles.[67]

William fitz Duncan's death is not recorded in any surviving chronicle but he ceases to appear in the witness lists of charters issued between 1147 and 1151. He was certainly dead by the time Alice de Rumilly established a community of Augustinian canons at Bolton in Wharfedale in 1151.[68] There is, however, a curious reference by John of Hexham in his chronicle under the year 1152. John associates the visit of the papal legate, John Paparo, cardinal-deacon of St Adrian, in that year with an expedition in which David had 'confirmed his nephew William fitz Duncan in the honour of Skipton and Craven'.[69] William fitz Duncan, we know, was already dead by this time, but his recognised heir in his northern English lands was his son by Alice, also named William, and we should probably see in John's account the confirmation of this younger William's rights following the final suppression of Wimund.

For David, then, the death of William fitz Duncan caused a protracted crisis for the security of his acquisitions in northern England. It was not, however, simply a question of the challenge presented by Wimund, but also one of the loss of a man who was among David's principal military commanders and lord of a series of key frontier territories at the southern edge of the Scottish advance. Certainly, William had a son by Alice de Rumilly and three daughters whose marriages could be used to bind the de Rumilly/fitz Duncan heritage ever more closely to the Scots, but, given that William and Alice only married in the mid-1130s, all were still young.[70] The younger William in particular was significantly under age, and although the king would have moved swiftly to entrust the wardship of the boy's lands to a reliable agent, William's extreme youth would have deprived David of effective leadership in place at a critical moment. Wimund, we can assume, had capitalised on that weakness, but were there others in a position to make a move also?

William fitz Duncan's possession of the lordship of Craven and the castle of Skipton gave the Scots a powerful presence within Yorkshire. In 1141, it had not been able to provide them with a springboard from which to launch a successful assault on York itself, or the means to influence the archiepiscopal election in the city, but in the late 1140s the whole political complexion of Yorkshire and the remains of 'English' northern England had changed dramatically and David again saw an opportunity to capitalise on these developments. The main changes were twofold. In the north-west, the uneasy relationship between Stephen and Ranulf, Earl of Chester, had broken down in the late summer of 1146, while at York in early 1147 the Pope had declared the deposition of Stephen's nephew, William fitz Herbert, as archbishop, and in July, Henry Murdac, Abbot of Fountains, had been elected in his place.[71]

David had played no direct part in the expulsion of fitz Herbert from his see and the advancement of Henry Murdac. The main challenge to the archbishop had come from the Cistercians, who saw him as a symbol of simoniacal corruption within the Church that needed to be purged, and his intrusion by King Stephen as tainted with the vexed issue of investiture and the freedom of the Church in elections from secular interference. Henry Murdac enjoyed a high reputation within the Cistercian order and was a friend of Bernard of Clairvaux. Once Bernard had been mobilised on Henry's behalf, Archbishop William's days were numbered, for the abbot mounted a sustained, vitriolic attack on him in a campaign of letter-writing and sermons.[72] In many ways, Stephen played into Bernard's hands, for his

failure to control his supporters in what was becoming an increasingly acri-
monious dispute. First, he managed to lose the support of William of Ste
Barbe, Dean of York and Bishop of Durham, a development which cost him
influence in what had been a decidedly anti-Scottish see down to that date;
then his supporters had mounted a violent assault on Fountains itself and
attacked several prominent members of the diocesan clergy of York, castrating
the archdeacon. With this mounting evidence for fitz Herbert's unsuitability
laid before him, the Cistercian Pope, Eugenius III, declared the archbishop
deposed and ordered a fresh election to be held. On 24 July 1147 at
Richmond, far removed from the centres of pro-Stephen influence around
York, a minority of the diocesan clergy – led by the reformist Cistercian and
Augustinian monasteries – elected Henry Murdac in William's place and on 7
December the new archbishop received papal approval. While William almost
immediately withdrew from his see and eventually went into exile, his
remaining supporters steadfastly refused to accept Henry Murdac into York
and, with Stephen's backing, kept him from his see. Basking in his reputation
as a great patron of the Cistercians, David saw in this dispute the potential to
extend his political influence under the guise of pious support for a member
of a persecuted order and committed ecclesiastical reformer. Throughout
1148, it can be assumed, David courted the archbishop-elect assiduously.

In late May 1149, David's great nephew, Henry of Anjou, arrived at the
king's court in Carlisle. His arrival permitted David to display again his
mastery of political opportunism by turning the young man's presence fully
to his advantage. According to John of Hexham, David staged a lavish court
ceremony in which he, aided by Earl Henry and Ranulf, Earl of Chester,
knighted his great nephew.[73] As a precursor to the knighting ceremony,
David extracted an oath from Henry of Anjou that, should he succeed in
gaining the English throne, he would formally recognise Scottish possession
of Newcastle and all of Northumbria,[74] an oath which probably extended to
cover the western territories also. Too much significance has been placed on
this agreement by virtue of the events of 1157, when Henry of Anjou
reneged on his agreement and took back all of David's acquisitions from the
young King Malcolm IV,[75] but in 1149 it may only have been seen by David
as an additional safeguard. At the time of the Carlisle ceremony, Stephen
had successfully reasserted his authority in southern England and the
Matildine cause there was effectively dead. To most observers, the possibility
of Henry of Anjou mounting a successful challenge for his grandfather's
throne must have seemed nil, and the expected successor to Stephen was
most likely to be his elder son, Eustace. Far more important to David was

the presence in his court of several key dignitaries from the south, headed by Ranulf, Earl of Chester, and Henry Murdac, Archbishop of York.

Ranulf's presence at Carlisle, the city which he had sought to regain since he had inherited his father's claim to it in 1129, marked a radical shift in the political relationships in the north-west. According to John of Hexham, Ranulf had performed homage to David as part of a deal whereby David secured Carlisle and, in return for giving up his claim, Ranulf gained the honour of Lancaster and the promise of marriage to one of Earl Henry's daughters.[76] We do not know the terms of Ranulf's homage, but it appears that for his new lordship in Lancaster he became the man of the King of Scots with no acknowledgement of any overriding lordship of the English crown. David was again showing unequivocally that his direct lordship – his kingdom – extended at least as far south as the Ribble and, by reaching this settlement with Ranulf he had strengthened his hold over his English provinces and provided himself with a new frontier lord to replace William fitz Duncan.

The attendance of Henry Murdac at David's court was highly significant also, for the archbishop's dispute with Stephen was reaching a new pitch of bitterness. Stephen still refused to accept his nephew's deposition from the archbishopric and was adamant that Henry, despite the support for him among the increasingly influential Yorkshire Cistercians and from the Pope, was to be barred from admission to his see. In 1149, Henry, therefore, while recognised by the wider Church establishment as archbishop, was excluded from York by Stephen and had not performed homage to the English king.[77] David clearly saw the possibilities for the advancement of his own interests in the stand-off at York and, while the archbishop may have been persuaded to come to Carlisle by the presence of Henry of Anjou, it is possible that Henry Murdac had already come to recognise that David offered him the only real chance of securing his see. David's interest in supporting Henry Murdac's claims to York is transparently obvious. While it is possible that support for the Angevin cause lay behind David's actions, given his decidedly self-interested pursuit of territory in northern England from 1141 onwards it seems more probable that it was his own political and ecclesiastical needs that he was serving.[78]

David used the gathering at Carlisle to devise a new strategy for securing control of England north of the Humber. Its objective was the capture of York itself and the establishment of Henry Murdac as archbishop under David's protection. David himself, accompanied by Henry of Anjou and the cream of the Anglo-Scottish nobility, would come down to Lancaster to meet with Ranulf and his men, then push east through the Pennine passes. It was, for Ranulf, a very attractive proposition, for Scottish control of York would also have provided him with a springboard from which to launch his efforts to regain control of his lands around Lincoln.[79] The whole operation depended on careful timing to co-ordinate the attacks and on maintaining the element of surprise. Stephen, however, somehow got word of David's scheme from loyalists at York and managed to pre-empt the Scots by leading a strong force in person into the city.[80] Faced with the choice of mounting an assault on a city that Stephen had now won over with concessions to its citizens or withdrawing with his forces intact, David chose to fall back. Stephen, however, while strong enough to risk crossing the Humber from his heartland in southern England and entering York, was not sufficiently strong to mount a challenge to David, who sat glowering in Carlisle.[81] Satisfied that York was securely in his hands, Stephen withdrew southwards and David disbanded his army. The moment of crisis was past and the chance to re-draw radically the political map of the British Isles lost forever.

While 1149 did not represent quite the last military operation in the Scottish occupation of northern England, it represented the high-tide mark. By August 1149, David had secured peace and stability within his domain, and obtained recognition of his lordship from the last would-be challengers to his control of English Cumbria, Lancaster and Northumberland. The bishopric of Durham, too, while not in his direct possession, was not ill-disposed towards him. This domination of northern England, more complete on the west coast than on the east, gave David an extended sphere of authority that embraced the northern part of the Irish Sea. With success came power and wealth, and David was probably at no time more secure within the heartland of Gaelic Scotland that now lay far to the north of the provinces where he most regularly based himself. Concentration on his southern frontier had only been possible as a result of his triumphs over Máel Coluim mac Alasdair and Óengus of Moray, and his successful relationships with his great Gaelic lords beyond the Forth, but it was victory in England that won him lasting acceptance among these Gaelic magnates and secured his grip over his inherited kingdom. A strong and unifying kingship within Scotland had been underpinned by its successful extension far to the south of its Gaelic core.

CHAPTER ELEVEN

David the Venerable
1149–53

By 1149, David was by the standards of his time a very old man and was surely preparing himself for the death that would soon come and the reward that would follow in the hereafter. He could, however, look to the future of the extended kingdom which he had created with a great degree of confidence. Between Cleveland and Caithness, there seemed to be no realistic threat to the authority which he had so painstakingly assembled and consolidated. Possession of Northumberland and English Cumbria had been, it seemed, confirmed as the inheritance of his heirs by Henry of Anjou, securing a southern frontier far to the south of the traditional heartland of the kingdom which he had inherited. Anglo-Norman nobles whose principal political ties were to Scotland and its ruling house were in possession of lordships throughout the southern gains and the second rank of the regional nobility was bound closely into the service of the king and his son. In Henry, too, David had a mature and experienced adult heir to succeed him in the near future, a man with proven experience in government and administration, skilled in warfare, a respected patron of the Church, and popular with his subjects. There was every prospect that under 'King Henry' of Scotland David's achievements would be consolidated and built upon to effect a permanent realignment of power in mainland Britain.

The concession extracted from Henry of Anjou at Carlisle in May 1149 revealed how radically the political structures within Britain had been redrawn by David. Down to 1141, David had still been required to accept that all his gains in northern England were held of the English crown: they were under Scottish control but were not part of the kingdom of the Scots. By 1149, however, all pretence of acknowledging English superiority for these lands had been dropped and David was ruling them as an integral part of his kingdom. Naturally, this was not a position that Stephen was likely to recognise, but Henry of Anjou's pledge to maintain the *status quo* should he succeed to the English throne underscored the reality of the situation. Stephen might yet consider the northern lordships and shires rightfully to be part of his realm, and as recently as 1146 had sought to grant his former lordship of Lancaster to Ranulf, Earl of Chester.¹ But Stephen lacked the ability to make real his grant to Ranulf, for Lancaster was firmly in David's hands, and when the earl finally gained possession it was by the gift of the Scottish king and it was to him, not to either Stephen or Henry of Anjou, that Ranulf gave homage. It is in situations such as this that we can see the actuality of David's power and the effectiveness of his absorption of his acquisitions into an enlarged Scottish kingdom. By 1149–50, the 'Scoto-Northumbrian' realm, although still lacking full control of Durham and possession of York, was a reality rather than the chimaeric fantasy pursued by David's forefathers.

At the close of the 1140s, then, David could look with some considerable satisfaction on his achievements. He had turned his inheritance from what, in contemporary European terms, was an underdeveloped society into a state that could hold its own among the states of western Europe. Starting with limited resources, he had carefully nurtured his interests and gradually expanded on this small foundation to a point where development and growth became self-sustaining. Income from Huntingdon and, probably, Teviotdale and the Merse, enabled him to attract more men to his service and begin the capital investment which would turn at least the eastern portion of his southern Scottish principality into an economic generator. Once trade began to flow through his burghs and port of Roxburgh and Berwick, further stimulated by his monastery at Selkirk and its economic development of the central Borders uplands, and by the beginnings of Bishop John's organisation of his diocesan administration, so too had flowed his income. With this core territory firmly in his grasp, David was provided with the basic resources that would enable him to make the step from Prince of Cumbria to King of Scots. Of course, the kingdom which he had inherited was perhaps less economically sophisticated in 1124 than had been the former Northumbrian territories in the south where he had first tasted independent power, but, once he had succeeded in imposing his lordship over it, Scotland would provide him with an abundance of resources, human and material, which could be turned with great effect to the business of state-building.

What David needed to 'jump-start' the economic development of his kingdom was a significant injection of the raw substance by which wealth was measured in medieval Europe: silver. England possessed an important source of that precious metal at Alston to the east of Carlisle, where it had been discovered in lead-workings. The mines had started to produce silver in around 1130 and were an important generator of revenue for the English crown through the last years of Henry I's reign.[2] David cannot but have been aware of this rich resource located in territory to which he believed he had a right and his anxiety to retain control of Cumberland must surely in part have been driven by desire to control the mines. For a decade, the silver from the Alston mines had been flowing into David's coffers, providing the substance to fuel his ambitious programmes of castle-building, monastic foundations and burgh development.[3] This new and dependable source of income more than amply replaced what had been forfeited with the loss of Huntingdon to his St Liz stepson, and replenished royal resources that had been depleted significantly by his generous patronage of the Church and lavish infeftment of Anglo-Norman lords with Scottish estates. Most importantly, however, Alston silver permitted him to mint his own coins, one of the chief symbolic acts of medieval kingship and statehood. David's coins were an unequivocal statement of the independence and integrity of his kingdom. Down to about 1141, the coins minted in the north had been produced using Stephen's dies, an arrangement which served to emphasise the continuing, albeit notional, inclusion of Cumberland and Northumberland in the territories of the English crown. After that date, the silver pennies minted at Carlisle, like those produced at Berwick, Roxburgh, Edinburgh, Perth and Aberdeen, were to a uniform – Scottish – pattern, and, although Earl Henry's mints at Corbridge and Newcastle issued coins in his own name, they conformed to the design and quality of his father's issues.[4] In contrast to the increasingly debased coins being produced in the royal and baronial mints in southern Britain, the Scottish coins were of high silver content and production standard. Fuelled by this injection of bullion, the economy of David's new kingdom boomed while it languished in the south.

The importance of the Cumbrian silver to David's revolution in Scotland should not be understated. At a fairly basic level, it transformed the position of the crown. While much of the revenue of the kings of Scots into the later Middle Ages continued to be paid in kind, David also now received cash payments and could also dispose of surplus food renders on the open market for silver. With a native, high-quality currency available to him, David could now act like the ruler of any of the major, modern, European states. Building projects could be funded on a lavish scale to provide the king with a suitably impressive physical setting in which to parade his new majesty and regal authority, setting the monarchy on a plane above the magnates. It was probably David who built, or at least completed, the great keep which dominates the castle at Carlisle, and possibly also that at Lancaster, while Earl Henry may have built that at Bamburgh and started the construction of the immense motte-and-bailey at Warkworth.[5] Likewise, David could divert money into religious building projects, again making an ostentatious statement of his kingship's place among the monarchies of Europe. Such major capital projects as the building of royal castles, abbeys and cathedrals, however, represented only one facet of a spending boom which would propel the Scottish economy from the margins to the mainstream of European economic trends. Alongside masonry-and-mortar investment came purchase of high-value commodities to furnish and embellish those structures and to give sophistication to the court and household. Just as his mother, Margaret, had encouraged foreign traders to come to Scotland with their exotic wares and thereby help to enrich the cultural fabric of the kingdom, so too did David attract an increased volume of trade to his kingdom as merchants responded to the new demand for their goods from king, magnates and clergy. With his new disposable income, David could also attract ambitious men to his service, retaining them on fees paid in cash rather than having to further alienate his landed resources to provide them with a means of support. From household knights to the clerks of his writing-office and household administration, the flow of bullion enabled the king to construct around himself a following modelled on Anglo-Norman practice. Royal government in Scotland had moved from the rudimentary and small-scale to the sophisticated and grand, and with its expansion so too did royal authority grow.

From the outset of his reign, David had well understood the link between monarchical power and prestige and economic development. Before 1124, he had granted the status of burgh to Roxburgh and probably also to Berwick, establishing the two settlements as privileged trading centres with monopolies over trade in carefully defined hinterlands.[6] As the reign progressed, burgh status was awarded to other important settlements clustered around the chief royal residences: Edinburgh, Lanark, Stirling, Dunfermline, Perth and Aberdeen. Other burghs were probably planned or existed, especially north of the Tay. For David, these market centres were the key to wealth generation and their distribution provides a telling insight on where the bulk of the king's revenue was concentrated. But David was not content with the economic exploitation of the country south of the Tay, and the mints located at Perth and Aberdeen emphasise his intention that the economic modernisation of his kingdom would be wholesale. Both were ports and formed conduits through which the produce of vast agricultural hinterlands were exported and where the king's agents could dispose of his own surpluses from his renders in kind and from royal estates. It was a shift from what was essentially little more than a subsistence or barter-based economy to a full-blown monetised market economy, and it was achieved in its basics in little more than a decade. By the late 1140s, money income from the burghs and their related trade was a fixed and important component in crown revenue.[7] David had provided his successors with a source of income that would survive the exhaustion or loss of the Alston mines or the depletion of royal landed estates in the later twelfth and thirteenth centuries.

Of course, when we talk of the 'Davidian revolution' it would be entirely false to give the impression that the king carried through this radical reconstruction of his kingdom single-handedly. From soon after 1113, he had been introducing aristocratic colonists from England and northern France, clerics from England and the near continent, and, to provide the skills and know-how to make the new burghs flourish, ordinary townspeople from England, Flanders and elsewhere.[8] These newcomers had different expectations based on different cultural backgrounds, and their demands alone served to stimulate the economy and push forward the development of trade, commerce and the use of money. These new elements had presented David with tremendous new opportunities but also confronted him with new challenges, for they required to be fitted into the complex structures of the traditional legal practices of his kingdom. They were outsiders, lacking kin connections to protect or avenge them in a society that was still essentially kin-based and regulated in its social interactions through the exercise of such relationships. David, therefore, was obliged to legislate in a manner unlike any of his predecessors and on subjects hitherto unheard of in Scotland. Everything from inheritance practice to the regulation of trade fell within the competence of royal legislation. Many of the laws attributed to David were probably not formulated in his reign, but what is significant is that it was to his reign that later generations of lawyers looked for the origins of the Scottish legal tradition.[9]

One central theme in David's supposed legal innovations is his alleged introduction of the form of land tenure that has come to be known as feudalism.[10] David has been represented in Scottish history as the man who converted Scotland into a 'feudal' state and introduced a wholly new system of law founded upon 'feudal' principles. By the late 1140s, certainly, it was evident that there were differing modes of land tenure and different forms of relationship between David and his Anglo-Norman colonial lords and his Gaelic magnates, but there is little evidence for a widespread policy of infeftment of colonial lords in the heartland of his kingdom beyond the Forth. There, his one significant achievement is claimed to be the resignation of Fife into his hands by Earl Donnchad I in around 1136 and its re-grant to him as a fief.[11] Geoffrey Barrow has emphasised the significance of this legal change in respect of the most senior of the Gaelic earldoms, which would have given formal definition to the relationship between earl and king, but there is no sign that it had any deeper ramifications as far as the earl and his successors were concerned. Indeed, the act, if it in fact ever occurred, did not transform Donnchad or his heirs into 'feudal' lords and the earls of Fife continued to exercise their social and political role as Gaelic magnates quite unchanged by the nominal effect of any parchment-based deal.[12] If the Fife surrender took place, it clearly had little impact on David's other Gaelic magnates, for none beat a path to court to receive confirmation of their possession of their earldoms by royal charter. Some infeftments did take place within Fife, but on royal lands not on portions of the earls' estates. Robert the Burgundian, for example, received land around Lochore and to the south of Loch Leven,[13] while Alan Lascelles, whose family emerge later in the twelfth century as lords of Naughton and Forgan, may have been established in Fife late in David's reign.[14] Even in Moray, where David is viewed traditionally as having underpinned his conquest with a feudal settlement of at least the Laich district, only one colonist can be identified as being infefted in land there in David's reign. If the 'feudalisation' of Scotland had been one of David's aims after 1124, a quarter of a century later he had made no significant progress in establishing it in the country north of the Tay. Developments there, it seems, had been left on the drawing-board while David and his lieutenants concentrated on affairs in the south.

Once the high drama of the summer of 1149 was over, David could turn once more to the settlement of still pressing business elsewhere in his kingdom. Moray, since the death of William fitz Duncan, probably lay at the forefront of his concerns and it was towards the northern provinces of his kingdom, where he had never before ventured, that he made his way in 1150. As discussed in Chapter Six, David had been obliged to consider a radical reconstruction of his arrangements for the peace and stability of the north in both the mid-1130s when William had turned his main focus towards securing Alice de Rumilly's heritage and in the late 1140s after William's death. There is, however, no evidence to suggest that David had done anything more than issue instructions to his lieutenants as to what arrangements he expected to be made, and certainly nothing to indicate that he considered it necessary or personally desirable to visit the region in person. At the very least, the continuing instability on the frontier with Stephen in the south required the king to remain close to the centres of his power. By early 1150, however, with the southern frontier stabilised, the threat from Wimund eradicated, and his Angevin great nephew safely back on the continent, David could finally turn his personal attention towards the north of the kingdom.

On 21 May 1150, David was at Kinloss in Moray for the foundation of Melrose's third colony.[15] As discussed earlier, we should not fail to acknowledge the pious motives which lay behind this foundation, but it, like the recent foundation of Holmcultram in Cumberland, also carried a strong political purpose. Far removed from the other Cistercian monasteries in the kingdom and the northernmost royal foundation in Scotland of any religious order, Kinloss was as much a political as a religious symbol. Planted in the heart of lowland Moray in the centre of what had probably been comital demesne under Óengus and William fitz Duncan, it was a bold proclamation of royal power and a statement of confidence in the security of Scottish royal authority. It is, however, unlikely to have been the only business that David undertook while in the region and it is possible that the administrative mechanisms which emerge in the Laich of Moray in the reigns of Malcolm IV and William the Lion had their origins around this time.[16] There is no sign of sheriffdoms at so early a date, but it is likely that David strengthened or established the line of royal castles that stretched along the southern side of the Moray Firth from Banff to Inverness. It is possible also that it was in the course of this northern tour that David secured the installation of his former chancellor, Edward, as Bishop of Aberdeen, placing a man with strong court connections in charge of a territorially strategic bishopric at a critical moment[17]

Northern affairs seem still to have dominated David's time in June, when he and a great gathering of leading clerics and nobles assembled at Dunfermline for the dedication of the new abbey church.[18] Among those present were the bishops of St Andrews, Glasgow, Caithness, Aberdeen and Ross, the abbots of Kelso, Holyrood and Cambuskennth, Duncan, Earl of Fife, Gartnait, Earl of Buchan, and Morgrund, Earl of Mar, plus a host of other Gaelic and Anglo-Norman lords. While such a gathering of the kingdom's elite could be expected at the dedication of what was still the premier royal monastery, the prominence of northern bishops and earls suggests that other business might have been under consideration at the time. Sadly, we have no record of business discussed at this gathering, nor at the council held by David in Edinburgh towards the end of the year.[19] At the close of 1150, therefore, David appears to have been preoccupied still with arrangements for the security of his regime in the northern mainland, and events the following year would show that his preoccupation was not without justification.

It was perhaps in 1150 on his way to or from Moray, but possibly in 1151, that David made his one recorded visit to Aberdeen. The importance of this expedition into the north is underscored by the men who attended on him at Aberdeen. With him were Gregory, Bishop of Dunkeld, Andrew, Bishop of Caithness, Samson, Bishop of Brechin, Donnchad, Earl of Fife, Máel Muire, Earl of Atholl, and Gille Brigte, Earl of Angus, plus a number of Gaelic magnates from the north-east.[20] It was a significant group of men, with Gregory being possibly the former Bishop of Moray of that name,[21] Andrew representing David's political establishment in the north mainland, Donnchad being lord of extensive estates in highland Moray, and Máel Muire both a kinsman of Harald Maddadsson of Orkney and Caithness and also holder of an earldom which had been central to David's policies in the north since the 1120s. Their accompanying David at this time is unlikely to have been simple coincidence. The business to which they were called as witness, moreover, suggests that David was undertaking a radical reconstruction of arrangements for the future policing of the northern part of the kingdom, for the act to which their names were appended freed the brethren of the abbey of Old Deer in Buchan from any obligation to perform secular service and other demands in respect of their extensive estates in the region. Clearly, military service and crown rights in the north were at the forefront of David's concerns. The reasons for that concern with military arrangements may have lain in Orkney, where David's two decades of careful nurturing of a pro-Scottish government had been overthrown by an unforeseen development.

In 1151, King Eystein of Norway, the overlord of the earldom of Orkney but with whom Harald Maddadsson had no formal political relationship and to whom Harald had not performed homage, arrived in the islands with a powerful fleet. It was immediately apparent that Eystein had arrived intent on receiving Harald's obedience and was prepared to force him militarily into submission. The teenage earl, who had been left in nominal control of both Orkney and Caithness by Rognvald while his older kinsman undertook an extended pilgrimage to the Holy Land, was at his residence in Thurso in Caithness when the Norwegians arrived suddenly and captured him, forcing his submission and homage as the price for his release.[22] It was a bold and decisive stroke which undid at a blow the Scottish domination of the earldom that David had secured in the 1130s. Having achieved his primary objective with unexpected ease, Eystein demonstrated his superior power in what seems a rather aimless cruise down the eastern coasts of Scotland and England, raiding as he went, but apparently with no clear purpose other than to win plunder.[23] Among the victims of this gratuitous display of strength was Aberdeen, which Eystein's men plundered and burned, and it may have been in response to this clear indication of the unpreparedness of his vassals in the north-east that David again came north to reorganise its defences. That, however, was not the full extent of David's response and he quickly showed that he was not prepared to accept Eystein's coup in Orkney and Caithness.

Later in 1151, clearly in a move designed to counter this reverse, David threw a wild card into the equation by supporting the claims of another member of the Orkney dynasty, Erlend Haraldsson, grandson of Earl Håkon and the son of the man disposed of by Harald Maddadsson's kin in around 1123, to a share in the rule of the northern earldoms. Like Harald before him, Erlend had no formal ties to Norway and was untainted by any submission to Eystein. David granted him half of Caithness, thereby re-emphasising the vassalic relationship between the Orkney dynasty and the kings of Scots in respect of the mainland earldom. Eystein, however, responded by making a grant to Erlend of Harald Maddadsson's half of Orkney in a move which showed how much faith the Norwegian king placed in Harald's earlier submission. Far from retrieving the position in the north for the Scottish crown, David's intervention produced a three-cornered conflict between Erlend, Harald and Rognvald, who returned from his travels in the midst of the upheavals, which ended only in 1154 with the death of Erlend.[24] At the end of his life, David was faced with the knowledge that his carefully nurtured schemes for the domination of Orkney and Caithness had miscarried badly, but he would not know that his failure there presented his successors with over half a century of debilitating conflict in which Harald Maddadsson, free from Scottish or Norwegian interference, pursued his own empire-building dreams and supported a new generation of challengers for the Scottish throne.

In the early summer of 1152, any remaining hopes on David's part for a tranquil end to his reign vanished with the arrival of shocking news. On 12 June, possibly at Newcastle or at Roxburgh, Earl Henry had died. The prince could have been no more than thirty-eight years old and had been an active and vigorous man in his teens and twenties, but it is possible that his health had deteriorated in the 1140s. In his *vita* of St Malachy, Bernard of Clairvaux mentions a visit by the archbishop to David's court at Carlisle and his curing of Henry from a serious malady which had brought him to the point of death.[25] That incident apart, however, there is no indication that Henry's health had been a cause for serious concern, and David had clearly assumed that he would be handing on his kingdom to his son. Already aged and evidently preparing for his own death, David instead found himself having to plan for an unlooked for future where his crown passed not to a mature and experienced adult ruler in his son but to an untried child in his eldest grandson, Malcolm. After the burial of Henry at Kelso Abbey, therefore, David had to give urgent consideration to the succession. Unlike Henry I and the death of William in the sinking of the White Ship, the death of Earl Henry did not precipitate a crisis within the Scottish royal house, for the earl had fathered three healthy sons. David's line, therefore, would continue, but there remained the possibility of challenge from older members of the alternative lines of descent from Máel Coluim mac Donnchada. There was also the question of the security of Earl Henry's northern English lands. The mature Henry would have been more than capable of defending his position in those, but a child ruler lacked the personal bonds with his potential vassals which had been forged by his father in his decade and a half of control. For these reasons, David felt obliged to shift his focus from the remote north of his kingdom and take active steps to settle the succession firmly on Malcolm and mark out the future for Earl Henry's Northumbrian domain.

David understood well that although there was no real question that anyone other than Malcolm would succeed him, the likelihood that the accession of a mere boy to the throne would pass without any challenge was remote. To minimise the risk of political disturbance, therefore, he arranged for his grandson to be presented to his future subjects as his designated heir and also provided him with a guardian in the person of Donnchad, Earl of Fife, the most senior of the Gaelic magnates.[26] According to John of Hexham, David decided to send his grandson on a tour around his future kingdom so that he might be seen and acknowledged as heir to the kingship by his future subjects, and gave Donnchad an army with which to overawe the reluctant.[27] In John's account, Donnchad is titled *rector*, possibly indicating only that he was to be Malcolm's guardian during this extended circuit of the kingdom but more likely signifying that David intended the earl to exercise an office similar to regent. As his eldest grandson headed north into Scotland, David turned to the question of Northumberland and personally escorted his second grandson, William, to Newcastle. There, he presented the nine-year-old boy to the barons of the earldom as their future lord and, in a bitterly ironic move which demonstrated how little trust he placed in the pledges of men, took hostages from the Northumbrians as surety for their oaths.[28] Surely, he had his own career of broken promises rising in his conscience like ghosts to haunt him. He had done what he could to smooth the path ahead; he could only have prayed that it was sufficient.

Through this time, the business of securing the kingdom and the routine of government continued. It was clearly with an eye to the threat of disturbance that in 1152 David secured the appointment of one of his chaplains, William, to the See of Moray,[29] thereby completing his designs for the establishment of firm government in a province where challenge to his grandson might emerge. William rose to the occasion and was to prove a pillar of the royal establishment in the north through the critical early years of Malcolm IV's reign. In the south, too, David was still looking to consolidate his hold over the gains of the last decade and pin them ever more firmly into the Scottish orbit. In September 1151, David had undertaken an expedition into Craven and Skipton to secure the honour for his great-nephew William, son of William fitz Duncan, taking and destroying a fortification built there by Stephen loyalists.[30] Clearly, he had not given up on his ambitions to secure tighter control of western Yorkshire and, probably, to extend that control over the rest of the shire. That aim, however, was finally blocked that same year when Henry Murdac made his peace with Stephen and was admitted by him into his see. David's dream for a Scottish archdiocese with its seat at York evaporated with that reconciliation along with his aspirations for a more secure Scoto-Northumbrian realm with its southern frontier on the Humber. The old potential threat to Scottish sovereignty posed by the metropolitan claims of an English archbishop had re-emerged.[31] It was surely no coincidence that at Easter 1152, when the papal legate John Paparo returned to David's court after his visit to Ireland, David raised the question once again of the elevation of the See of St Andrews to the rank of metropolitan for Scotland.[32] His request that the archdiocese of St Andrews which he envisaged should embrace Orkney and the Western Isles as well as all of mainland Scotland reveals the extent of the kingdom over which he held effective sway, and the territory which he was determined not to yield to foreign interests.

At the close of David's reign there were clear signs that the long period of stability which he had established for his kingdom and the extended sphere of authority which he had created were threatened. The challenges, however, were external and remote and David was taking active steps to neutralise or eliminate them. How successful he would have been we can only conjecture, for in the spring of 1153 his health began to deteriorate sharply. Knowing that his end was approaching, David made his peace with God and prepared for death.[33] At length, on the morning of 29 May, he was found dead in his bed in his chamber in the great tower at Carlisle.[34] From Carlisle, his body was carried to Dunfermline for burial in the abbey which he had built there, interred alongside the tombs of his father, mother and brothers. John of Hexham tells how when cortège reached the crossing of the Forth at Queensferry, the water appeared to be uncrossable on account of the wild raging of gale-force winds. When his coffin was placed in the boat, the wind subsided and the vessel was able to cross in safety, but raged again with unabated fury when its cargo was lifted safely ashore. Intended as a sign of his saintliness and worth in God's eyes, the story neatly symbolises David and the Scottish kingdom. He had brought security and stability; without him, who knew what lay on the path ahead?

CHAPTER TWELVE

Saint and Sinner – the Historical Reputation of David I

A generation ago, most Scottish school children still learned a little at primary school about the king who 'revolutionised' twelfth-century Scotland. David I was the king who introduced 'feudalism'; who began the development of the sheriffdoms and shires that were still a feature of the modern administrative map of Scotland; who introduced French and English monks in an effort 'to make Scotland more religious and more civilised'; and converted 'certain villages into royal burghs' to encourage the development of industry and trade. In the final judgement, 'David I made Scotland a more advanced country, and gave it a pattern of life which was to last for four hundred years'.[1] It was a simple, if not simplistic message, but one which managed to summarise the achievement of the 'Davidian Revolution' and present it in the language of the Brave New World of the late twentieth century. David was a moderniser, an innovator, a revolutionary who dragged Scotland from the ignorance and darkness of suspicion and thrust it, blinking, into the brilliant sunlight of Modernity. It has a very contemporary ring to it, redolent of late twentieth-century, post-War optimism, but it is an image that had formed even before its subject was in his grave.

David's reputation has, since the twelfth century, consisted of two almost opposing strands. On the one hand, he has been presented very much in the mould of the secular revolutionary, a king who enhanced and entrenched the authority of his office, instituted a radical policy of social and economic reconstruction, and waged aggressive and particularly brutal wars. On the other, we have the very powerful image of David as the pious, priest-like

king, penitent for the suffering which he caused, patron of the Church, pro-
tector of the poor, the weak and the oppressed. Although the two images
went hand in hand in the twelfth-century accounts of the king, by the
modern period the war-mongering and atrocities of the 1136–38 campaigns
and his many tortuous shifts and twists as he manoeuvred himself out of
oath and treaty obligations had been lost in the manufacture of the icon of
the perfect king. David, the venerable, serene patriarch ruling over a kingdom where peace, justice and prosperity flourished, altogether overshadowed
the ambitious and expansionist ruler who projected his authority at spear-
point over all of Scotland and northern England. Careful propaganda –
'spin' in modern terms – was already perfected as a black art eight centuries
before Alasdair Campbell and Charlie Wheelan took up their profession.

Warrior and priest were two sides of the royal image in the later eleventh
and twelfth centuries, developed to its peak by the Capetian kings of
France,[2] whose model the kings of Scots were to emulate in respect of succession practice and royal style.[3] That the warrior was down-played in
preference for the priest required a deliberate choice in presentation, and
the shift occurred very rapidly in the last years of David's life and in the first
decade after his death. Down to the later 1140s, David is accorded all the
attributes of kingship in records of his actions, and it was not simply critical
or hostile writers such as Richard and John of Hexham who were keen to
stress the king's military credentials and secular powers. Orderic, Ailred and
William of Malmesbury, for example, all report his warlike activities more
or less uncritically as part and parcel of his necessary royal behaviour. Even
authorities critical of the conduct of his army in northern England either
deflect personal responsibility for the excesses from the king, or excuse his
invasion on the grounds that he was forced into the war by his moral obligation to uphold his oath to support Matilda's right to the English throne.[4]
David's warrior reputation was further underscored by his knighting of
Henry of Anjou in 1149. That Henry sought knighthood from his great-
uncle was not simply determined by the young pretender's need to bind the
Scottish king back into the Angevin cause after the debacle of 1141, but was
a reflection of David's prestige as one of the foremost – if elderly – knights
of the day who had, perhaps most importantly for the young man, himself
been knighted by Henry I.[5] It needs to be recognised that David was considered a chivalric figure and his ability to attract men into his service was
based on more than simply his ability to reward them with cash or land.
David was a leader of knights, a commander of stature, in whose service
fame and fortune could be won by aspiring young aristocrats.

The image of the king as warrior or knight had, by the beginning of David's reign, become a standard element in royal iconography. On reverse side of their seals, Scottish kings from Donnchad II onwards had been portrayed as knights, armoured in Norman style, mounted on a war-horse, providing a potent image of one dimension of the power upon which crown authority was founded. David, too, employed the same image on his seal,[6] but it was the representation given on the obverse which came to be regarded as more typical of him than the knight on the reverse. The obverse depicts the king enthroned in majesty, the dispenser of justice arrayed with the full panoply of symbols of his kingship. The seated figure of the king is shown crowned, carrying a sword in his right hand and a cross-surmounted orb in his left. It is a very similar image to the only near-contemporary por-trait which we possess of David, where he is depicted enthroned in majesty under the left-hand arch of the capital M of Malcolmus in his grandson's great charter issued to the monks of Kelso in 1159.[7] In it, the king is pre-sented very much in the mould of a Biblical patriarch, presumably modelled on contemporary representations of the Biblical King David, bearded and aloof. He is shown in 'civilian' dress: red mantle fastened at the neck and dropping in folds over his knees; green tunic with decorated hem and cuffs; blue leggings and short boots. In his right hand he wields a drawn sword, in his left is an orb. The majesty and authority of the figure is obvious, and its gravitas is rendered all the greater by its juxtaposition with the representa-tion of his grandson, Malcolm, to his left. The young king is shown as a beardless youth, sceptre in his right hand and sheathed sword laid across his knees, perhaps symbolic of his perhaps not yet having come into his full powers as an adult ruler. Beside his grandfather, he is an altogether less than impressive figure and, it could be argued, the inclusion of David's image in what was a document issued solely in Malcolm's name and six years after David's death is intended to underscore the source of the young king's authority and the nature of the power on which its was based: here is David marking out Solomon as his successor.[8] When popular depictions of David began to be produced in the Victorian era it was this 'civil' presentation of royal authority, with the benign patriarch dispensing peace and love, which established itself as the stock image of the king.[9]

Stripping David of his military attributes – the sword is as much a symbol of justice as of coercive force – served to emphasise his spiritual qualities. In modern historical assessments, the spiritual dimension to David's ecclesi-astical policies is often lost behind a focus on the material and political benefits which flowed from the restructuring of the Church and the

introduction of reformed Benedictine monasticism. In part, this is a consequence of modern secular cynicism or discomfort with acceptance or
discussion of individual personal beliefs, but it is also a consequence of a
more basic failure to recognise the centrality of religion to everyday life in
the past. The late eleventh and twelfth centuries were witnessing a religious
revival – a reformation of religion as far-reaching in its consequences as the
Protestant Reformation of the sixteenth century – in which laymen as well
as ecclesiastics played pivotal roles. With the spiritual credentials of his
mother, sister and two elder brothers behind him, coupled with his own
manifest displays of personal piety from around 1113 onwards, David was
evidently a well-known figure in continental reforming circles by the 1130s.
Even quite early in his reign, David clearly enjoyed an established reputation as Christian king and defender of the Church. In around 1134, St
Bernard of Clairvaux, the charismatic but to modern eyes sanctimonious
Cistercian theologian and clerical reformer, wrote to David seeking his support for the fledgling Cistercian foundation at Fountains in Yorkshire. 'I
have long since learned to love you, most illustrious king', he wrote,

> your fair renown has for long stirred in me the desire to meet you in person.
> This is my desire and relying on the words, 'The Lord has heard the desire of
> the poor', I am confident in the Lord that one day I shall see you in the body
> whom even now I delight to gaze upon in spirit and imagination, and who I
> constantly think of with such pleasure and joy.[10]

Although the language may be too over-the-top for most modern tastes,
within the conventions of the twelfth century it showed how the king's
reputation as a patron of religious reform had already gained widespread
currency in mainland Europe. In 1134, David was not yet a patron of the
Cistercian order, but in the remaining two decades of his reign he established himself as one of its chief royal supporters in Europe.

It was not distant admiration of a patron of the Cistercian order, however,
that inspired Abbot Ailred of Rievaulx to produce his description of David
in an extended eulogy that came to form the basis of most subsequent
character-portraits of the king.[11] Written probably little more than a year
after David's death as part of an address from the abbot to the new King
Henry II of England,[12] it is the best known and most quoted of the accounts
which focus on David's qualities rather than on his political achievements.
Ailred emphasises a whole series of attributes in David which would be
recognised at once as the characteristics of a Cistercian monk as set out in

works such as the *Mirror of Charity*, where emphasis is placed particularly on patience, chastity, humility and obedience.[13] His opening statement sets the tone of the rest of the account: 'The religious and pious king David has departed from the world'.[14] David is then presented as a bringer of peace and progress – a far cry from Ailred's comments in his *Relatio de Standardo*, where the 1136–38 war in northern England was given a 'warts-and-all' treatment – and painted as a 'gentle king, just king, chaste king, humble king', whose reign conferred great benefit on humanity. The image built by Ailred is that of a man suited by character and temperament to a life of contemplation as a monk, a point emphasised by Ailred's claim that he had to be coerced into accepting the kingship and even had qualms about undergoing the king-making ritual on account of its distinctly unchristian character. Here was a man who hungered after higher things than worldly fame or power.

Having established that David was more monk than king, Ailred went on to outline the benefits which the rule of such a man brought to the Scots. His manner was an example to his subjects and through it 'the whole barbarity of that nation was softened',[15] with the result that they gave up their warlike ways and accepted the rule of law and justice. There are clear echoes of William of Malmesbury's comment on his civilising influence on the Scots.[16] The focus on justice intensifies with the presentation of the king as law-giver and judge, who would forgo his hunting in order to listen to the plea of a poor man who caught him just as he was about to mount, and who would sit at the door of his hall to give justice to all comers, regardless of their station. Again, his patience and diligence in dealing with business which consumed so much of his time is stressed, underscoring that monkish attribute. The main portion of the account, however, deals with the king's preparations for death, and the comparison with his mother's arrangements and actions as recorded by Turgot are very clear.[17] His personal involvement in the services, where he corrected the priests who were rushing through the orders, serves to underscore his superior priestly character.

David as more monk than king again dominates the account offered by William of Newburgh. In William's eulogy of David in his *Historia Rerum Anglicarum*, however, it is the comparison of David of Scotland with the Biblical King David which was made first and most explicitly. William drew direct parallels between the king and the Biblical David.[18] Both he presented as virtuous but touched by sin: flawed paragons. The Biblical king, God's anointed who had brought the Ark of the Covenant to Jerusalem, had fallen from virtue through his adultery with Bathsheba, wife of Uriah the Hittite, and arranged for Uriah's death when she became pregnant, adding murder to his sins.[19] David of Scotland, 'in other ways pious and good', had been driven by his support for the cause of his niece to unleash death and destruction on the innocent people of England, an act which stood as a bloody blemish on an otherwise spotless record. William, who was writing in the context of Angevin England, sought to exculpate the great-uncle of his king by carefully recording David's attempts to prevent the unnecessary bloodshed, but he recognised that the war waged by David had sullied the king's reputation. Just as the Biblical king had regained God's grace through 'pious humility', however, so too had the Scottish king purged his guilt through penitence and good works:

> Therefore not only in the performance of pious works but also in the making of fruitful repentence did this new David, a king not barbarous of a barbarous nation, reflect the royal image of the David of old.[20]

The parallels between the two David's did not, however, end there, for William also saw similarities between the Biblical king's punishment for his former sins by the rebellion of his favourite son, Absalom, while the Scottish king had been similarly punished by the rebellion of Wimund. In other respects, however, William of Newburgh offers a fairly conventional picture of the saintly king, painting him as worldly yet otherworldly, a powerful temporal ruler but also a religious and pious man. David's saintly credentials are clearly set out, with his nearly priestly qualities – priest-like celibacy after the death of his wife, careful observation of the divine offices, good works and alms-giving – listed surely with an eye towards future canonisation.

After the flurry of activity which followed David's death and the first possible moves towards canonisation, the king somewhat slips from focus in Scotland. Later twelfth- and thirteenth-century Scottish sources such as the *Chronicle of Melrose* present a starkly prosaic picture of the king, and only one quite late account offers more than a basic narrative of his reign. It follows the by then stock presentation of David, the man of religion, who 'obtained victory over his enemies more by entreaties poured out to God than by weapons of war'.[21] Given the central role which the king had played in building the prestige of the ruling dynasty and in winning an albeit temporary domination of the political structure of mainland Britain, it is a rather odd relegation to account for. Certainly, at the beginning of the fourteenth century his place as the founder of the Scottish legal tradition and, in general, father of the kingdom, was widely recognised,[22] but throughout the thirteenth century there appears to have been no acknowledgement of the king's significance nor any use of his example as a defence against English claims to the overlordship of Scotland. Neither Alexander II nor Alexander III, both of whom mounted robust defences of their independence against such claims, used David's consistent avoidance of submission to either Henry I or Stephen as a tool in their arguments. Quite possibly, his possession of Huntingdon and initial homage for the northern counties was seen as weakening the Scottish case more generally.

David's low profile in the historical record is maintained through the early part of the Wars of Independence. No use appears to have been made of him in the Bruce propaganda offensive either domestically or externally. The naming of Robert Bruce's son and successor, David II, harks back to the founder of that line's royal claims, Earl David of Huntingdon, the youngest of David I's three grandsons, and not to the king himself. Part of this reluctance to use the very powerful image of David I may lie in what appears to have been a peculiar reticence on the part of the Bruce kings in their propaganda against England. While Edward I is consistently vilified in person, there is little or nothing that can be seen as particularly anti-English and certainly nothing to equal the gleeful abuse of the later medieval Scottish writers.[23] But David I can hardly be labelled anti-English, given his West Saxon ancestry alongside his Scottish, his education and upbringing in the south and close personal relationship with English kings and nobles. While those very facts may have been seen as weakening his value to the Scots, his shift from vassal of the English king to stern defender of Scottish independence must surely have counterbalanced the effect.

In the second half of the fourteenth century, David finally emerges from the shadows and restakes a key place in the grand historical narrative of Scotland. The chronicles completed by John of Fordun provide the first detailed presentation of David and his achievements from a Scottish perspective.[24] They are, for the most part, a disappointingly bland offering, and play down the causes of the wars against England and the defeat at the Standard, but play up the territorial gains made by David.[25] In his assessment of the king, however, Fordun is distinctly more forthcoming. David was 'blessed through all generations; for there never, from time immemorial, arose a prince like him'.[26] Most of what follows, however, was derived from Ailred, William of Newburgh and the Hexham tradition, with the emphasis being placed especially upon his piety and spirituality. The bulk of the account is a verbatim rehearsal of Ailred's eulogy, but that is followed by pedigrees of the king on both his father's and mother's sides.[27] The stated purpose behind the genealogies, which Fordun claimed to have obtained from Walter Wardlaw, Bishop of Glasgow (1367–87), in itself an indication of the current interest in Scottish royal genealogy, was to make it known to contemporary kings and to all other readers of the work

> of how old, how noble, how strong and invincible a stock of kings he came (whereof ye also are come) – kings who have, until now, through the blessed King Most High, been keeping the kingly dignity unspotted for a longer time, with freer service, and what is more glorious, with a stronger hold of the Catholic faith than all other kings, save only a few, if any.[28]

David's blood was once again being presented as especially virtuous and his reputation as a pious defender of the Christian faith re-established. His maternal pedigree is prefaced with an unashamed celebration of his saintly lineage but, interestingly, also sets out 'to show you the line of our English kinship'.[29] This statement rests oddly with the common perception of the outright and unremitting hostility of later medieval Scots chroniclers towards the English, but may point to attempts at rapprochement made in the 1350s and 1360s. David appears to have been used as a possible bridge between the Scots and the English, and it is possible that this presentation of him may be a carry-over into Fordun's work of an earlier compilation pro-duced during the reign of David II, who explored various schemes for transmitting the succession to the Scottish throne to a Plantagenet prince, ranging from Edward III himself, to his sons Lionel, Duke of Clarence, and John of Gaunt, Duke of Lancaster.[30] Was the earlier portion of the work attributed to 'Fordun' a dossier of information compiled in Scotland to brief a possible Plantagenet heir to David? Such an origin would certainly explain the very neutral attitude towards the English displayed in the chronicle, and would also explain why the part-English and culturally Anglophile David I emerges suddenly again to prominence after two centuries in the shadows.[31]

Having re-established his place in Scottish historiography, David remained a prominent figure in the works of later fourteenth- and fif-teenth-century chroniclers. His values and attributes were regarded as particularly useful by writers who were seeking to extol the merits of strong kingship in a period where monarchical authority in Scotland had been eroded through the internal conflicts of the Stewart family during the reigns of the first two Stewart kings, Robert II (1371–90) and Robert III (1390–1406), and the long period of captivity in England (1406–24) of

James I. David clearly had powerful attractions to men who considered strong, centralising monarchical power as a good thing, for he showed the leadership skills required to impose authority on a fractious and rebellious people (for whom in late fourteenth- and early fifteenth-century Scotland we should read 'over-mighty' noblemen), and who, through his firm government at home, was able to project his authority decisively abroad. As clerics, too, in an increasingly anti-clerical world, David provided them with an exemplar of proper Christian kingship, with great emphasis placed on his support for organised religion and the established hierarchy. At a time when Christendom was beset by schism, with rival popes based in Rome and Avignon, he could be used as a symbol for how a truly Christian ruler should behave in such perilous times. Andrew of Wyntoun concentrated again on David's virtues as an ideal king. For him, 'He was the beylde of his kyn/with uertu he suppressit syn'.[32] He presented David as a virtuous ruler who attacked evil-doers wherever he found them, yet at the same time a meek and righteous man who did not glory in his power and authority. No sin of pride for David, nor was he subject to lust, neither sexual nor for property and power. These were the qualities which Wyntoun highlighted before all others, the attributes of Christian kingship. Underpinning these, however, were David's active traits. He was a lover of justice, yet a merciful and reluctant judge. The Church flourished under his active patronage and his achievement was to banish the darkness of spiritual ignorance from his realm – 'He illumynyt in his dayis/His landis with kyrkis and abbayis'. David brought the light of religion to his people. In his final assessment of David, Wyntoun portrayed him as king, knight and monk, who lived as an earthly ruler by day, but 'A monk dewote he was on nycht'.[33] It is an image of semi-sacral kingship with which David could probably have identified very closely, and which near-contemporary rulers, such as Henry V of England, sought to appropriate for themselves. Closer to home, it was also a model which the freed James I was to embrace after 1424.

It is in the work of Walter Bower, Abbot of Inchcolm (1417–49), known as *Scotichronicon*, that the medieval representations of David reach their peak and where his reputation as governor, warrior and priest achieve their fullest development. Twenty-one out of the sixty-two chapters of Book V of Bower's monumental work are given over to David,[34] a length of treatment otherwise accorded only to Robert Bruce and, especially, James I.[35] While his work is largely a development of the material already assembled by Fordun, Bower also articulates very clearly his views on ideal kingship and the benefits of strong monarchy. He starts with the usual recitation of

David's manifest virtue, but embellishes it with the simple statement that he prospered in all things through his piety and godliness. Following Fordun, the war with England is made a conflict driven by his refusal to break the oath which he had given in 1127, and the Battle of the Standard is presented twice as two separate conflicts, first in such ambivalent terms as to make it appear a victory for David, then as a Scottish defeat.[36] Unlike Fordun, however, Bower gives an extended account of the lineage of David's children on the maternal side, starting with Queen Matilda.[37] Bower thus establishes the saintly pedigree of the Scottish royal house, with David and Margaret on one side, and Matilda's father, Waltheof, on the other. Like Fordun, he extends into a detailed exploration of the English lineage of the Scottish royal house, and all the elements together form a powerful articulation of Scottish superiority over the English royal house. Not only does the line of kings descended from David have the blood of three saints flowing in its veins, but it represents the senior, legitimate line of the Old English kings. There is, then, a nationalist, if not supremacist, tone to Bower's presentation of David I, but he is also being presented by the abbot as a model of kingship to be followed by the Stewarts in the fifteenth century. Recent studies of Bower's historiography have shown how the first David headed a series of kings upon whom the young James II was urged to model himself, including also Alexander II, Robert I, David II and James I.[38] David I was here recognised by Bower as the founder of a tradition of strong monarchy under which Scotland in the past had flourished.

In the manufactured history of post-Wars of Independence Scotland, the work of Fordun, Wyntoun and Bower had propelled David back into the national consciousness. Among ecclesiastics, David's legacy may not have been forgotten over the intervening centuries, but the heightened sense of nationhood that emerged in the later fourteenth and fifteenth centuries among a far wider lay community required iconic or talismanic figures around whom to build their image of a perfect kingdom, and the neglected rulers of past centuries were resurrected to fill that void. David fulfilled just such a role, for the picture built of him from the production of Ailred's eulogy onwards was of the perfect king who gave ideal government to a people basking in his reflected glory and enjoying the fruits of peace and prosperity which his firm government, exercise of justice and, above all, devotion to religion, yielded. In an era bristling with handbooks exhorting princes to good government, David had again become the king to emulate.

Such was the power and authority of David's fifteenth-century image, which saw him fixed as one of a trinity of Scottish 'paladins' from whom the contemporary Scottish state drew its legitimacy,[39] that his reign displaced that of Alexander III as the 'Golden Age' of medieval Scotland in elite perspectives. The evidence is ambivalent, but it has been argued that the re-emergence of the round-headed arch in late fifteenth- and early sxteenth-century Scottish architectural vocabularies was a conscious hearkening back to the late Romanesque tradition of David's time.[40] If this is the case, then it is perhaps unsurprising that the style should be redeveloped during the reigns of James III and James IV, one the originator and the other the developer of an 'imperial' style in Scotland. For kings active in the articulation of an exalted idea of their own kingship and the absolute sovereign status of their kingdom, who better to look back to for inspiration than David I? As the Scottish monarchy developed in the later Middle Ages under James IV in particular, so too were the attributes of David's kingship subtly shifted and given fresh emphasis to give added authority to their policies or to criticise their deficiencies. Two differing views which use the same basic image were offered by two of the leading historians of early sixteenth-century Scotland, John Major or Mair, and Hector Boece.

Major, the slightly earlier of the two, was writing a history with a strongly unionist agenda. His *History of Greater Britain*, published in 1521,[41] was a ground-breaking study in that it attempted to offer a view of the history of the islands as a whole – or, at least, the histories of Scotland and England – and argued strongly in favour of a full union of the two kingdoms. Given David's staunch defence of his status as an independent ruler, he was an unlikely model for Major the unionist. David, however, is given a glowing eulogy. He is 'that most excellent King of Scots, in whom are found wonderful examples of all virtues', and 'a more excellent man than his two brothers'.[42] His first virtue is given as his strength of leadership, where

> the proud he tamed, beating them down with a hammer, but to all that submitted duly to his authority he showed himself merciful and gracious... and here I will make my frank confession that it transcends my feeble powers accurately to take the measure of this man...[43]

He ends his account of the king with an extended discourse on his other virtues, emphasising above all his 'temperance, fortitude, justice, clemency, and regard for religion'.[44] It is not, however, an entirely uncritical portrait, Major introducing for the first time a strongly negative view of the implications of David's religious reforms and, especially, what he considered to be his profligate generosity to the monasteries. It is Major who gives us the original account of James I's visit to his ancestor's tomb at Dunfermline and the fifteenth-century king's comment that David should 'there abide, king most pious, but likewise to Scotland's state and king's most unprofitable'.[45] This anti-clerical attitude is picked up and developed by Hector Boece, whose own *History* appeared only six years after the publication of Major's work.

When Hector Boece was producing his *History* in 1520s, it was against a backdrop of the criticism faced before 1513 by James IV for his manipulation of the judicial system and especially his use of remissions for crimes committed as a means of boosting royal revenues, and the continuation of such practices under the minority regimes for the child, James V. David provided a powerful tool with which to attack that policy. For Boece, David's principal legacy was his reputation as a dispenser of justice. This attribute is the first aspect of his rule commented upon in the narrative of David's reign. As Bellenden's translation puts it, he

> ...did grete iustice eftir his coronacioun in all parties of his realme... and was sa piteous that he satt in daylye iugement to caus his pure [poor] commonis haif iustice, and causir the accioun of his nobillis to be decernit be his vther iugis. He gart ilk iuge refound the skaith that come to the party be his wrang sentence, throw quhilk he decorit the realme with mony nobill actis...[46]

Default of justice and the undermining of the rule of law by arbitrary action were seen as discreditable acts that sullied the reputation of the monarch at home and abroad, and, more importantly, reduced the moral standing of the kingdom itself. David, as an exemplar, was being used to criticise contemporary practice and encourage reform in government. His religious reputation, however, enabled him to be used in an altogether different way.

Bellenden's 1533 translation of Hector Boece provides one of the most memorable descriptions of David, which became a central image in most accounts of the king and his life produced in the nineteenth and twentieth centuries. Referring to David's munificence towards the Church at the expense of the Crown, Boece used Major's claim that James I, on visiting his ancestor's tomb at Dunfermline, had commented negatively on his profligate alienation of royal revenues, translated by Bellenden that David was 'ane sair sanct for the Croune'.[47] Usually misquoted and misattributed to James VI and I rather than to his early fifteenth-century predecessor,[48] the label is part of an extended criticism of David for his overly generous benefactions to the Church, which impoverished his kingdom for centuries thereafter. It is worth reproducing the whole of the section here, for it reveals strikingly the changed perceptions of religious value-for-money between the earlier twelfth century and the early sixteenth century.

> He biggit xv abbais in Scotland, and dotate thaim with sindry landis, rentis and possessionis… [provides a list of the names of the monasteries]… and by thir abbayis foundit foure bischoprikkis, Ross, Brechin, Dunkeld and Dunblane, and dotaitt thame sa richelie that he left the croun sa indigent and pure [poor] that his successouris mycht nocht sustene thair emperiall estaitt eftir him, as thai did afoir; throw quhilk it gaif thame occasioun to bring grete houses to nocht, to get the landis to sustene the croun, howbeit he did the samyn for the best. And thairfor King James the First, quhen he come to his sepulture at Dumfermeling, said that he was ane sair sanct for the Croune, as he wald signify that he dotat the Kirk our richelie and left the Croune our pure. For in weritie he tuke fra the Croune xl thousand libri Scottis, quhilk is possedit now be the Kirk, to na less damage of commoun wele than perdicioun of gude relligioune. For gif he had considerate prudentlie the maner of deuote religion, he had nother dotat the kirkis with sic riches nor yit biggit thame with sik cost and magnificence…[49]

Boece, like Major, while being very careful to say that David's intentions in his generosity to the Church had all been simply for the best – a morally good action – offers a very critical view that calls into question the wisdom of his actions. The criticism is aimed both at David, for his beggaring of the crown which forced later kings to take unpopular and unjust actions to appropriate the resources of others to support their regal state, but more particularly at the senior clergy of Boece's own time, whom he accused of misappropriation and misuse of the revenues from the properties given by David. The message within Boece is being cried very much in the language of Reform, but always with an eye cast back to the basic fact that the position in the late fifteenth and early sixteenth centuries had arisen as a consequence of David's enthusiastic support for an earlier round of reform.

The Boece/Bellenden image of David is, however, concerned with more than just the religious dimension. The king is in all other ways a paragon of princely virtue. He was 'nocht litill commendit in his tyme for his singulare vertew', which surpassed that of any man in his realm. His great achievements not only including the purging of Scotland of 'corruppit & vicious lymmaris' but also ensuring that his servants were also men of virtue. His style of government and personal living was such that all excesses were cut away and, by his careful control of his person and the manners of the men around him, he secured peace and stability in his rule and brought his people 'under ane mynde and amite'.[50] For the divided Scotland of the 1520s, when Boece originally wrote his work, and for its would-be rulers, it was a powerful message, and it was one that carried added resonance as the sixteenth century progressed.

Bishop John Leslie of Ross's Latin *History* of Scotland, published in 1578, translated into Scots by James Dalrymple in 1596,[51] offers a rather brief overview of David and his reign. The principal emphasis, as usual, is on the king's virtuous behaviour, stressing first his prudence and wisdom, commenting that 'throuch that singular virtue he nevir brack the band of peace ance confirmet wt Henrie king of Ingland', and following with the usual account of his justice, benevolence and patience.[52] As should perhaps be expected in a history written by a senior cleric, it is David's support for the Church that is highlighted, but without any of the criticism evident in the works of Major and Boece. Like a true Christian monarch, David burned with the love of God, and such was his zeal to glorify Him and 'to amplifie the boundes of Religioune', that he founded and richly endowed no less than fourteen monasteries and four bishoprics. Leslie also places great emphasis on David's dependence on counsel and advice from his bishops, clearly a reaction against the criticism that episcopal involvement in royal government had drawn in the earlier sixteenth century.[53] Here, we are confronted with a counter-Reformation use of David as the saintly king, devotee of Holy Mother Church, and model for modern monarchs. It was surely with an eye to the king's semi-sacral role, emphasised so recently by Leslie, and so compatible with James VI and Charles I's views of the relationship between the Church and Crown, that Archbishop Laud included David in his calendar of saints in his Scottish Prayer Book of 1637. David so clearly fitted into the royal agenda of the early seventeenth century, with his active personal role in promoting religious reform and his close relationship with his episcopate, that it is surprising that a greater use was not made of him by apologists for episcopacy in seventeenth-century Scotland.

It is equally surprising to find George Buchanan, a scholar whose views on monarchy were decidedly jaundiced, extolling David's virtues as superior before all other kings. In his history of Scotland, produced largely as an extended critique on the past failures of monarchical government and the nature of the relationship between Church and State, however, he opined that 'a more perfect exemplar of a good King is to be found in the reign of David I than in all the theories of the learned and ingenious'.[54] For

Buchanan, however, David was a monarch who successfully combined strong and lawful government with piety and support for religion without him becoming tyrannical or attempting to exert earthly control over the ecclesiastical state. This was the kind of king that he had tried to ensure James VI would become, who supported and deferred to the spiritual order while exercising godly government of his people. Indeed, in the dedication of his work to James, Buchanan stressed the qualities of David's rule and enjoined James to follow his example.

By the beginning of the seventeenth century, then, we can see that something of a dualist view of David had emerged in historical writings. He was presented as a state-builder and staunch defender of Scotland's independent status, a man whose strength brought stability and – in an observation by Sir Thomas Craig which foreshadows the later 'Whiggish' view of British history – through his resistance of attempts to conquer his kingdom by the English, ensured that Scotland was set on a path to maturity that led ultimately to the dynastic union of the early seventeenth century.[55] Furthermore on the credit side of the balance-sheet, he was a wise and just ruler, whose firmness and personal example helped breed a strength of character in his subjects and servants and, through their following of his example, brought peace and harmony to his realm. Finally, he was a godly man, whose recognition of his position under God and of his Christian duties as a ruler to his people could be praised by supporters of Divine Right kingship or of a Godly Commonwealth in equal measure. On the negative side, however, David was identified closely with the 'Roman' Church and his 'prodigal' endowment of monasteries in particular was regarded as ultimately harmful to the interests of both the monarchy and the people of Scotland. A slave to superstition, he beggared his descendants to feed the coffers of a corrupt institution and forced later kings to unjustly oppress their subjects to compensate for the lost revenues. Both sides of the equation, however, only considered David in a starkly black-and-white vision of his actions. Historiographically, there was no setting of David into a wider context and, certainly, no consideration of the actual implications – positive or negative – for Scotland which his policies entailed.

Both views of David remained unchallenged until late in the eighteenth century, when there was the beginning of a revival of interest in Scottish history as a subject for serious academic endeavour. Perhaps the shrewdest analysis of David and his achievements, one which has shaped most modern views of the king, was constructed at this time. It was offered by David Dalrymple, Lord Hailes, whose *Annals of Scotland*, first published in 1776, set a new standard in critical historical writing.[56] In it, Dalrymple applied his lawyer's mind and forensic skills to a careful dissection of the existing interpretations of Scottish history and the various stresses and biases within earlier writings. 'We ought to judge of the conduct of men according to the notions of *their* age, not of *ours*,'[57] he observed in what is still a telling judgement on the historian's craft. His comment was directed principally at criticism of David's lavish endowment of monasteries, which he argued should be viewed in the spirit of the age in which the gifts were made, not of the post-Reformation era in which they were seen as 'prodigal superstition'. Dalrymple offered the first substantial defence of David's monastic policy which argued from a fundamentally secular and practical standpoint rather than from a spiritual one. His principal argument was founded on the material benefits that accrued to Scotland from the king's 'investment'. It was a very straightforward analysis founded on the principals of cost and benefit, very much the product of the Age of Reason. Dalrymple presented a simple case. In return for the initial endowment, the monks brought learning, provided educated men, cultivated letters, promoted agriculture, architecture and engineering. They were, in Dalrymple's presentation, Improvers in the late seventeenth- and eighteenth-century sense of estate management and economic development. He is not adopting a counter-Reformation stance as apologist for the religious orders – they were, he states, utterly corrupted over time – but he defends David against any charge of responsibility for either the misuse of the investment or for the corruption which resulted. Adopting John Major's words, Dalrymple argues that 'It was devotion... that produced opulence; but the lewd daughter strangled her parent'.[58]

Given the stress placed on David as the founding figure of the medieval kingdom, and the prominent place given to him in Dalrymple's work, it still comes as a surprise to find that Patrick Fraser Tytler, in the preface to his monumental *History of Scotland*, dismissed the pre-1250 period as being of interest to specialists only. 'I have commenced the *History of Scotland*', he stated, 'at the accession of Alexander the Third, because it is at this period that our national annals become particularly interesting to the general reader.'[59] Tytler neatly side-stepped the controversy of the period, avoiding both the religious controversies surrounding David and the whole issue of earlier relations with England. Despite, or perhaps because of Tytler's failure to examine the pre-1250 period, the remainder of the nineteenth century saw an explosion of interest in the historical record of the formative era of the kingdom. The historiographical trends of the century were dominated by particular issues which were coloured by the politics and religious controversies of the time, and David, as a great patron of the 'Roman' Church, experienced in some aspects the nadir of his reputation. He, with his mother, had the whole responsibility for the destruction of the 'Celtic' or 'Columban' Church heaped on his head. This dimension extended through into one key issue in later Victorian historiography: the emergent notion of a clash of cultures over which David presided.

As far back as Sir Thomas Craig in 1605, a cultural or racial dimension had been introduced into the presentation of Scottish history. Craig had placed great stress on the introduction to Scotland from the time of Malcolm III of a significant English or Norman-French element in the aristocratic population, foreshadowing the later peaceful unions between the kingdoms. It was only in the nineteenth and earlier twentieth centuries that this issue became the centrepiece in a new presentation of Scotland's history. While in the past it had been David's achievements as a state-builder and his religious reputation that had formed the central component of any discussion of his reign, in the later 1800s the balance shifted markedly towards the implications of his colonial and 'feudal' policies. By the time that Andrew Lang published his *History of Scotland* in 1900, David's reign had acquired symbolism as the moment of decisive cultural change in the kingdom: 'With Alexander, Celtic domination ends; with David, Anglo-Norman and English dominance is established'.[60] With this simple statement, Lang fixed firmly into place one of the most persistent paradigms in the historiography of medieval Scotland; that David was the man who hammered the nails into the coffin of 'Celtic' Scotland and set a pattern of development that has moulded the internal dynamics of the country for ever after. Three-quarters of a century later, it still exercised a powerful hold over Archie Duncan, who saw kings Edgar and Alexander I as the last gasp of the 'Old Scottish state' and that a New World Order dawned in April 1124 with the accession of David I.[61] Even at the tail end of the twentieth century, Lang's seismic cultural shift still exercised a powerful hold, filtered through the added lens of Barrovian feudalism, where David was the feudalising, Anglo-Normanised innovator, imposing his vision on a culturally conservative Gaelic nobility.[62] Even although we can recognise that this view of a Celtic twilight rudely snuffed out by the brash modernity of Anglo-Norman modernity is a product of the upsurge of Celtophilism in the second half of the nineteenth century and was, in part, a lament for the 'noble savage' whose impoverished descendants and seemingly dying culture loomed large in the consciences of Victorian intellectuals, it has preserved a tenacious hold long after the wider thesis had been discredited.[63]

The basic argument presented by Lang is that David was thoroughly anglicised from the outset and displayed a marked antipathy towards 'the ancient race'. He brought with him to Scotland feudalism, and a flood of 'Englishmen, Normans and Norman ideas', and in the face of this tide 'Celtic men and ideas retreated to their congenial glens'.[64] It was only when the pressures became too much to bear that the 'Celts' rebelled, and David responded by waging against them a war of conquest and, in Lang's presentation, racially-fuelled colonisation. The same tone of Celt *v.* Norman is carried through into his discussion of the campaign of 1138 and the Battle of the Standard, where he presents the failure of the Celts in the conflict in the same light as their slaughter at Culloden, their fierce nobility in Britain's eighteenth-century imperial wars, and a clear connection is drawn between the men who died at Northallerton and their descendents who built the Empire in the nineteenth century.[65] These men, whose loyalty and service to the crown was so necessary in David's empire-building, were the same men against whom he employed his Norman and English friends. There is in Lang's work a lament for the Highlander, but it is the oppressed and abused Highlander of the nineteenth-century Clearance rather than the 'Celt' of twelfth-century Scotland.

Lang's critique of the reign developed on another emergent criticism of David; that his acquisitions in northern England were a disastrous adventure that led Scotland nearly to ruin.[66] The language employed is strongly negative in tone, and the down-side of David's actions is considered before any positive dimension. Thus, for example, his choice of wife was questioned, for she was 'unfortunately' the daughter of Earl Waltheof. It was unfortunate because, as Waltheof's daughter, she was heiress to his claims to Northumbria. David's pursuit of Matilda's heritage led to the disasters of William the Lion's reign, his captivity and submission to English overlordship. That was the direct consequence, Lang argued, of David's dreams of empire, that 'blood was shed, and money was spent in vain' trying to secure an extended kingdom. From being the far-sighted state-builder of Dalrymple and earlier observers, Lang's assessment presented David instead as a man who delivered Scotland and the Scots into subjection to foreign interlopers in his own time, and to a foreign king in the time of his grandsons. Far from advancing Scotland's interests, the end result of David's policies had been a narrow escape from national oblivion.

Presentation of David's reign as a pivotal point in national development is again the central theme in Hume Brown's thesis.[67] Rather than a straightforward cultural clash as presented by Lang, he saw its significance in terms of consolidation of statehood. Yes, there was a racial dimension to the process, with David being presented as the man who substituted the Saxon influence that had prevailed since the time of his father for Norman influence. Hume Brown, however, considered that 'the most potent influence that sustained him in all his undertakings was the disciplined strength of the Norman knights and barons behind him'.[68] Change was delivered by the mailed fist. Yet Hume Brown presented a much more subtle and richly-textured analysis than this bold statement might lead us to expect. David's reign was presented as 'most memorable in every aspect of the life of a people',[69] and in the profundity of the changes brought about he likened it to that iconic period in the defining of modern Scottish character, the sixteenth-century Reformation. His religious reforms, as with the Reformation, brought Scotland into a new set of international relationships. This aspect, and the recasting of social conditions for the people of Scotland which he set in train, made David's reign in Hume Brown's view 'an epoch in the national development'. Directly contrary to the view expressed by Lang, where David's reign was presented as ultimately destructive to Scotland's native culture, Hume Brown positively enthuses over the scale and significance of what David achieved. It is a presentation that verges on the nationalistic, proclaiming the entry of Scotland into the ranks of the European brotherhood of states, a positive rather than a negative image of progress.

Hume Brown, however, was no mere panegyrist, and his assessment of the king starts out with a critical review of his policy.[70] He cuts through the claims of highmindedness which have surrounded David's policy towards England after 1135. While he acknowledged the wisdom of much of what David did, he questioned the manner of its pursuit: 'of the highmindedness of a St Louis, with whom he has sometimes been compared, there is little trace'.[71] Instead, he considered his conduct of Anglo-Scottish diplomacy to have been 'purely selfish' and, most damning yet, that he 'had recourse to methods which place him precisely on the level of the average ruler of his time', a stinging indictment.

Having set out these basic premises, Hume Brown then offered a systematic analysis of how David brought about change, and here he introduces a notion that became a *leitmotif* of most twentieth-century assessments of the reign: what David achieved was more than simply change, he 'performed it on a scale which converted it into a revolution'.[72] Thus was born the idea of the 'Davidian Revolution' which Geoffrey Barrow developed into one of the most powerful theses in late twentieth-century Scottish historiography. The revolution, in Hume Brown's eyes, however, was not the result of gradual integration and an emerging hybridity of practice between old and new: it was confrontational and compulsive. This recognition, however, is the nearest that Hume Brown came to agreement with the racial conflict presentation of Andrew Lang, and he tempered his discussion of the profundity of the change taking place with acknowledgement that there were wide regional variations in degree and extent of change; some areas were affected at only the most superficial of levels. There is also a clear recognition that the significance of what David achieved can only be understood properly from a retrospective view. Most importantly for modern historiography, Hume Brown offered the first comprehensive overview which looked at more than simply his 'feudalising' and religious policies. From the field of land tenure and law generally, through to the development of burghs and trade, the impact of the revolution was given a careful consideration. It is a grand vista which Hume Brown opened out before his readership, and one in which the few negative aspects are confronted and explained alongside the manifold positive dimensions.

From the time of the publication of Hume Brown's history in 1909 until the second half of the twentieth century, there was little development in either study of David I and analysis of his reputation, or in historical study of the Scottish Middle Ages generally. The sea-change occurred in the 1950s with the emergence of a new trend in Scottish historiography which was spearheaded by a group of young scholars who had reacted against the stagnation scholarship which had gripped their subject for nearly half a century. Led by Geoffrey Barrow and Archie Duncan, this group set about producing a 'new history' which was founded on the fruits of critical analysis of the contemporary documentary sources. Geoffrey Barrow in particular made the twelfth century his specialist field and, down to the present, established himself as the most influential historian of earlier medieval Scotland. Starting from what can be described as originally an integrationist approach under the umbrella of 'British History', Barrow offered a view of Scotland that allowed the main historical trends and developments to be viewed from a wider perspective and not curtailed by narrow, national boundaries.[73] His first detailed study of David I, therefore, presents him within the wider context of insular British developments and sets his reign and its achievements into a context that all earlier studies effectively lacked.[74] From the outset, while Barrow stressed the degree and the nature of the changes which David wrought, he was careful to stress that the king was able to hold a balance between the forces of change and those of tradition. This image of a balance between old and new, continuity and change, runs as a subtext through all of his subsequent analyses of aspects of David's reign, climaxing with his 1984 study, 'David I of Scotland: The Balance of New and Old'.[75]

Barrow's presentation of David marked a decisive shift in interpretation of his achievement, away from a purely 'shock of the new' approach to a more even-handed analysis that avoided the emotive Celtic Gotterdamerung imagery of Andrew Lang. Its weakness, however, was that while continuity from the Gaelic past was an accepted fact, it was utterly submerged beneath his analysis of the evidence for change. While this imbalance has been addressed to a considerable extent in some of his more recent work, the tide of 'feudalisation' and the wave of Anglo-Norman colonists introduced by David into Scotland has become the most enduring image of his research and has imbedded itself deeply in the consciousness of lay and academic communities. Echoing Hume Brown, but with a subtly different emphasis, Barrow identified the lordships created for the Anglo-Norman lords as the decisive factor in the process of change; 'the achievement of David I and his two grandsons would hardly have been possible unless they had been able to use these lordships as a principal instrument in imposing a much enhanced royal authority'.[76] Although he stressed the scale of continuity that existed alongside this apparently overwhelming change, that side of the argument failed to make the impact in the public perception that the image of Anglo-Norman knights, castles, monks and all the other symbols of the 'Davidian Revolution' achieved. David's achievement, as presented by some of Barrow's interpreters, is still highly coloured by a view of die-hard Celtic conservatism mown down by the Young Guns of continental innovation.

The strength of the Barrovian thesis can be seen at its sharpest in Michael Lynch's analysis of the reign in his *Scotland: a New History* (1991).[77] This is a masterful presentation in summary form of the forty-year output of his predecessor in the chair of Scottish History at Edinburgh. Throughout it, Lynch offers a carefully considered view of the two sides of the coin, attempting to stress the Janus-like image of the king and the methods which he employed. It is in his final observation that Lynch makes what is possibly one of his most trenchant comments. While past historians have ended with the upbeat image of modernity, looking forward to the 'feudal' kingdom of later twelfth and thirteenth century Scotland, Lynch looks in the other direction. David's campaigns in northern England, while enmeshed in the 'feudal' world, were also a continuation of the policies of his ancestors; 'the longer the reign went on, the more it might be claimed that David had become a Celtic king'.[78]

Throughout all of these studies, one theme which carried through from the work of Lang was a lingering sense that the end result of David's campaigns had been a negative one for Scotland. Failing to pay heed to David Dalrymple's warning from 1776, David was judged guilty of the weakness of his successors. His successes in northern England involved Malcolm IV, William the Lion and Alexander II in a struggle which they could not have hoped to win, and exposed Scotland to a threat to its independence from which it escaped only after centuries of debilitating struggle. It took until 1993 for that view to be challenged with any degree of success by Keith Stringer, who has reversed a century of negativism and stressed the degree of David's achievement.[79] Stringer has shown convincingly that what David was attempting to create was an entirely new prescription for power in the British Isles, a radical realignment that would have seen a Scoto-Northumbrian realm stretching northwards from the Humber, with 'England' confined to the Midlands and south. Perhaps it was the failure of that dream within four years of his death that has persuaded previous generations of historians that it was just a mirage, a false dream that distracted then nearly destroyed the Scots, but Stringer has shown that what David set in place had the ingredients for permanence. Just as dynastic accident had brought about the circumstances whereby David could build his extended kingdom, so it was only a series of dynastic accidents that contributed to its demise.

Despite Stringer's powerful argument, the most recent general histories of Scotland can still present a somewhat distrustful outlook on David, coloured by concern at the cultural consequences of his 'Davidian Revolution' and still singularly dismissive of his extension of Scottish authority into northern England. Murray Pittock, for example, sees David's stake in England as a source of weakness as much as it was a symbol of his power,[80] a view which harks back a century to Andrew Lang's criticisms. The implication which Pittock makes is that David's English lands exposed his successors to generations of demands from English kings for their homage for those properties, which led to an undermining of their independent authority as kings. That point, rather than David's achievements as a moderniser, state-builder and ecclesiastical reformer, is the only aspect of his reign to receive any developed discussion. The politics of post-Union Britain and early devolutionary Scotland are writ large in this presentation. A contrasting view is offered by Christopher Harvie, whose principal focus is on David the secular ruler and moderniser. Harvie places David higher in the national pantheon than Robert the Bruce, accolade indeed for any other medieval Scottish king, and states that 'his reign and its achievements would for centuries be a benchmark for the national estates: nobility, church and burghers'.[81] Each of those estates is touched on briefly, but as to exactly what benchmarks were set in David's reign we are left to guess.

In the end, we are left with a chameleon-like image of David I. There have been few historians who have discounted the scale of his achievement or the profundity of what he achieved, but there have been many who have questioned the methods and the desirability of the results. What is clearest, however, is that his legacy is one which can be adapted to suit the needs of a whole range of widely different agendas. He is both saint and sinner, a man who destroyed one culture to build another, monster or messiah. Eight hundred and fifty years after his death he can still arouse strong passions, yet little of the heat expended on assessing him brings us any closer to the complex creature that was David the man.

Notes

INTRODUCTION

1   G.W.S. Barrow, *David I of Scotland: the Balance of New and Old* (Reading, 1985), reproduced in G.W.S. Barrow, *Scotland and Its Neighbours in the Middle Ages* (London, 1992), 45–65.

2   A.A.M. Duncan, *Scotland: the Making of the Kingdom* (Edinburgh, 1975), 142.

CHAPTER ONE: THE FOUNDING OF THE CANMORE DYNASTY

1   A.A.M. Duncan, *The Kingship of the Scots 842–1292* (Edinburgh, 2003), 51–2. The nickname appears to date from no earlier than the thirteenth century.

2   Duncan, *Kingship of the Scots*, 35–43.

3   *Anglo-Saxon Chronicle*, versions C and D, s.a. 1054.

4   *Annals of Ulster*, s.a. 1054.

5   William of Malmesbury, *Gesta Regum Anglorum*, ed. W. Stubbs (London, 1887), 236–37.

6   For discussion of this point and its consequences for Scottish historiography, see Duncan, *Kingship of the Scots*, 35–53.

7   See, for example, G.W.S. Barrow, *Kingship and Unity: Scotland 1000–1306* (London, 1981), 26–27.

8   A.O. Anderson, *Scottish Annals from English Chroniclers AD 500–1286* (London, 1908), 86.

9   Duncan, *Kingship of the Scots*, 35–43.

10 For the known later kings of Strathclyde, see A. MacQuarrie, 'The Kings of Strathclyde *c.*400–1018', in A. Grant and K.J. Stringer (eds), *Medieval Scotland: Crown, Lordship and Community* (Edinburgh, 1993), 1–19. The suggestion that Donnchad mac Crinain was made King of Strathclyde by his grandfather, King Máel Coluim II mac Cináeda, is based on fourteenth-century tradition, articulated by the chronicler John of Fordun, which presented Strathclyde as an apanage held by the designated successor of the King of Scots.

11 F. Barlow, *Edward the Confessor* (London, 1970), 211–12.

12 I am grateful to Alex Woolf for first suggesting this alternative to me.

13 Duncan, *Kingship of the Scots*, 41.

14 *Vita Ædwardi Regis*, ed. F. Barlow, second edition (London, 1992).

15 Anderson, *Scottish Annals from English Chroniclers*, 86.

16 Symeon of Durham, *Historia Regum*, ii, 174–75.

17 Symeon of Durham, *Historia Dunelmensis Ecclesiae*, i, 84; Symeon of Durham, *Historia Regum*, ii, 155–56.

18 For an excellent and innovative discussion of the relationship of Moray to Scotland that requires a radical reassessment of the traditional interpretations, see A. Ross, *The Province of Moray c.1000–1230* (unpublished PhD thesis, University of Aberdeen, 2003).

19 See A. Forte, R. Oram and F. Pedersen, *Viking Empires* (forthcoming Cambridge, 2004) for a new discussion of the relationship between Scotland and Orkney.

20 Anderson, *Early Sources*, ii, 4.

21 Anderson, *Early Sources*, ii, 22–26 note 2.

22 *Annals of Ulster*, s.a. 1085 records the death of Domnall son of Máel Coluim, King of Scotland. This is the only record of his existence.

23 Anderson, *Scottish Annals*, 88.

24 *Anglo-Saxon Chronicle*, C, s.a. 1066.

25 Anderson, *Scottish Annals*, 88.

26 *Chron. Melrose*, s.a1069.

27 Anderson, *Scottish Annals*, 88.

28 William of Malmesbury, *Gesta Regum*, ii, 307–08.

29 Duncan, *Kingship of the Scots*, 44.

30 Pedersen, Forte and Oram, *Viking Empires*.

31 Symeon of Durham, *Historia Regum*, ii, 190–92.

32 Symeon of Durham, *Historia Regum*, ii, 190–92.

33 Kapelle, *Norman Conquest of the North*, 123.

34 Douglas, *William the Conqueror*, 22122.

35 *Anglo-Saxon Chronicle*, D, s.a. 1070; Douglas, *William the Conqueror*, 222.

36 *Anglo-Saxon Chronicle*, D, s.a. 1067 = ?1070.

37 Anderson, *Scottish Annals*, 93–94 and note 4.

38 Anderson, *Early Sources*, ii, 25.

39 See, for example, Duncan, *Making of the Kingdom*, 124.

40 D.E.R.Watt (ed.), *Fasti Ecclesiae Scoticanae Medii Aevii ad annum 1638* (Scottish Record Society, 1969), 70.

41 Turgot, Life of Queen Margaret, in Anderson, *Early Sources*, ii, 5888.

42 Turgot, Life of Queen Margaret, in Anderson, *Early Sources*, ii, 65, 76, 77.

43 Turgot, Life of Queen Margaret, in Anderson, *Early Sources*, ii, 6974.

44 Duncan, *Making of the Kingdom*, 122–23.

45 G.W.S.Barrow,'Benedictines,Tironensians and Cistercians', in *The Kingdom of the Scots* (London, 1973), 188–211 at 191.

46 Anderson, *Early Sources*, ii, 31–32.

47 Turgot, Life of Queen Margaret, in Anderson, *Early Sources*, ii, 64–65; Barrow, 'Benedictines, Tironensians and Cistercians', 194–95.

48 For example, G. Donaldson, *Scotland: Church and Nation Through Sixteen Centuries* (Edinburgh, 1960), 18.

49 Duncan, *Making of the Kingdom*, 123.

50 Barrow, 'Benedictines, Tironensians and Cistercians', 196.

51 Turgot, Life of Queen Margaret, in Anderson, *Early Sources*, ii, 66.

52 Turgot, Life of Queen Margaret, in Anderson, *Early Sources*, ii, 68–69.

53 Margaret, despite her supposed asceticism, displayed a very worldly love of finery and elaborate court ceremonial. See Turgot's comments, 68–69.

54 *Anglo-Saxon Chronicle*, E, s.a. 1072; *Chron. Melrose*, s.a1072; *Annals of Ulster*, s.a. 1072.

55 Symeon of Durham, *Historia Regum*, ii, 196.

Gospatric appears to have gone first to Flanders, whose count was a bitter enemy of Duke William of Normandy, but, having failed to secure the aid he wanted there, headed for Scotland (Symeon of Durham, *Historia Regum*, ii, 199).

56 Symeon of Durham, *Historia Regum*, ii, 199.

57 Symeon of Durham, *Historia Regum*, ii, 199–200.

58 William of Malmesbury, *Gesta Regum*, ii, 309; *Anglo-Saxon Chronicle*, D, s.a. 1075 = 1074.

59 *Anglo-Saxon Chronicle*, s.a. 1075 = 1074.

60 Forte, Oram and Pedersen, *Viking Empires*; Kapelle, *Norman Conquest of the North*, 135–37.

61 *Anglo-Saxon Chronicle*, E, s.a. 1079.

62 Kapelle, *Norman Conquest of the North*, 139–40.

63 *Chron. Melrose*, s.a. 1080; Symeon of Durham, *Historia Regum*, ii, 211.

64 Kapelle, *Norman Conquest of the North*, 142–46.

65 De Miraculis et Translationibus Sancti Cuthberti, in Symeon of Durham, ii, 338.

66 *Anglo-Saxon Chronicle*, E, s.a. 1091; Duncan, *Kingship of the Scots*, 46.

67 *Anglo-Saxon Chronicle*, E, s.a. 1091.

68 Kapelle, *Norman Conquest of the North*, 148–49.

69 *Anglo-Saxon Chronicle*, E, s.a. 1091.

70 Symeon of Durham, *Historia Regum*, ii, 218.

71 *Anglo-Saxon Chronicle*, E, s.a 1092.

72 Barrow, *Kingship and Unity*, 31. Compare this with Kapelle, *Norman Conquest of the North*, 150–51.

73 *Anglo-Saxon Chronicle*, E, s.a. 1093.

74 Kapelle, *Norman Conquest of the North*, 150–52.

75 *Anglo-Saxon Chronicle*, E, s.a 1093. For other possible contributing factors in this confrontation, see below p.54.

76 *Anglo-Saxon Chronicle*, E, s.a. 1093. William Rufus's altogether conciliatory behaviour may have been a consequence of the serious illness which had struck him down earlier in the year. The king appears to have believed that he was dying and for a while seemed to have turned over a new leaf. After the scare of the spring had passed, however, he reverted quickly to his old character.

77 Symeon of Durham, i, 195.

78 Florence of Worcester, *Chronicon*, ii, 31.

79 *Anglo-Saxon Chronicle*, E, s.a. 1093.

80 Duncan, *Making of the Kingdom*, 121.

81 *Anglo-Saxon Chronicle*, E, s.a. 1093.

82 For Morel and Máel Coluim see Barlow, *William Rufus*, 316–317. For Morel's later reputation, see *ibid.*, 347, 351, 355–57.

83 Kapelle, *Norman Conquest of the North*, 152–53.

Kapelle's conviction that Máel Coluim's ultimate objective was Carlisle is scarcely
compatible with the fatal fight occurring on
the Scots' homeward route from their plundering raid, nor does his complex scenario
involving armies kept in the field on William
Rufus's instructions bear up to scrutiny. Based
only on Symeon of Durham's account of the
king's five raids on Northumbria, whose reli-
ability he had called in to question previously,
the set-piece battle which it implies occurred
does not receive mention in any other contemporary text, all of which instead speak of a
skirmish, ambush, or treachery at a parley.

CHAPTER TWO: THE STRUGGLE FOR SCOTLAND

1   Symeonis Opera, ii, 222, describes Edward as
    'heir of the kingship after him'. In the Anglo-
    Saxon Chronicle, s.a. 1093, it is stated that
    Edward 'should have been king after [his
    father] if he had survived'.
2   Life of Margaret, c.13.
3   Chron. Fordun, ii, 209.
4   Life of Margaret, c.13.
5   Anglo-Saxon Chronicle, s.a. 1093.
6   Chron, Fordoun, ii, 209–10.
7   Anderson, Early Sources, ii, 59.
8   Anglo-Saxon Chronicle, s.a. 1072; Annals of
    Ulster, s.a. 1072; Chron. Melrose, s.a. 1072.
9   Anglo-Saxon Chronicle, s.a. 1087; Chron. Melrose,
    s.a. 1087.
10 Anglo-Saxon Chronicle, s.a. 1093.
11 Duncan, Kingship of the Scots, 54.
12 Florence of Worcester, ii, 32.
13 A.A.M. Duncan, 'Yes, the Earliest Scottish
    Charters', Scottish Historical Review, lxxviii
    (1999), 1–35.
14 Anglo-Saxon Chronicle, s.a. 1093; Chronicle of the
    Kings of Scotland in W.F. Skene (ed.), Chronicles
    of the Picts, Chronicles of the Scots (Edinburgh,
    1867), 175.
15 Duncan, 'Yes, The Earliest Scottish Charters',
    3–4.
16 Oram, Lordship of Galloway, 41.
17 Lawrie, Early Scottish Charters, no.XII.
18 Duncan, Kingship of the Scots, 55.
19 Anglo-Saxon Chronicle, s.a. 1093.
20 Florence of Worcester, Chronicon ex Chronicis,
    ii, ed. B.Thorpe, English History Society (1849),
    32.
21 Chronicle of the Kings of Scotland, in Skene, Picts
    and Scots, 175.
22 Annals of Ulster, s.a. 1085.
23 Annals of Ulster, s.a. 1094; William of
    Malmesbury, Gesta Regum Anglorum, ii, 477.

24 For the events of 1095, see Barlow, William
    Rufus, 337–55.
25 Duncan, 'Yes, The Earliest Scottish Charters',
    Scottish Historical Review, lxxviii (1999), 135.
26 Duncan, Kingship of the Scots, 56–57.
27 Duncan, 'Yes, The earliest Scottish Charters',
    22–23.
28 Barlow, William Rufus, 357–69.
29 Anglo-Saxon Chronicle, s.a. 1097.
30 William of Malmesbury, Gesta Regum
    Anglorum, ii, 476.
31 Chron. Melrose, s.a. 1097; Anderson, Early
    Sources, ii, 99.
32 Anderson, Early Sources, ii, 100.
33 William of Malmesbury, Gesta Regum
    Anglorum, ii, 477.
34 Chronicle of the Kings of Scotland, E, 131–33.
35 Heimskringla, Magnus Bareleg's Saga, c.10.
36 Duncan, Kingship of the Scots, 59.
37 Lawrie, Early Scottish Charters, no. XIV.

CHAPTER THREE: BROTHER OF THE QUEEN

1   For Henry's probable date of birth, see
    Hollister, Henry I, 30–32.
2   Hollister, Henry I, 107–15.
3   Hermann of Tournai (Herimannus
    Tornacensis), Narratio Restaurationis abbatiae S
    Martini Tornacensis, ed. G. Waitz, Monumenta
    Historica Germaniae, Scriptores, xiv, 274–317.
4   Eadmer, Historia Novorum, 121–26.
5   Honeycutt, Matilda of Scotland, 21.
6   See, for example, Duncan, Making of the
    Kingdom, 120–21.
7   Eadmer, Historia Novorum, 121–26; Herman of
    Tournai, Liber de Restaurationis, 281–82.
8   Orderic Vitalis, Historia Ecclesiastica, viii, 20.
9   Eadmer, Historia Novorum, 122.
10 Barlow, William Rufus, 313. Barlow identifies
    the would-be husband as Alan Niger rather
    than his younger brother and heir, Alan Rufus.
11 Anselm, Letters, no. 177.
12 Barlow, William Rufus, 315–16.
13 Honeycutt, Matilda of Scotland, 21–22.
14 Hermann of Tournai, Liber de Restaurationis,
    281.
15 Anselm, Letters, no. 177.
16 Orderic Vitalis, Historia Ecclesiastica, viii, 20.
17 From the time of her first reappearance in the
    historical records in 1100, Edith is referred to
    as Matilda, the name by which she was to be
    known as Henry's wife and queen. When and
    why the name change occurred is a matter of
    conjecture (for discussion of this point see
    Honeycutt, Matilda of Scotland, 26). For con-

venience, I shall here continue to refer to her
as Edith until the time of her marriage and
thereafter refer to her as Matilda.

18 William of Malmesbury, *Gesta Regum*, ii,
    493–94; Eadmer, *Historia Novorum*, 120–21.

19 Eadmer, *Historia Novorum*, 121–26; Herman of
    Tournai, *Liber de Restaurationis*, 282.

20 *Anglo-Saxon Chronicle*, s.a. 1100.

21 'David, the queen's brother', for example, wit-
    nessed one of Matilda's acts in 1103 or 1105 x
    1107 (Honeycutt, *Matilda of Scotland*, Appendix
    1 no. xix). From 1113, he is referred to as Earl
    David.

22 Orderic Vitalis, *Historia Ecclesiastica*, iv, 274–75.
    The term 'household young bloods' is Archie
    Duncan's rendering of Orderic's 'domestici
    pueri' (Duncan, *Kingship of the Scots*, 63).

23 Hollister, *Henry I*, 331–32

24 Ailred of Rievaulx, 'Genealogia regum anglo-
    rum', *Patrologia Latina* 195, 736.

25 William of Malmesbury, *Gesta Regum*, ii, 476.
    The translation is from Anderson, *Scottish
    Annals*, 157.

26 Hollister, *Henry I*, 338.

27 *RRAN*, ii, no. 648.

28 *RRAN*, ii, nos 689, 701, 703, 706, 828, 832, 833,
    occurring between 29 August 1105 and August
    1107, show him beginning to witness charters
    on a more regular basis.

CHAPTER FOUR: PRINCE OF THE CUMBRIAN REGION

1   *Annales Monastici*, ii, 40.

2   Duncan, *Kingship of the Scots*, 59.

3   Symeon of Durham, ii, 236.

4   Duncan, *Kingship of the Scots*, 59–60, discusses the
    identity of the 'nepos regis Alexandri' who wit-
    nessed the king's charter to the canons of Scone
    (*Scone Liber*, no 1).

5   Anderson, *Early Sources*, ii, 141. An alternative
    version suggests that he died in Dundee, and
    later tradition locates his place of death as
    Invergowrie.

6   Duncan, *Kingship of the Scots*, 60.

7   Ailred of Rievaulx, *De Standardo in Chronicles
    of Stephen, Henry II* etc, iii, 192–95.

8   *RRAN*, ii, no. 883.

9   See the comments of Duncan, *Kingship of the
    Scots*, 63.

10 Hollister, *Henry I*, 199–201.

11 Ibid., 209–11.

12 Ibid., 213–14.

13 The argument, set out in *RRAN*, ii, p.xxx, is
    that Henry was at Westminster in June 1109,
    following his return from Normandy, at
    Nottingham for a council on 17 October, and
    back at Westminster for Christmas. One char-
    ter of Henry issued at Nottingham was
    witnessed by Robert Bruce. Robert witnessed
    two other charters of Henry I, both at York,
    which have then been assigned to 1109 on no
    stronger grounds than Robert's witnessing of
    the securely dated Nottingham document. If
    the York charters do date to 1109, then this
    would require Henry to have either travelled
    north to arrange support for David between
    June and mid-October or between mid-
    October and Christmas, leaving very little
    operating leeway.

14 J. Wilson, 'Foundation of the Austin Priories of
    Nostell and Scone', *Scottish Historical Review*,
    vii (1910), 157–58.

15 Kapelle, *Norman Conquest of the North*, 207.

16 Duncan, *Kingship of the Scots*, 63–64.

17 Lawrie, *Early Scottish Charters*, no. LII; A.A.M.
    Duncan, 'The Bruces of Annandale, 1100-
    1304', *TDGNHAS*, lxix (1994), 89-102 at
    89–90.

18 *Early Yorkshire Charters*, i, 385–86; ii, v., 11–12,
    326; ibid., iii, 23, 143, 148; for a discussion of
    these grants, see Kapelle, *Norman Conquest of
    the North*, 198–99.

19 Duncan, *Kingship of the Scots*, 64.

20 Lawrie, *Early Scottish Charters*, 45, 46. See also
    the discussion of his titles by Duncan, *Kingship
    of the Scots*, 60–61.

21 '...non vero toti Cumbrensi regioni dom-
    inabatur', Lawries, *Early Scottish Charters*, 46.

22 Lawrie, *Early Scottish Charters*, nos XXVI
    (where Alexander expressly affirms that he and
    his brother David together warrant the alms
    given by King Edgar to the monks of
    Durham), XXVII, XXXI and XXXII.

23 Ailred of Rievaulx, *De Standardo in Chronicles
    of Stephen, Henry II* etc, iii, 192–95.

24 Duncan, *Kingship of the Scots*, 61–65.

25 *Life of Waltheof* in Anderson, *Early Sources*, ii,
    145–47 and notes.

26 Duncan, *Kingship of the Scots*, 65 comments that
    the establishment of David in Cumbria should
    be seen as part of Henry I's 'conquest' of north-
    ern England, the last piece of unfinished
    business from the two previous reigns. This
    theme is explored at length by Kapelle in *The
    Norman Conquest of the North*, especially in
    chapter 7.

27 *Anglo-Saxon Chronicle*, E, s.a. 1107; Duncan,
    Kingship of the Scots, 60.

28 *Brut y Tywyssogion: or, The Chronicle of the Princes,*

ed. J. Williams ab Ithel (London, 1860), 115.

29 The date of the marriage is unknown, William of Malmesbury, our sole twelfth-century source for it, stating simply that the match occurred after Edgar's death to establish an alliance between Henry and Alexander (*Gesta Regum Anglorum*, ii, 476).

30 The most recent and best translation of Ailred's account of Robert Bruce's 1138 speech is given in Ross, *The Province of Moray c. 1000–1230*, 182. The speech states that Máel Coluim mac Alasdair, Alexander's bastard son, inherited his father's animosity towards David.

31 Translation from the Gaelic of 'A Verse on David Son of Máel Coluim (*c.*1113)', in T.O. Clancy (ed.), *The Triumph Tree* (Edinburgh, 1998), 184.

32 Duncan, *Kingship of the Scots*, 61–62.

33 *Liber Ecclesie de Scon* (Bannatyne Club, 1843), no.1; Lawrie, Early Scottish Charters, no.XXXVI; Duncan, *Kingship of the Scots*, 59–60.

34 *Liber Sancte Marie de Calchou* (Bannatyne Club, 1846), no. 1. For discussion of this act and David's religious patronage more generally, see below chapter nine.

35 D.E.R. Watt, *Fasti Ecclesiae Scoticanae Medii Aevii ad annum 1638* (Edinburgh, 1969), 144–45.

36 *Charters of David I*, no. 15 (discussion); Lawrie, *Early Scottish Charters*, no. L (full text of 'notitia' and 'inquisitio').

37 N.F. Shead, 'The origins of the medieval diocese of Glasgow', *Scottish Historical Review*, xlviii (1969), 220–25; H.H.E. Craster, 'A contemporary record of the pontificate of Ranulf Flambard', *Archaeologia Aeliana*, vii (1930), 33–56.

38 *Charters of David I*, 60.

39 *Charters of David I*, 61.

40 *RRAN*, ii, no. 1062.

41 *Charters of David I*, nos 2–4, 6–7. No. 1, David's confirmation of the Querqueville property granted to St Mary's abbey at York by Robert Bruce, appears also to belong to this group.

42 *Charters of David I*, no. 4.

43 *Charters of David I*, no. 8.

44 *Charters of David I*, 38.

45 *RRAN*, ii, no 1180.

46 Duncan, *Kingship of the Scots*, 63

47 Laynesmith, *Matilda of Scotland*, 145.

48 *Charters of David I*, no. 13.

49 J. Green, 'Anglo-Scottish Relations, 1066–1174' in M. Jones and M. Vale (eds), *England and Her Neighbours, 1066–1453* (London, 1989),

53–72 at 60–61.

50 Symeon of Durham, *Historia Dunelmensis Ecclesia*, i, 140.

51 Symeon of Durham, *Historia Regum*, ii, 261–62.

52 Duncan, *Kingship of the Scots*, 63–64.

53 Symeon of Durham, *Historia Regum*, ii, 267.

54 Green, 'Anglo-Scottish Relations', 64.

55 Oram, *Lordship of Galloway*, 61.

56 *Charters of David I*, 38.

57 Green adopts an altogether less dramatic interpretation of the events of 1121–22 in her later study of David's relations with Henry I. See J.A. Green, 'David I and Henry I', *Scottish Historical Review*, lxxv (1996), 1–19.

58 Symeon of Durham, *Historia Regum*, ii, 265.

59 William of Malmesbury, *Gesta Regum*, ii, 476.

60 Walter Bower, *Scotichronicon*, iii, ed. D.E.R. Watt and others (Edinburgh, 1995), 109. For Alexander's grant of the island to the canons of Scone, see *Scone Liber*, no. 3, and for the evidence for the priory see Lawrie, *Early Scottish Charters*, 294–95.

61 Duncan, *Kingship of the Scots*, 65.

62 *Charters of David I*, 38.

63 Hollister, *Henry I*, 292–305.

CHAPTER FIVE: STRANGER IN A STRANGE LAND?

1 See, for example, the *Chronicle of Melrose*, where there is no stigma attached to Donnchad's legitimacy in the original chronicle entry for 1094, but an insertion based on the later *Chronicle of Huntingdon* describes him unequivocally as illegitimate. For the fifteenth-century view, see Bower, *Scotichronicon*, iii, 85.

2 For a fuller discussion of this issue, see D. Broun, 'Contemporary perspectives on Alexander II's succession: the evidence of king-lists' in R.D. Oram (ed.), *The Reign of Alexander II* (forthcoming, Brill, 2005).

3 Ailred of Rievaulx, Epistola, in Anderson, *Scottish Annals*, 232–37.

4 Geoffrey Barrow, in *Charters of David I*, 62, notes to no. 16, suggests that David was inaugurated on 23 or 25 April, which would require him to have been sitting at his dying brother's bedside ready for a dash to Scone for immediate enthronement as king. *Anglo-Saxon Chronicle*, E, s.a. 1124, however, says that Alexander only died on the ninth day before the kalends of May, i.e. 23 April, while Symeon of Durham, *Historia Regum*, ii, 275 places his death on 26 April. There is no indication of an extended illness and later sources indicate that his death was comparatively sudden, which makes it unlikely that

David was in attendance and ready to assume the kingship.

5   *Charters of David I*, no. 16.

6   Duncan, *Making of the Kingdom*, 135; Barrow, *Kingship and Unity*, 32.

7   William of Malmesbury, *Gesta Regum*, ii, 476.

8   J.G. Scott, 'The Partition of a Kingdom: Strathclyde 1092–1153', *Transactions of the Dumfriesshire and Galloway Natural History and Antiquarian Society*, lxxii (1997), 11–40 at 24–26.

9   G.W.S. Barrow, *The Anglo-Norman Era in Scottish History* (Oxford, 1980), 12, 70; Barrow, *Kingship and Unity*, 32

10 Orderic Vitalis, Historia Ecclesiastica, viii, 20 (Migne, Patrologia Latina, 188, col. 622).

11 *Charters of David I*, 39–40 for a skeleton itinerary of the king in this period.

12 *Charters of David I*, nos 17–22.

13 John of Crema's commission was issued by the Pope on 13 April 1125 and he was back in London for a council of the English Church by 8 September.

14 *Anglo-Saxon Chronicle*, E, s.a 1126.

15 Hugh Sottewain, *Archbishops of York*, in *Historians of the Church of York*, i, ed. J. Raine (London, 1879), 217.

16 Ibid.

17 Symeon of Durham, *Historia Regum*, ii, 281–82.

18 Anderson, *Scottish Annals from English Chroniclers*, 164–66; General Letter of Archbishop Thurstan, in *Historians of York*, iii, 51–52. For discussion of this subject, see *Charters of David I*, 68.

19 *Liber Vitæ Ecclesiæ Dunelmensis*, ed. J. Stevenson (Surtees Society, 1841), 67–68. There is also a thirteenth-century version of the event recorded on page 59. For Bishop Robert's act, which dates the event, see Lawrie, *Early Scottish Charters*, no LXXIII.

20 For a discussion of this possibility, see *Charters of David I*, 68-69, notes to nos 29 and 30.

21 *Charters of David I*, no. 30.

22 See *Kelso Liber*, no.1 and the annotated text in *Charters of David I*, no.14. David granted the monks 'a toft in the burgh of Roxburgh, the seventh part of the mill, 40 shillings from the burgh ferme, and a fishery'.

23 *Dunfermline Registrum*, no. 1; *Charters of David I*, no. 33.

24 Symeon of Durham, *Historia Regum*, ii, 281.

25 *Charters of David I*, no. 22; Anderson, *Scottish Annals from English Chroniclers*, 166.

26 *Dunfermline Registrum*, no. 1.

27 *Charters of David I*, 72.

28 Henry of Huntingdon, *Historia Anglorum*, 252; Orderic Vitalis, *Historia Ecclesiastica*, viii, 20; *RRAN*, ii, no. 1639.

29 Gervase of Canterbury, *Historical Works*, i, *The Chronicles of Stephen, Henry II and Richard I*, ed. W. Stubbs (London, 1879), 96. Sadly, Gervase only tells us that David was attended by a multitude of his nobles, but not who those nobles were.

30 For early material detailing Matilda's life, see Anderson, *Early Sources*, ii, 33–34. She figured so infrequently in David's acts that very few hard facts about her life are known. Anderson, in his earlier work, *Scottish Annals from English Chroniclers*, believed that she died after as late as 1147 (Anderson, *Scottish Annals*, 157 note).

31 *Charters of David I*, nos 3, 7, 8, 14 and 47.

32 Walter Bower, *Scotichronicon*, ed. D.E.R. Watt and others, iii (Edinburgh, 1995), 135.

33 Robert of Torigni, *Chronica*, in *Chronicles of Stephen etc.*, iv, 118.

34 Orderic Vitalis, *Historia Ecclesiastica*, viii, 20.

35 A. Williams, *The English and the Norman Conquest* (Woodbridge, 1995), 95–96. I am grateful to Alex Woolf for drawing my attention to this evidence.

36 The location of the battlefield is not recorded in any of the surviving early sources, but it appears in the *Gesta Annalia* portion of Fordun, which implies that it appeared in a now-lost early chronicle (*Chron. Fordun*, ii, 224).

37 *Annals of Ulster*, s.a. 1130; Orderic Vitalis, *Historia Ecclesiastica*, viii, 20.

38 *Annals of Ulster*, 1130.

39 Robert of Torigni, *Chronica*, s.a. 1130.

40 *Annals of Ulster*, s.a. 1130.

41 *Chron. Melrose*, s.a. 1134.

42 Ailred of Rievaulx, *De Standardo*, in *Chronicles of Stephen, Henry II and Richard I*, ed. R. Howlett (London, 1886), iii, 193. I am grateful to Alasdair Ross for permission to reproduce his translation of the speech, given in his as yet unpublished PhD thesis, and for the following commentary on the manuscript and the text. 'Howlett, the editor, noted that in one of the manuscript versions, the Rievaulx copy, the word proderent had been expunged. Therefore he did not include it in the main text. In the translation I have provided two versions of the section where this word was expunged in the Latin. Although it is not usual to restore expunged words to a text I have chosen to do so on this occasion for two reasons. Firstly, if the word is restored the meaning of the text

actually becomes clearer. Secondly, the restored word fits in beautifully with the rhetoric. Unfortunately, it has not proved possible on this occasion to examine the original MS. to see if the expunction of this word was done by the scribe or at a later date. This obviously needs further investigation' (Ross, Thesis, 186 and note 46).

43 *Chron. Holyrood*, s.a. 1153.

CHAPTER SIX: THE CONQUEST OF THE NORTH

1   See R.D. Oram, 'David I and the Conquest and Colonisation of Moray', *Northern Scotland*, 19 (1999), 1–19 at 1–4.

2   A. Grant, 'Thanes and Thanages from the Eleventh to the Fourteenth Centuries', in A. Grant and K.J. Stringer (eds), *Medieval Scotland: Crown, Lordship and Community* (Edinburgh, 1993), 39–81. For the Moray and Ross thanages see 46–47 and 72–73.

3   *Orkneyinga Saga: The History of the Earls of Orkney*, trans H. Pálsson and P. Edwards (Harmondsworth, 1978), 76–78.

4   Anderson, *Scottish Annals*, 100 and note 1.

5   *Anglo-Saxon Chronicle*, D, s.a. 1078.

6   *Annals of Ulster*, s.a. 1085; Duncan, *Making of the Kingdom*, 165.

7   *Chron. Melrose*, s.a. 1134.

8   See, for example, the view of events offered by G.W.S. Barrow, *Kingship and Unity: Scotland 1000–1306*, first edition (London, 1981), 33.

9   See the critique offered in 'David I and the Conquest and Colonisation of Moray', 67.

10 Lawrie, *Early Scottish Charters*, no. cclv and notes; *Registrum de Dunfermelyn* (Bannatyne Club, 1842), 33.

11 Lawrie, *Early Scottish Charters*, no. cx; *Registrum de Dunfermelyn*, 34; D.E. Easson, *Medieval Religious Houses. Scotland* (London, 1957), 55.

12 *The Heads of Religious Houses in Scotland from Twelfth to Sixteenth Centuries*, edd. D.E.R. Watt and N.F. Shead (Edinburgh, 2001), 179, 215–16; S.R. Macphail, *History of the Religious House of Pluscardyn* (Edinburgh, 1881).

13 Douglas, *William the Conqueror*, 199, 328; R. Midmer, *English Medieval Monasteries* (London, 1979), 59–60.

14 Lawrie, *Early Scottish Charters*, no. cclv; *RRS*, i, 44 and note 4. For Holyrood, see *Holyrood Liber*, no. 1; Kelso, see *Kelso Liber*, nos 1 and 2; Melrose, see *Melrose Liber*, nos 1 and 2.

15 Lawrie, *Early Scottish Charters*, nos cx and cclv.

16 See Duncan, *Making of the Kingdom*, 298.

17 Barrow, *Kingship and Unity*, 51–52.

18 Stringer, *Reign of Stephen*, 34–35; G.W.S. Barrow, 'The Reign of William the Lion', in *Scotland and Her Neighbours in the Middle Ages* (London, 1993), 78; A.L. Poole, *Domesday Book to Magna Carta*, second edition (Oxford, 1955), 271, note 3.

19 D. Broun, 'Contemporary perspectives on Alexander II's succession: the evidence of king-lists' in R.D. Oram, *The Reign of Alexander II* (forthcoming, Brill, 2005).

20 Barrow, *Kingship and Unity*, 51–52.

21 *Regesta Regum Scotorum*, ii, *The Acts of William I*, ed. G.W.S. Barrow (Edinburgh, 1971), 12.

22 William of Newburgh, *Historia Rerum Anglicarum*, in R. Howlett (ed.), Chronicles of Stephen etc, i, 7376.

23 Benedict of Peterborough, *Gesta Regis Henrici Secundi*, ed. W. Stubbs, i (London, 1867), 277–78.

24 My earlier proposed scenario in 'David I and the Conquest and Colonisation of Moray' on this point must be rejected.

25 Kapelle, *Norman Conquest of the North*, 191–230.

26 *Orkneyinga Saga*, 118. What the nature of the kinship between David and Maddad was is unclear. Traditionally, based on a statement in *Orkneyinga Saga*, Maddad's father, Máel Muire, has been called a son of King Donnchad I mac Crináin, and therefore a younger brother of David's father, Máel Coluim III. Maddad's son, Máel Coluim, Earl of Atholl, married Hextilda daughter of Bethoc daughter of Domnall Bán, the elder brother of Máel Muire by this proposed pedigree. Had Máel Muire been Domnall Bán's brother then this marriage would have been uncanonical, being within prohibited degrees of consanguinity. This marriage took place after around 1179 when Richard Cumin, Hextilda's first husband, disappears from the historical record. At this date, at the court of King William the Lion, it is unlikely that such an uncanonical marriage would have passed without comment or, indeed, been permitted.

27 McDonald, *Kingdom of the Isles*, 46.

28 *RRS*, i, 44; Barrow, 'Badenoch and Strathspey I: secular and political', *Northern Scotland*, 8 (1988), 1–15; Grant, 'Thanes and Thanages', 73.

29 Barrow, 'Badenoch and Strathspey I', 3–7.

30 Ross, Thesis, 211–12.

31 *Orkneyinga Saga*, 98, 119. For discussion of Frakkok and the feud between the rival lines of Orkney earls, see Pedersen, Oram and Forte, *Viking Empires* (Cambridge, 2004).

32 *Orkneyinga Saga*, 98. This supposed vassalic relationship between the Earl of Caithness and the King of Scots is probably a projection backwards from the changed political world of the late twelfth and earlier thirteenth centuries when the saga was composed.

33 *Orkneyinga Saga*, 100–01.

34 *Orkneyinga Saga*, 137–39; P. Topping, 'Harald Maddadson, Earl of Orkney and Caithness, 1139–1206', *SHR*, lxii (1983), 105–20 at 105–06 and 107–08.

35 For Frakkok's family connections, see *Orkneyinga Saga*, 97–98, 101.

36 W.P.L. Thomson, *History of Orkney* (Edinburgh, 1987), 61.

37 *Orkneyinga Saga*, 119, 138–39.

38 Topping, 'Harald Maddadson', 105–07.

39 *Orkneyinga Saga*, 143.

40 *Orkneyinga Saga*, 144–45.

41 Thomson, *History of Orkney*, 69.

42 The best recent discussions of the development of St Magnus Cathedral and the cult are collected in B.E. Crawford, (ed.), *St. Magnus Cathedral and Orkney's Twelfth-Century Renaissance* (Aberdeen, 1988).

43 *Orkneyinga Saga*, chapters 86 to 89.

44 Topping, 'Harald Maddadson', 105–20; Thomson, *History of Orkney*, 70.

45 *Orkneyinga Saga*, chapter 91.

46 *Orkneyinga Saga*, chapters 92–94.

47 *Chron. Melrose*, s.a. 1197.

48 *Chron. Fordun*, s.a. 1196.

49 William 'the prince', was considered in some quarters to be a candidate for the kingship. Flateyiarbók claimed that 'all Scots wished to take [him] as their king' (Anderson, *Early Sources*, ii, 5).

50 *RRS*, i, 43–44.

51 Only three mottes in lowland Moray can, with confidence, be assigned a twelfth-century date. See G.G. Simpson and B. Webster, 'Charter evidence and the distribution of mottes in Scotland', in K.J. Stringer (ed.), *Essays on the Nobility of Medieval Scotland* (Edinburgh, 1985), 1–24, Appendix 1, G. Stell, 'Provisional list of mottes in Scotland', 19. The sites in question are Duffus Castle, Knight's Hillock in Urquhart parish, and Tor Chastle in Dallas parish. Of these, only the first can be dated to the reign of David.

52 B. Jones, I. Keillar and K. Maude, 'Discovering the Prehistoric and proto-Historic Landscape', and I.A.G. Shepherd, 'The Picts in Moray', in W.D.H. Sellar (ed.), *Moray: Province and People* (Edinburgh, 1993), 47–74 and 75–90.

53 *RRS*, ii, no. 116; Duncan, *Making of the Kingdom*, 138.

54 See, for example, Kapelle, *Norman Conquest of the North*, 229.

55 *RRS*, i, no.181; L. Toorians, 'Twelfth-century Flemish Settlement in Scotland', in G.G. Simpson (ed.), *Scotland and the Low Countries 1124–1994* (East Linton, 1996), 1–14 at 4–5, 13–14; Duncan, *Making of the Kingdom*, 138. The use of agents who found potential colonists on behalf of a landowner, referred to as *locators* or *populators*, was common in the German colonisation of the Slav lands east of the Elbe, and in Iberia and, possibly, Ireland. For discussion of their role, see Bartlett, *Making of Europe*, 121–22, 142–43, 145.

56 Watt, *Fasti*, 214. The earliest secure dating evidence for Bishop William in Moray places him there in 1152.

57 Ross, Thesis, 208 discusses the possible role of the bishops of Moray as replacements for the temporal powers of the earls or mormaers.

58 Anderson, *Early Sources*, ii, 210.

59 The main evidence for the structure of the diocesan administration in Moray dates from the early 1200s, when Bishop Brice Douglas fixed his see at Spynie, but it is inconceivable that his predecessors had functioned without a core of senior clerical officials to aid in the running of their sprawling diocese. See Watt, *Fasti*, 218 and following.

60 Bartlett, *Making of Europe*, 228; T.E. McNeill, *Anglo-Norman Ulster: the History and Archaeology of an Irish Barony, 1177–1400* (Edinburgh, 1980), 46–50.

61 *Chron. Melrose*, s.a. 1148.

62 Other dimensions of this pioneering image are discussed in chapter 9.

63 Watt, *Fasti*, 58.

64 See, for example, R. Fawcett, *Scottish Cathedrals* (London, 1997), 32.

65 I.B. Cowan, *The Medieval Church in Scotland*, ed. J. Kirk (Edinburgh, 1995), 35; K. Veitch, 'The Scottish material in *De domibus religiosis*: date and provenance', *Innes Review*, xlvii (1996), 14–23; G.W.S. Barrow, '*De domibus religiosis*: a note on Dornoch', *Innes Review*, xlviii (1997), 83–84.

66 Duncan, *Making of the Kingdom*, 266; Barrow, *Kingship and Unity*, 68.

67 Bartlett, *Making of Europe*, chapter 6.

68 Ross, Thesis.

69 See Oram, 'A Family Business?'; Oram, 'Earldom of Mar'.

70 Ross, Thesis, 125–33

71 Barrow, 'Badenoch and Strathspey I', 4–5.

72 Ross, Thesis, 208–15.

73 Oram, *Lordship of Galloway*, 210–213; Oram, 'Earldom of Mar', 56–57.

CHAPTER SEVEN: LORD OF THE WEST

1 Oram, *Lordship of Galloway*, 39–44.

2 Oram, *Lordship of Galloway*, xxii

3 Oram, *Lordship of Galloway*, 61.

4 For the later impact of that alliance, see Oram, *Lordship of Galloway*, chapters 3 and 4.

5 *Charters of David I*, no.16.

6 Kapelle, *Norman Conquest of the North*, 206–07.

7 *Chron. Holyrood*, s.a. 1153.

8 R.A. McDonald, *The Kingdom of the Isles. Scotland's Western Seaboard, c.1100–c.1336* (East Linton, 1997), 42–43, 65–67.

9 *Charters of David I*, no.15.

10 Oram, *Lordship of Galloway*, 10, 16.

11 *Charters of David I*, no. 14.

12 *RRS*, i, no.131.

13 *Charters of David I*, no. 57.

14 Oram, *Lordship of Galloway*, xxiii.

15 *Charters of David I*, no. 17.

16 *Charters of David I*, no. 37.

17 Oram, *Lordship of Galloway*, 122 and notes 80 and 81.

18 Ross, *The Province of Moray c.1000–1230*, 182.

19 *Charters of David I*, no.37. A connection with David's campaigns against his nephew would narrow the timeframe of this document to 1128 x 1134, when Máel Coluim mac Alasdair was betrayed and imprisoned.

20 G.W.S. Barrow, *The Anglo-Norman Era in Scottish History* (Oxford, 1980), 72 and note 64.

21 Ailred of Rievaulx, *De Standardo*, 191.

22 *Charters of David I*, no.147.

23 *Chron. Man*, s.a. 1144 = 1154.

24 These ties are particularly evident in the religious connections of the kingdom of the Isles. In 1134, Óláfr brought a colony of monks from Stephen's own foundation at Furness in the northern portion of the honour of Lancaster and established them at Rushen in Mann (*Chron. Mann*, s.a. 1134). Sometime after the foundation of Rushen, he gave the monks of Furness the right to elect the Bishop of the Isles.

25 Oram, *Lordship of Galloway*, 61.

26 *Charters of David I*, no.56.

27 *Charters of David I*, no.57.

CHAPTER EIGHT: WAR IN ENGLAND

1 Matthew, *King Stephen*, 59–60.

2 *John of Hexham*, in Symeon of Durham, ii, 287.

3 Matthew, *King Stephen*, 70.

4 Richard of Hexham, Historia de gestis Regis Stephani et de bello de Standardo, in *Chronicles of Stepehn, Henry II and Richard I*, ed. R.Howlett, iii (London, 1886), 145.

5 Henry of Huntingdon, *Historia Anglorum*, ed. T. Arnold (London, 1879), 258–59.

6 Ailred of Rievaulx, *Saints of Hexham* in J. Raine (ed.), *The Priory of Hexham*, i (Surtees Society, 1864), 183.

7 For the bad reputation of the Galwegians, see D. Brooke, *Wild Men and Holy Places* (Edinburgh, 1994), 94–99.

8 Fergus's career is discussed in detail in Oram, *Lordship of Galloway*, 51–86.

9 Matthew, *King Stephen*, 79.

10 Richard of Hexham, 145–46.

11 Henry of Huntingdon, *Historia Anglorum*, 259.

12 Richard of Hexham, 146.

13 Matthew, *King Stephen*, 78.

14 Richard of Hexham, 146.

15 John of Hexham, 287.

16 *Gesta Stephani Regis Anglorum*, in Howlett (ed.), *Chronicles of Stephen*, etc., iii, chapter 25.

17 *Historians of the Church of York*, ed. J.Raine, iii, 66–67.

18 *Chron. Holyrood*, 119. The date of this event given by Holyrood, 7 July 1136, has recently been questioned and may arise from a mistranscription in the chronicle (*Charters of David I*, 81 notes to no. 56).

19 *Registrum Episcopatus Glasguensis* (Bannatyne Club, 1843), no. 3.

20 *Registrum Episcopatus Glasguensis*, nos 9 and 10.

21 *Gesta Stephani*, 20–21.

22 Richard of Hexham, 150–51; John of Hexham, 288.

23 Matthew, *King Stephen*, 79.

24 Poole, *Domesday Book to Magna Carta*, 270.

25 Ibid.

26 *Gesta Stephani*, 34.

27 *Gesta Stephani*, 34; Kapelle, *Norman Conquest of the North*, 198–9.

28 John of Hexham, 289; for Walter's lordship of Carham and castle at Wark, see Kapelle, *Norman Conquest of the North*, 197, 205.

29 Anderson, *Scottish Annals*, 179–80.

30 For a discussion of this northern English chronicle tradition and its presentation of the Scots and Galwegians in 1138 see R.D. Oram, 'The Mythical Picts and the Monastic Pedant: the Origin of the Legend of the Galloway Picts', *Pictish Arts Society Journal*, 4 (1993), 14–27.

31 Richard of Hexham, *De Gestis Regis Stephani*, 152–53.

32 Richard of Hexham, *De Gestis Regis Stephani*, 153.

33 Richard of Hexham, *De Gestis Regis Stephani*, 153; John of Hexham, 289.

34 John of Hexham, 290.

35 Matthew, *King Stephen*, offers a radical reassessment of the whole reign.

36 John of Hexham, 290.

37 Richard of Hexham, *De Gestis Regis Stephani*, 155.

38 Richard of Hexham, *De Gestis Regis Stephani*, 155.

39 Richard of Hexham, *De Gestis Regis Stephani*, 155–56.

40 Ibid.

41 John of Hexham, 291.

42 Richard of Hexham, *De Gestis Regis Stephani*, 156–57.

43 Ibid., 157–58.

44 John of Hexham, 292.

45 See for example, Ailred of Rievaulx, *De Standardo*, in *Chronicles of Stephen, etc.*, iii, 181.

46 John of Hexham, 292. For Stephen's arrest of Eustace and deprivation of his castles, see Ailred of Rievaulx, *De Standardo*, 190.

47 John of Hexham, 292; Richard of Hexham, *De Gestis Regis Stephani*, 158.

48 Richard of Hexham, *De Gestis Regis Stephani*, 158–59.

49 *Anglo-Saxon Chronicle*, E, s.a. 1138.

50 Richard of Hexham, *De Gestis Regis Stephani*, 159. For the backgrounds of these men, see Kapelle, *Norman Conquest of the North*, 198-9, 221–22, 223

51 Ailred of Rievaulx, *De Standardo*, 182; Richard of Hexham, *De Gestis Regis Stephani*, 161–62.

52 Richard of Hexham, *De Gestis Regis Stephani*, 161–62; Duncan, 'Bruces of Annandale', 90–91.

53 Ailred of Rievaulx, *De Standardo*, 192–95.

54 Ailred of Rievaulx, *De Standardo*, 195.

55 John of Worcester, 111.

56 Henry of Huntingdon, 262; Ailred of Rievaulx, *De Standardo*, 18589.

57 Ailred of Rievaulx, *De Standardo*, 189–90.

58 Ailred of Rievaulx, *De Standardo*, 190–91.

59 Richard of Hexham, *De Gestis Regis Stephani*, 162–63; Ailred of Rievaulx, *De Standardo*, 191–92.

60 Ailred of Rievaulx, *De Standardo*, 196.

61 For an expression of this view, see Richard of Hexham, *De Gestis Regis Stephani*, 164.

62 Richard of Hexham, *De Gestis Regis Stephani*, 165.

63 Richard of Hexham, *De Gestis Regis Stephani*, 166.

64 Richard of Hexham, *De Gestis Regis Stephani*, 170, makes it clear that the blockade of the castle continued after David's departure from Wark in September.

65 Richard of Hexham, *De Gestis Regis Stephani*, 169.

66 Richard of Hexham, *De Gestis Regis Stephani*, 169–70. John of Hexham, 298, indicates that the Scottish clergy and magnates had gathered at Carlisle by David's decree.

67 John of Hexham, 298; Richard of Hexham, *De Gestis Regis Stephani*, 170.

68 Richard of Hexham, *De Gestis Regis Stephani*, 170.

69 Richard of Hexham, *De Gestis Regis Stephani*, 171.

70 Richard of Hexham, *De Gestis Regis Stephani*, 171–72.

71 Richard of Hexham, *De Gestis Regis Stephani*, 176.

72 Matthew, *King Stephen*, 81.

73 Richard of Hexham, *De Gestis Regis Stephani*, 177–78. The names of the two earls are only recorded as 'Mal…' and 'Mac…'.

74 E.g., R.H.C. Davis, *King Stephen 1135–54*, third edition (London, 1990), 46. For recent discussions of the historiography and a more positive interpretation see K.J. Stringer, *The Reign of Stephen: Kingship, Warfare and Government in Twelfth-Century England* (London, 1993), 32–33; Matthew, *King Stephen*, 81–82.

75 Stringer, *Reign of Stephen*, 33.

CHAPTER NINE: THE SAINTLY KING

1 Honeycutt, *Matilda of Scotland*, especially chapter 5.

2 D.H. Farmer, *The Oxford Dictionary of Saints*, fourth edition (Oxford, 1997), 129. St David of Scotland remains in the Calendar of the Scottish Episcopal Church.

3 *Life of Margaret*, chapter 5, in Anderson, *Early Sources*, ii, 66–67.

4 Anderson, *Scottish Annals from English Chronicles*, 126–27.

5 Symeon of Durham, *Historia Regum*, ii, 204.

6 Symeon of Durham, *Historia Regum*, ii, 204.

7 Symeon of Durham, *Historia Regum*, ii, 205.

8 Eadmer, *Historia Novorum*, 279–88

9 Symeon of Durham, *Historia Regum*, ii, 275.

10 Duncan, *Making of the Kingdom*, 131; Barrow, *Kingship and Unity*, 78–79.

11 Watt, *Fasti*, 144–45.

12 *Anglo-Saxon Chronicle*, H, s.a. 1114.

13 Watt, *Fasti*, 145.

14 Hugh the Chantor, *History*, 76; Raine, *Historians of York*, iii, 4041.

15 Symeon of Durham, *Historia Regum*, ii, 264. Calixtus II's judgement against John, in the form of a letter, is given in Raine, *Historians of York*, iii, 44. His order to the Scottish bishops to submit to Thurstan, sent in a letter to King Alexander, is in ibid. 45. The Pope informed Thurstan of John's departure for Jerusalem in May 1122, Raine, *Historians of York*, iii, 46–47.

16 Symeon of Durham, *Historia Regum*, ii, 269.

17 *Charters of David I*, no.15.

18 Symeon of Durham, *Historia Regum*, ii, 277–78. For the legation of John of Crema, see P.C. Ferguson, *Medieval Papal Representatives in Scotland: Legates, Nuncios, and Judges-Delegate, 1125–1286*, Stair Society 45 (Edinburgh, 1997), 31–34.

19 Hugh Sottewain, Archbishops of York, in Rain, Historians of York, ii, 214–15.

20 Ferguson, *Papal Representatives*, 34.

21 Hugh Sottewain, Archbishops of York, in Raine, *Historians of York*, ii, 215.

22 Duncan, *Making of the Kingdom*, 259.

23 See above p.79–81. Hugh Sottewain, Archbishops of York, in Raine, *Historians of York*, ii, 217.

24 Raine, *Historians of York*, iii, 51–52; Duncan, *Making of the Kingdom*, 261.

25 Oram, *Lordship of Galloway*, 170–74.

26 Duncan, *Making of the Kingdom*, 260.

27 John of Hexham, 285.

28 Raine, *Historians of York*, iii, 66–67; Duncan, *Kingship of the Scots*, 89.

29 Duncan, *Kingship of the Scots*, 90–91.

30 Richard of Hexham, *Gesta Regis Stephani*, 169–70; John of Hexham, 298; Ferguson, *Papal Representatives*, 36–37.

31 John of Hexham, 298.

32 Richard of Hexham, *Gesta Regis Stephani*, 176.

33 Green, 'Aristocratic Loyalties on the Northern Frontier', 97.

34 For discussion of the Durham election and the York contovorsy, see below p.153–55.

35 John of Hexham, 321.

36 Watt, *Fasti*, 145.

37 The foregoing is a summary of the discussion offered by Keith Stringer in *Reign of Stephen*, 67–68.

38 Stringer, 'State-Building in Twelfth-Century Britain', 58–59.

39 John of Hexham, 326; Ferguson, *Papal Representatives*, 38–39.

40 John of Hexham, 327.

41 Ferguson, *Papal Representatives*, 39 n.66.

42 Duncan, *Making of the Kingdom*, 257.

43 Barrow, *Kingship and Unity*, 66–67.

44 Watt, *Fasti*, 39; Cowan, *Medieval Church*, 33.

45 Watt, *Fasti*, 1; Cowan, *Medieval Church*, 98–99.

46 *Charters of David I*, 33; Watt, *Fasti*, 1.

47 *Scone Liber*, nos.1 and 4; Watt, *Fasti*, 214.

48 Barrow, *Kingship and Unity*, 68.

49 Watt, *Fasti*, 94.

50 Watt, *Fasti*, 214.

51 Watt, *Fasti*, 266; Barrow, *Kingship and Unity*, 268.

52 Watt, *Fasti*, 94.

53 Anderson, *Early Sources*, ii, 193.

54 Watt, *Fasti*, 94.

55 Oram, *Lordship of Galloway*, 170 and note 35; Craster, 'Ranulf Flambard', 39.

56 Barrow, *Kingship and Unity*, 68; Duncan, *Making of the Kingdom*, 257.

57 The first Dean of Glasgow, for example, is recorded only in the reign of Malcolm IV, but an archdeacon is on record by around 1126 (Watt, *Fasti*, 152, 170). At St Andrews, an archdeacon is recorded 1147 x 1152 (Watt, *Fasti*, 304). At Dunkeld, however, the earliest dean is recorded in 1178 x 1188 and archdeacon in 1177 (Watt, *Fasti*, 102, 119).

58 Barrow, *Kingship and Unity*, 73.

59 Duncan, *Making of the Kingdom*, 144.

60 Duncan, *Making of the Kingdom*, 145.

61 C. Brooke, *The Age of the Cloister* (Stroud, 2003), 159; Duncan, *Making of the Kingdom*, 149.

62 Midmer, *English Medieval Monasteries*, 10 and Appendix 1.

63 The Mesolithic site at Rink Farm, which dates from before around 4500BC, lies at the confluence of the rivers Tweed and Yarrow just three miles north of Selkirk.

64 *Kelso Liber*, i, no.1.

65 Watt, *Fasti*, 145.

66 Brooke, *Age of the Cloister*, 153–57 gives a very useful summary of the development of the Augustinian rule and attitudes towards the Augustinian canons.

67 Duncan, *Making of the Kingdom*, 150.

68 Duncan, *Kingship of the Scots*, 91.

69 *Chron. Melrose*, s.a. 1128.

70 Duncan, *Making of the Kingdom*, 150.

71 R.D. Oram, 'Prayer, property and profit: Scottish monasteries *c.*1100–*c.*1300', in S.Foster, A.I. Macinnes and R. MacInnes (eds), *Scottish Power Centres from the Early Middle Ages to the Twentieth Century* (Glasgow, 1998), 79–99.

72 *Charters of David I*, no. 90.

73 Bartlett, *Making of Europe*, 227–29, 256–60.

74 Fawcett and Oram, *Melrose Abbey*, 20–22.

75 Bartlett, *Making of Europe*, 153–55.

76 Turgot, *Life of Margaret*, in Anderson, *Early Sources*, ii, 72.

77 R.R. Davies, *Domination and Conquest: the Experience of Ireland, Scotland and Wales 1100–1300* (Cambridge, 1990), 16–18.

78 Walter Daniel, *The Life of Ailred of Rievaulx*, ed. and trans. F.M. Powicke (London, 1950), 45; Bartlett, *Making of Europe*, 153–55.

79 Duncan, *Making of the Kingdom*, 145, quoting Knowles, *Monastic Order in England*.

CHAPTER TEN: THE 'SCOTO–NORTHUMBRIAN' REALM

1 For the use of this term, see G.W.S. Barrow, 'David I of Scotland: The Balance of New and Old', in *Scotland and Her Neighbours in the Middle Ages* (London, 1992), 45–65; K.J. Stringer, *The Reign of Stephen: Kingship, Warfare and Government in Twelfth-Century England* (London, 1993), 36–37.

2 Henry of Huntingdon, *Historia Anglorum*, 265.

3 John of Hexham, 300.

4 Chronicle of the Canons of Huntingdon, in Anderson, *Early Sources*, ii, 201.

5 Matthew, *King Stephen*, 143 and note 63.

6 Stringer, *Reign of Stephen*, 33.

7 John of Hexham, 306.

8 John of Hexham, 309.

9 *Charters of David I*, nos 102 and 103.

10 John of Hexham, 309.

11 Matthew, *King Stephen*, 106.

12 Historia Dunelmensis Ecclesiae, in Symeon of Durham, i, 162.

13 John of Hexham, 309.

14 Gesta Stephani regis Anglorum, in *Chronicles of Stephen* etc., iii, 3–136 at 74–75.

15 Matthew, *King Stephen*, 108.

16 Henry of Huntigdon, *Historia Anglorum*, 275.

17 Historia Dunelmensis Ecclesiae, continuatio altera, 162; John of Hexham, 311.

18 Historia Dunelmensis Ecclesiae, continuatio prima, 145–46.

19 Historia Dunelmensis Ecclesiae, continuatio prima, 144.

20 John of Hexham, 309.

21 Historia Dunelmensis Ecclesiae, continuatio prima, 145.

22 Historia Dunelmensis Ecclesiae, continuatio prima, 145.

23 Historia Dunelmensis Ecclesiae, continuatio prima, 146.

24 Historia Dunelmensis Ecclesiae, continuatio altera, 162; Historia Dunelmensis Ecclesiae, continuatio prima, 146.

25 Lawrie, *Early Scottish Charters*, 366–67.

26 Historia Dunelmensis Ecclesiae, continuatio prima, 153–55.

27 John of Hexham, 314; Historia Dunelmensis Ecclesiae, continuatio prima, 157, 159.

28 Stringer, 'State-building in Twelfth-Century Britain', 49.

29 Matthew, *King Stephen*, 114, 131.

30 Historia Dunelmensis Ecclesiae, continuatio altera, 167.

31 See, for example, Barrow, *Anglo-Norman Era*, 97–99.

32 G.W.S. Barrow, 'The Charters of David I', *Anglo-Norman Studies*, 14 (1991), 25–37 at 34–36.

33 Matthew, *King Stephen*, 131.

34 William of Newburgh, Historia Rerum Anglicarum, in *Chronicles of Stephen* etc, i, 70.

35 For example, *Charters of David I*, nos 59, 60, 65, 74, 81, 102.

36 *Charters of David I*, no. 82.

37 See comments in Kapelle, *Norman Conquest of the North*, 283–84 note; *Charters of David I*, 20.

38 Stringer, 'State-Building in Twelfth-Century Britain', 55.

39 For the Umfravilles and Earl Henry see *Charters of David I*, 20 and nos 52, 61, 62, 65, 73, 74, 78, 79, 80, 82, 101, 102, 103, 104, 121, 163, 169, 170, 199.

40 Stringer, 'State-building in Twelfth-Century Britain', 51; *Kelso Liber*, i, no.92 (Keith); *RRS*, ii, no.292 (Kinnaird); *Registrum Monasterii Sancte Marie de Cambuskenneth AD 1147–1535* (Grampian Club, 1872), nos 80 and 86 (Dunipace).

41 Stringer, 'State-building in Twelfth-Century Britain', 52–53.

42 Duncan, *Making of the Kingdom*, 222. For Alston, see I. Blanchard, 'Lothian and Beyond: The Economy of the "English Empire" of David I' in R.H. Britnell and J. Hatcher (edd), *Progress and Problems in Medieval England* (Cambridge, 1996), 23–45.

43 John of Hexham, 298.

44 Stringer, 'State-Building in Twelfth-Century Britain', 49.

45 *Charters of David I*, 86, 91, 101, 122, 132, 150–1.

46 G.W.S. Barrow, 'The pattern of lordship and feudal settlement in Cumbria', *Journal of Medieval History*, i (1975), 117–137 at 122; Kapelle, *Norman Conquest of the North*, 200.

47 For a discussion of David's possession of the honour of Lancaster, see G.W.S. Barrow, 'King David I and the Honour of Lancaster', *English Historical Review*, lxx (1955), 85–89.

48 *Charters of David I*, nos 111 and 112.

49 Stringer, *Reign of Stephen*, 33.

50 Stringer, *Reign of Stephen*, 34–35.

51 This effort to detach Anglo-Norman barons from their loyalty to Stephen is evident from at least 1138 (Stringer, 'State-Building in Twelfth-Century Britain', 44).

52 Simeon of Durham, ii, 326; Stringer, *Reign of Stephen*, 34–35.

53 Barrow, *Anglo-Norman Era*, 71–72 and note 64.

54 Barrow, *Anglo-Norman Era*, 73; Stringer, *Reign of Stephen*, 35.

55 *Charters of David I*, 36 and no.96.

56 Barrow, *Anglo-Norman Era*, 70–76; K.J. Stringer, 'Periphery and core in thirteenth-century Scotland: Alan son of Roland, Lord of Galloway and Constable of Scotland', in A. Grant and K.J. Stringer (eds), *Medieval Scotland: Crown, Lordship and Community* (Edinburgh, 1993), 82–113 at 89–92.

57 J. Green, 'Aristocratic Loyalties on the Northern Frontier of England, c. 1100–1174', in D. Williams (ed.), *England in the Twelfth Century* (Woodbridge, 1990), 83–100 at 94.

58 Hollister, *Henry I*, 235.

59 For discussion of the Bishops of Man generally, see A. Woolf, 'The Diocese of the Sudreyar', in S. Imsen (ed.), *Saertrykk fra Ecclesias Nidrosiensis 1153–1537: Sokelys pa Nidaroskirkens og Nidarosprovinsens historie* (Senter for Middelalderstudier, 2003), 171–181. I am grateful to Alex for having given me sight of an earlier draft of this paper, where the career of Wimund is discussed in detail, and from which this present account has benefited greatly.

60 William of Newburgh, *Historia Rerum Anglicarum*, 73–76.

61 Oliver, *Monumenta*, ii, 1–3.

62 Oliver, *Monumenta*, ii, 4–6.

63 Raine, *Historians of the Church of York*, ii, 372.

64 E. van Houts, (ed.), *The gesta Normannorum ducum of William of Jumièges, Orderic Vitalis, and Robert of Torigni*, (Oxford 1992), OV, 8.xxx. See Anderson, *Scottish Annals from English Chroniclers*, 223–26 and notes; Duncan, *Making of the Kingdom*, 166.

65 For Scandinavian and Isles-based connections with English Cumbria, see N. Higham, 'The Scandinavians in North Cumbria: Raids and Settlement in the Later Ninth to Mid Tenth Centuries', in J.R. Baldwin and I.D. Whyte (eds), *The Scandinavians in Cumbria* (Edinburgh, 1985), 37–51; R.N. Bailey, 'Aspects of Viking-Age Sculpture in Cumbria', in *ibid.*, 53–63; G. Fellows-Jensen, 'Scandinavian Settlement in Cumbria and Dumfriesshire: the Place-Name Evidence', in ibid., 65–82; S. Dickinson, 'Bryant's Gill: Another "Viking-Period" Ribblehead?', in ibid., 83–88; and especially A.J.L. Winchester, 'The Multiple Estate: A Framework for the Evolution of Settlement in Anglo-Saxon and Scandinavian Cumbria', in ibid., 89–101.

66 *The Register of the Priory of St Bees*, ed. J. Wilson, (Surtees Society, 1915) 532, discussed in *RRS* ii, 12–13.

67 Oram, *Lordship of Galloway*, 72–73.

68 Lawrie, *Early Scottish Charters*, 271–73.

69 Symeon of Durham, ii, 326.

70 Anderson, *Early Sources*, ii, 91–92 note 5. William apparently died while still under age, but witnessed a charter of Malcolm IV in 1162 x 1164, *RRS*, i, no 256. This would imply that he was born only in the mid to late 1140s.

71 Stringer, *Reign of Stephen*, 65, 77.

72 *Letters of St Bernard*, 259–61 and nos 187–208.

73 John of Hexham, 322–23.

74 Roger of Howden, *Chronica*, ed. W. Stubbs (London, 1868), i, 211.

75 *RRS*, i, 9; Green, 'Anglo-Scottish Relations', 68.

76 John of Hexham, 323.

77 Stringer, *Reign of Stephen*, 36.

78 W.L. Warren, *Henry II* (London, 1973), 36–37.

79 John of Hexham, 323.

80 Henry of Huntingdon, *Historia Anglorum*, 282.

81 John of Hexham, 323; Henry of Huntingdon, *Historia Anglorum*, 282.

CHAPTER ELEVEN: DAVID THE VENERABLE

1 Stringer, 'State-Building in Twelfth-Century Britain', 52, 53.

2 R. Bartlett, *England Under the Norman and Angevin Kings 1075–1225* (Oxford, 2000), 367. The mines were still producing significant revenue in the 1180s, but the metal-bearing seams were almost exhausted by the start of the thirteenth century.

3 Carpenter, *Struggle for Mastery*, 183.

4 Stringer, 'State-Building in Twelfth-Century Britain', 55.

5 Carpenter, *Struggle for Mastery*, 183.

6   David refers to 'my burgh' of Roxburgh in his foundation charter of Selkirk Abbey (*Kelso Liber*, no.1).

7   For a discussion of the money revenue from the burghs and trade, see Duncan, *Making of the Kingdom*, 156–57, 159.

8   Barrow, *Kingship and Unity*, 92–93.

9   H.L. MacQueen, *Common Law and Feudal Society in Medieval Scotland* (Edinburgh, 1993), 86–89.

10 This is not the place to embark upon a detailed exploration of the pros and cons of the feudal *v.* non-feudal debate, which would require a systematic examination of the charter evidence. For an exploration of the basics of the argument, see R.D. Oram, 'Gold into Lead? The State of Early Medieval Scottish History', in T. Brotherstone and D. Ditchburn (eds), *Freedom and Authority* (East Linton, 2000), 32–43.

11 *Charters of David I*, no.267; Barrow, *Kingship and Unity*, 44.

12 J. Bannerman, 'MacDuff of Fife', in Grant and Stringer, *Medieval Scotland*, 20–38. The charter by which David supposedly re-granted the earldom to Donnchad does not survive and the tradition of Fife's surrender to the crown and re-grant to its earl may be part of later medieval efforts to secure control of this politically symbolic earldom for a member, or close supporter, of the royal house.

13 R.D. Oram 'Patterns of Lordship, Secular and Ecclesiastical, *c.*1100–1300', in D. Omand (ed.), *The Fife Book* (Edinburgh, 2000), 105–15 at 110–11; Duncan, *Making of the Kingdom*, 167; *Charters of David I*, nos 33, 88, 89, 90 and 98 for Robert as a witness to royal charters.

14 Alan witnesses one surviving charter datable to post 1150: *Charters of David I*, no.197.

15 *Chron. Melrose*, s.a. 1150.

16 Duncan, *Making of the Kingdom*, 189–91.

17 *Charters of David I*, 33 and no.171 note.

18 *Charters of David I*, no.171.

19 *Chron. Holyrood*, s.a. 1150.

20 *Charters of David I*, no.136.

21 Watt, *Fasti*, 94 and 214; *Charters of David I*, no.33.

22 Topping, 'Harald Maddadson'; Thomson, *History of Orkney*, 70.

23 *Orkneyinga Saga*, chapter 91.

24 *Orkneyinga Saga*, chapters 92–94.

25 Bernard of Clairvaux, *St Bernard's Life of St Malachy of Armagh*, ed. and trans H.J. Lawlor (London, 1920), 76–79.

26 Duncan, *Kingship of the Scots*, 70–71.

27 John of Hexham, 327.

28 John of Hexham, 327.

29 *Charters of David I*, no.212; Watt, *Fasti*, 214.

30 John of Hexham, 327.

31 Stringer, 'State-Building in Twelfth-Century Britain', 58.

32 Ferguson, *Papal Representatives*, 39.

33 Ailred of Rievaulx, Epistola, in Anderson, *Scottish Annals from English Chronicles*, 232–36.

34 John of Hexham, 330.

CHAPTER TWELVE: SAINT AND SINNER

1   A.D. Cameron, *History For Young Scots*, i (Edinburgh, 1963), 57–60.

2   B. Schneidmüller, 'Constructing Identities of Medieval France', in M. Bull (ed.), *France in the Central Middle Ages 900–1200* (Oxford, 2002), 15–42 at 34–36; R. Fawtier, *The Captian Kings of France: Monarchy and Nation (987–1328)*, trans. L. Butler and R.J. Adam (London, 1962), 57–59.

3   Duncan, *Kingship of the Scots*, 68–69.

4   See, for example, John of Hexham, 287; Ailred of Rievaulx, *Saints of Hexham*, 183; *Gesta Stephani*, 34.

5   Orderic Vitalis, viii, 20.

6   For a summary description of the seals used by David, see *Charters of David I*, 30–32.

7   *Kelso Liber*, iii–vii. There is a full-scale, hand-coloured facsimile of the charter reproduced at the end of the introduction to volume I.

8   Barrow, 'David I of Scotland', 49.

9   See, for example, William Hole's mural presentation of the mounted king dispensing justice to the poor woman in the National Portrait Gallery in Edinburgh.

10 B. Scott James, *The Letters of St Bernard*, second edition (Stroud, 1998), no.172.

11 Ailred of Rievaulx, *Epistola*, in Anderson, *Scottish Annals from English Chroniclers*, 232–237.

12 Barrow, 'David I of Scotland', 47 and note 11.

13 Barrow, 'David I of Scotland', 47.

14 Ailred of Rievaulx, Epistola, 232.

15 Ibid., 23233.

16 William of Malmesbury, *Gesta Regum Anglorum*, 476–77.

17 Life of Margaret in Anderson, *Early Sources*, ii, 82–86; Ailred of Rievaulx, Epistola, 234–36.

18 William of Newburgh, *Historia Rerum Anglicarum*, 70–72.

19 2 Samuel 11.

20 The translation is A.O. Anderson's, *Scottish Annals from English Chronicles*, 230.

21 *Chronicle of the Kings of Scotland*, in Skene,

Chronicles of the Picts and Scots, 132–33.

22 Barrow, 'David I of Scotland', 46.

23 I am grateful to Michael Penman for discussing this point with me, which he elaborates upon in his paper to the 2004 Leeds Medieval Congress.

24 *John of Fordun's Chronicle of the Scottish Nation*, ed. W.F. Skene, (Edinburgh, 1872), ii, 221–48.

25 Ibid., 222–23.

26 Ibid., 225.

27 Ibid., 244–48.

28 Ibid., 244.

29 Ibid., 245.

30 For detailed discussion of the Scottish succession issue in the mid-fourteenth century, see M. Penman, *David II 1329–71* (East Linton, 2004), especially 153–174 and chapters 8 and 9.

31 I am indebted to Steve Boardman for drawing my attention to this possible interpretation of the structure and composition of Fordun, and to Michael Penman for his discussions with me of its potential significance in terms of the reign of David II.

32 *The Original Chronicle of Andrew of Wyntoun*, ed. F.J. Amours, *Scottish Text Society*, iv (Edinburgh, 1906), 385.

33 Chron. Wyntoun, iv, 411.

34 Walter Bower, Scotichronicon, ed. D.E.R. Watt and others, vol. 3 (Aberdeen, 1995), 126–77 and notes.

35 Walter Bower, Scotichronicon, ed. D.E.R. Watt and others, vol. 8 (Aberdeen, 1987), 303–41, for the presentation of the king and his qualities.

36 The confusion arises from the different names given to the battle. Some sources refer to it as the battle of Northallerton, after the nearest large settlement, others to Cowton Moor, after the field over which the conflict was waged, and others as 'the Standard' after the symbol around which the English force was rallied. Bower has clearly used different sources that employ the different names and has made two separate battled out of the one event.

37 Bower, Scotichronicon, 3, Book VI, 290–343.

38 S. Mapstone, 'Bower on kingship', in D.E.R. Watt and others (eds), Walter Bower, Scotichronicon, 9 (1998), 321–28.

39 Barrow, 'David I of Scotland', 46. The trinity comprised St Margaret, David and Robert Bruce.

40 I. Campbell, 'A romanesque revival and the early Renaissance in Scotland *c*.1380–1513', Journal of the Society of Architectural Historians, 54:3 (1995).

41 John Major, *A History of Greater Britain*, 1521, ed. and trans. A. Constable (Scottish History Society, 1892).

42 Major, *History*, 133, 134.

43 Major, *History*, 134.

44 Major, *History*, 138–139.

45 Major, *History*, 135–136.

46 Bellenden, *Chronicles*, ii, 184.

47 Bellenden, *Chronicles*, ii, 185.

48 See comments on this by David Hay Fleming, *Critical Reviews Relating Cheifly to Scotland* (London, 1912), 48.

49 Bellenden, *Chronicles*, ii, 185.

50 Bellenden, *Chronicles*, ii, 191.

51 *The Historie of Scotland written first in Latin by the Most Reuerend and Worthy Jhone Leslie Bishop of Rosse and Translated in Scottish by Father James Dalrymple*, ed. E.G. Cody, i (Scottish Text Society, 1888), 326–29.

52 Leslie, *History*, 326.

53 Leslie, *History*, 327.

54 George Buchanan, *The History of Scotland*, trans. G. Aikman (Glasgow, 1827-29). The quote is from the translation from the Latin given by David Dalrymple, Lord Hailes in his *Annals of Scotland*, i (Edinburgh, 1819), 109.

55 See, for example, Sir Thomas Craig in his *De Unione Regnorum Britanniae Tractatus*, ed. and trans. C.S. Terry (Scottish History Society, 1909), 245, 421.

56 Dalrymple, *Annals*, 74–116.

57 Dalrymple, *Annals*, 115.

58 Dalrymple, *Annals*, 116.

59 P.F. Tytler, *History of Scotland*, i (Edinburgh, 1828), preface, i.

60 A. Lang, *A History of Scotland*, i (Edinburgh, 1900), 102–09.

61 Duncan, *Making of the Kingdom*, 132 and chapter 7.

62 See, for example, McDonald, *Kingdom of the Isles*, chapter 2.

63 The Celtophile tradition received its bible with the publication in three volumes between 1876 and 1880 of William F. Skene's monumental *Celtic Scotland*. The foundation of societies devoted to the study of the cultural, language, literature and history of the Gaels began with the Highland Society of Edinburgh in 1784, but the upsurge in interest in the Highlands and Highlanders really followed the publication of Sir Walter Scott's *Waverley* in 1814, coupled with growing public concern at the impact of Clearance in the region in the early 1800s. Agitation for land reform in the later nine-

teenth century also served to heighten interest in Gaelic Scotland and stimulated the formation of new organisations, such as the Gaelic Society of Inverness (1871) and the Gaelic Society of Glasgow (1887). Crucial to the development of the 'Celtic' view of Scottish history was the appointment in 1882 of John Stuart Blackie to the first chair of Celtic at the University of Edinburgh,

64 Lang, *History*, 102.

65 Lang, *History*, 107. For a discussion of the late eighteenth- and nineteenth-century development of the myth of the Highland soldier, see A. McKillop, *More Fruitful than the Soil* (East Linton, 2001).

66 Lang, *History*, 102.

67 P. Hume Brown, *History of Scotland*, i (Cambridge, 1909), 7396.

68 Hume Brown, *History*, 73.

69 Hume Brown, *History*, 74.

70 Hume Brown, *History*, 86-87.

71 Hume Brown, *History*, 87.

72 Hume Brown, *History*, 88.

73 G.W.S. Barrow, *Feudal Britain* (London, 1956).

74 Barrow, *Feudal Britain*, 134–135.

75 Barrow, 'David I of Scotland', in *Scotland and its Neighbours*, 45–65.

76 Barrow, *Anglo-Norman Era*, 91.

77 M. Lynch, *Scotland: a New History* (London, 1991).

78 Lynch, *Scotland*, 83.

79 Stringer, *The Reign of Stephen*, 28–37. The argument presented there was significantly expanded in his 'State-Building in Twelfth-Century Britain'.

80 M. Pittock, *A New History of Scotland* (Stroud, 2003), 42.

81 C. Harvie, *Scotland: A Short History* (Oxford, 2002), 34.

Bibliography

UNPUBLISHED THESES

Ross, A., *The Province of Moray c. 1000–1230*. A thesis presented for the degree of PhD (University of Aberdeen, 2003).

PRIMARY SOURCES

A Scottish Chronicle Known as the Chronicle of Holyrood, ed. M.O. Anderson and A.O. Anderson (Scottish History Society, 1938).

Ailred of Rievaulx, *Saints of Hexham* in J. Raine (ed.), *The Priory of Hexham*, i (Surtees Society, 1864).

Anderson, A.O. (ed.), *Scottish Annals from English Chroniclers AD 500–1296* (London, 1908).

Anderson, A.O. (ed.), *Early Sources of Scottish History AD 500–1286*, 2 volumes (Edinburgh, 1922).

S. Anselmi Opera Omnia, ed. F.S.Schmitt (1946–52).

Benedict of Peterborough, *Gesta Regis Henrici Secundi*, ed. W. Stubbs, 2 vols (London, 1867).

Bernard of Clairvaux, *St Bernard's Life of St Malachy of Armagh*, ed. and trans H.J. Lawlor (London, 1920).

Brut y Tywyssogion: or, The Chronicle of the Princes, ed. J.Williams ab Ithel (London, 1860).

Chronica Regum Manniae et Insularum. The Chronicle of Man and the Isles. A Facsimile of the Manuscript Codex Julius A. VIII in the British Museum (Douglas, 1924).

Chronica Roger de Hovedon, ed. W. Stubbs (London, 1868–71).

Chronicle of Melrose (facsimile edition), eds A.O. Anderson and others (London, 1936).

Chronicles of the Picts, Chronicles of the Scots, ed. W.F. Skene (Edinburgh, 1867).

Chronicles of the Reigns of Stephen, Henry II and Richard I, ed. R. Howlett, (London 1884–89).

The Chronicles of Scotland Compiled by Hector Boece, translated into Scots by John Bellenden 1531, eds E.C. Batho and H.W. Husbands (Scottish Text Society, 1938–1941).

The Charters of David I: the Written Acts of David I King of Scots, 1124–53, and of his Son Henry, Earl of Northumberland, 1139–52, ed. G.W.S. Barrow (Woodbridge, 1999).

Clancy, T.O. (ed.), *The Triumph Tree: Scotland's Earliest Poetry AD 550–1350* (Edinburgh, 1998).

Dalrymple, D., (Lord Hailes), *Annals of Scotland*, i (Edinburgh, 1819).

Early Yorkshire Charters, eds W. Farrer and C.T. Clay, 12 volumes, Yorkshire Archaeology Society Record Series (Edinburgh, 1913-).

Florence of Worcester, *Chronicon ex Chronicis*, 2 volumes, ed. B. Thorpe, *English History Society* (1848–49).

George Buchanan, *The History of Scotland*, trans. G. Aikman (Glasgow, 1827–29).

Gervase of Canterbury, *Historical Works*, i, *The Chronicles of the Reigns of Stephen, Henry II and Richard I*, ed. W. Stubbs (London, 1879).

The gesta Normannorum ducum of William of Jumièges, Orderic Vitalis, and Robert of Torigni, ed. E. van Houts, (Oxford 1992).

Gesta Stephani Regis Anglorum, in Howlett (ed.), *Chronicles of Stephen*, etc., iii, 3–136.

Henry of Huntingdon, *Historia Anglorum*, ed. T. Arnold (London, 1879).

Hermann of Tournai (Herimannus Tornacensis), *Narratio Restaurationis abbatiae S Martini Tornacensis*, ed. G. Waitz, *Monumenta Historica Germaniae*, Scriptores, xiv, 274–317.

Historians of the Church of York, ed. J. Raine, (London, 1879–94).

The Historie of Scotland, Wrytten First in Latin by the Most Reuerend and Worth Jhone Leslie Bishop of Rosse and Translated in Scottish by Father James Dalrymple… 1596, ed. E.G. Cody, i (Scottish Text Society, 1888).

Hugh Sottewain, *Archbishops of York*, in *Historians of the Church of York*, i, ed. J. Raine (London, 1879).

John of Fordun's Chronicle of the Scottish Nation, ed. W.F. Skene (Edinburgh, 1872).

John Major, *A History of Greater Britain, 1521*, ed. and trans. A. Constable (Scottish History Society, 18982).

Lawrie, A.C., *Early Scottish Charters Prior to AD 1153* (Glasgow, 1905).

The Letters of St Bernard of Clairvaux, trans B. Scott James, second edition (Stroud, 1998).

Liber Cartarum Sancte Crucis (Bannatyne Club, 1840).

Liber Ecclesie de Scon (Bannatyne Club, 1843).

Liber Sancte Marie de Calchou (Bannatyne Club, 1846).

Liber Sancte Marie de Dryburgh (Bannatyne Club, 1847).

Liber Sancte Marie de Melros (Bannatyne Club, 1837).

Liber Vitæ Ecclesiæ Dunelmensis, ed. J. Stevenson (Surtees Society, 1841).

Macphail, S.R., *History of the Religious House of Pluscardyn* (Edinburgh, 1881).

The Original Chronicle of Andrew of Wyntoun, ed. F.J. Amours, *Scottish Text Society*, iv (Edinburgh, 1906).

Orkneyinga Saga: The History of the Earls of Orkney, trans H. Pálsson and P. Edwards (Harmondsworth, 1978).

Regesta Regum Anglo-Normannorum, ed. H.W.C. Davis, C. Johnson, H.A. Cronne and R.H.C. Davis, 4 volumes (Oxford, 1913–69).

Regesta Regum Scotorum, i, *The Acts of Malcolm IV*, ed. G.W.S. Barrow (Edinburgh, 1960).

Regesta Regum Scotorum, ii, *The Acts of William I*, ed. G.W.S. Barrow (Edinburgh, 1971).

The Register of the Priory of St Bees, ed. J. Wilson, (Surtees Society, 1915).

Registrum de Dunfermelyn (Bannatyne Club, 1842).

Registrum Episcopatus Glasguensis (Bannatyne and Maitland Clubs, 1843).

Registrum Monasterii S. Marie de Cambuskenneth (Grampian Club, 1872).

Registrum S. Marie de Neubotle (Bannatyne Club, 1849).

Richard of Hexham, Historia de gestis Regis Stephani et de bello de Standardo, in *Chronicles of Stephen, Henry II and Richard I*, ed. R. Howlett, iii (London, 1886).

Roger of Howden, *Chronica*, ed. W. Stubbs (London, 1868–71).

Symeonis Monachi Opera Omnia, ed. T. Arnold, (London 1885).

Thomas Craig, *De Unione Regnorum Britanniae Tractatus*, ed. and trans. C.S. Terry (Scottish History Society, 1909).

Vita Ædwardi Regis, ed. F. Barlow, secnod edition (London, 1992).

Walter Bower, *Scotichronicon*, ed. D.E.R. Watt and others, volume 3 (Aberdeen, 1995).

Walter Bower, *Scotichronicon*, ed. D.E.R. Watt and others, volume 8 (Aberdeen, 1987).

Walter Daniel, *The Life of Ailred of Rievaulx*, ed. and trans. F.M. Powicke (London, 1950).

William of Malmesbury, *Gesta Regum Anglorum*, ed. W. Stubbs (London, 1867).

William of Newburgh, *Historia Rerum Anglicarum*, in R. Howlett (ed.), Chronicles of Stephen etc., vols i and ii (London, 1884–85)

SECONDARY WORKS

Bailey, R.N., 'Aspects of Viking-Age Sculpture in Cumbria', in J.R. Baldwin and I.D. Whyte (eds), *The Scandinavians in Cumbria* (Edinburgh, 1985), 53–63

Baldwin, J.R. and Whyte, I.D., (eds), *The Scandinavians in Cumbria* (Edinburgh, 1985).

Bannerman, J., 'MacDuff of Fife', in A. Grant and K.J. Stringer (eds), *Medieval Scotland: Crown, Lordship and Community* (Edinburgh, 1993), 20–38.

Barlow, F., *Edward the Confessor* (London, 1970).

— *William Rufus* (London, 1983).

Barrow, G.W.S., 'King David I and the Honour of Lancaster', *English Historical Review*, lxx (1955), 85–89.

—, *Feudal Britain* (London, 1956).

—, 'Benedictine, Tironensians and Cistercians', in *The Kingdom of the Scots* (London, 1973), 188–211.

—, 'The pattern of lordship and feudal settlement in Cumbria', *Journal of Medieval History*, i (1975), 117–137.

—, *The Anglo-Norman Era in Scottish History* (Oxford, 1980).

—, *Kingship and Unity: Scotland 1000–1306*, first edition (London, 1981).

—., 'Badenoch and Strathspey, 1130–1312', *Northern Scotland*, 8 (1988), 1–15.

—, 'The Charters of David I', *Anglo-Norman Studies*, 14 (1991), 25–37.

—, 'David I of Scotland: The Balance of New and Old', in *Scotland and Her Neighbours in the Middle Ages* (London, 1992), 45–65.

—, 'The Reign of William the Lion', in *Scotland and Her Neighbours in the Middle Ages* (London, 1992), 67–90.

—, '*De domibus religiosis*: a note on Dornoch', *Innes Review*, xlviii (1997), 83–4.

Bartlett, R., *The Making of Europe: Colonisation, Conquest and Cultural Change 950–1350* (London, 1993).

Blanchard, I., 'Lothian and Beyond: The Economy of the "English Empire" of David I', in R.H. Britnell and J. Hatcher (eds), *Progress and Problems in Medieval England* (Cambridge, 1996), 23–45.

Boardman, S. and Ross, A. (eds), *The Exercise of Power in Medieval Scotland* (Dublin, 2003).

Brooke, C., *The Age of the Cloister: The Story of Monastic Life in the Middle Ages* (Stroud, 2003).

Brooke, D., *Wild Men and Holy Places* (Edinburgh, 1994).

Broun, D., 'Contemporary perspectives on Alexander II's succession: the evidence of king-lists' in R.D. Oram, *The Reign of Alexander II* (forthcoming, Brill, 2005).

Cameron, A.D., *History For Young Scots*, i (Edinburgh, 1963).

Campbell, J., 'A romanesque revival and the early Renaissance in Scotland *c*.1380–1513', *Journal of the Society of Architectural Historians*, 54:3 (1995).

Carpenter, D., *The Struggle for Mastery: Britain 1066–1284* (London, 2003).

Cowan, I.B., *The Medieval Church in Scotland*, ed. J. Kirk (Edinburgh, 1995).

Craster, H.H.E., 'A contemporary record of the pontificate of Ranulf Flambard', *Archaeologia Aeliana*, vii (1930), 33–56.

Crawford, B.E., (ed.), *St. Magnus Cathedral and Orkney's Twelfth-Century Renaissance* (Aberdeen, 1988).

Davies, R.R., *Domination and Conquest: the Experience of Ireland, Scotland and Wales 1100–1300* (Cambridge, 1990).

Davies, R.R., *The First English Empire: Power and Identities in the British Isles 1093–1343* (Oxford, 2000).

Davis, R.H.C., *King Stephen 1135–54*, third edition (London, 1990).

Dickinson, S., 'Bryant's Gill: Another "Viking-Period" Ribblehead?', in J.R. Baldwin and I.D. Whyte, *The Scandinavians in Cumbria* (Edinburgh, 1985), 83–88.

Donaldson, G., *Scotland: Church and Nation Through Sixteen Centuries* (Edinburgh, 1960).

Duncan, A.A.M., *Scotland: the Making of the Kingdom* (Edinburgh, 1975).

—, 'The Bruces of Annandale, 1100–1304', *TDGNHAS*, lxix (1994), 89–102.

—, 'Yes, the Earliest Scottish Charters', *Scottish Historical Review*, lxxviii (1999), 1–35.

—, *The Kingship of the Scots 842–1292. Succession and Independence* (Edinburgh, 2002).

Easson, D.E., *Medieval Religious Houses. Scotland* (London, 1957).

Farmer, D.H., *The Oxford Dictionary of Saints*, fourth edition (Oxford, 1997).

Fawcett, R., *Scottish Cathedrals* (London, 1997).

—, and Oram, R.D., *Melrose Abbey* (Stroud, 2004).

Fellows-Jensen, G., 'Scandinavian Settlement in Cumbria and Dumfriesshire: the Place-Name Evidence', in J.R. Baldwin and I.D. Whyte, *The Scandinavians in Cumbria* (Edinburgh, 1985), 65–82.

Ferguson, P.C., *Medieval Papal Representatives in Scotland: Legates, Nuncios, and Judges-Delegate, 1125–1286*, Stair Society 45 (Edinburgh, 1997).

Forte, A., Oram, R., and Pedersen, F., *Viking Empires* (forthcoming Cambridge, 2004).

Grant, A. and Stringer, K.J., (eds), *Medieval Scotland: Crown, Lordship and Community* (Edinburgh, 1993)

—, 'Thanes and Thanages from the Eleventh to the Fourteenth Centuries', in A. Grant and K.J. Stringer (eds), *Medieval Scotland: Crown, Lordship and Community* (Edinburgh, 1993), 39–81.

Green, J., 'Anglo-Scottish relations, 1066–1174' in M.Jones and M.Vale (eds), *England and Her Neighbours, 1066–1453* (London, 1989), 53–72.

—, 'Aristocratic Loyalties on the Northern Frontier of England, *c.*1100–74', in D. Williams (ed.), *England in the Twelfth Century* (Woodbridge, 1990), 83–100.

—, 'David I and Henry I', *Scottish Historical Review*, lxxv (1996), 1–19.

Harvie, C., *Scotland: A Short History* (Oxford, 2002).

Hay Fleming, D., *Critical reviews Reltaing Chiefy to Scotland* (London, 1912).

Higham, N., 'The Scandinavians in North Cumbria: Raids and Settlement in the Later Ninth to Mid Tenth Centuries', in J.R. Baldwin and I.D. Whyte (eds), *The Scandinavians in Cumbria* (Edinburgh, 1985), 37–51.

Hollister, C.W., *Henry I*, edited and completed by A.C. Frost (London, 2001).

Honeycutt, L.L., *Matilda of Scotland: A Study in Medieval Queenship* (Woodbridge, 2003).

Hume Brown, P., *History of Scotland*, i (Cambridge, 1909).

Kapelle, W.E., *The Norman Conquest of the North. The Region and Its Transformation 1000–1135* (London, 1979).

Lang, A., *A History of Scotland from the Roman Occupation*, i (Edinburgh, 1900).

Lynch, M., *Scotland: a New History* (London, 1991).

MacQuarrie, A., 'The kings of Strathclyde *c.*400–1018', in A. Grant and K.J. Stringer (eds), *Medieval Scotland: Crown, Lordship and Community* (Edinburgh, 1993), 1–19.

MacQueen, H.L., *Common Law and Feudal Society in Medieval Scotland* (Edinburgh, 1993).

McDonald, R.A., *The Kingdom of the Isles. Scotland's Western Seaboard c.1100–c.1336* (East Linton, 1997).

McNeill, T.E, *Anglo-Norman Ulster: the History and Archaeology of an Irish Barony, 1177–1400* (Edinburgh, 1980).

Mapstone, S., 'Bower on kingship', in D.E.R. Watt and others (eds), Walter Bower, *Scotichronicon*, 9 (1998), 321–28.

Marshall, H.E., *Scotland's Story: A History of Scotland for Boys and Girls* (Edinburgh, no date).

Matthew, D., *King Stephen* (London, 2002).

Midmer, R., *English Medieval Monasteries: A Summary* (London, 1979).

Oram, R.D., 'The Mythical Picts and the Monastic Pedant: the Origin of the Legend of the Galloway Picts', *Pictish Art Society Journal*, 4 (1993), 14–27.

—, 'Prayer, property and profit: Scottish monasteries, *c.*1100–*c.*1300', in S.Foster, A.I. Macinnes and R. MacInnes (eds), *Scottish Power Centres from the Early Middle Ages to the Twentieth Century* (Glasgow, 1998), 79–99.

—, 'David I and the Conquest and Colonisation of Moray', *Northern Scotland*, 19 (1999), 1–19.

—, *The Lordship of Galloway* (Edinburgh, 2000).

—, 'Gold into Lead? The State of Early Medieval Scottish History', in T. Brotherstone and D. Ditchburn (eds), *Freedom and Authority* (East Linton, 2000), 32–43.

—, 'Patterns of Lordship, Secular and Ecclesiastical, *c.*1100–1300', in D. Omand (ed.), *The Fife Book* (Edinburgh, 2000), 105–15.

—, 'Continuity, adaptation in integration: the earls and earldom of Mar, *c.*1150–*c.*1300', in S. Boardman and A. Ross (eds), *The Exercise of Power in Medieval Scotland* (Dublin, 2003), 46–66.

— (ed.), *The Reign of Alexander II* (forthcoming, Brill, 2005).

Penman, M., *David II 1329–71* (East Linton, 2004).

Pittock, M., *A New History of Scotland* (Stroud, 2003).

Poole, A.L., *Domesday Book to Magna Carta*, second edition (Oxford, 1955).

Schneidmüller, B., 'Constructing Identities of Medieval France', in M. Bull (ed.), *France in the Central Middle Ages 900–1200* (Oxford, 2002), 15–42.

Fawtier, R., *The Captian Kings of France: Monarchy and Nation (987–1328)*, trans. L. Butler and R.J. Adam (London, 1962).

Scott, J.G., 'The Partition of a Kingdom: Strathclyde 1092–1153', *Transactions of the Dumfriesshire and Galloway Natural History and Antiquarian Society*, lxxii (1997), 11–40.

Shead, N.F., 'The origins of the medieval diocese of Glasgow', *Scottish Historical Review*, xlviii (1969), 220–25.

Simpson, G.G. (ed.), *Scotland and the Low Countries 1124–1994* (East Linton, 1996)

Simpson, G.G. and Webster, B., 'Charter evidence and the distribution of mottes in Scotland', in K.J. Stringer (ed.), *Essays on the Nobility of Medieval Scotland* (Edinburgh, 1985), 1–24.

Stringer, K.J. (ed.), *Essays on the Nobility of Medieval Scotland* (Edinburgh, 1985),

—, *The Reign of Stephen: Kingship, warfare and Government in Twelfth-Century England* (London, 1993).

—, 'Periphery and core in thirteenth-century Scotland: Alan son of Roland, Lord of Galloway and Constable of Scotland', in A. Grant and K.J. Stringer (eds), *Medieval Scotland: Crown, Lordship and Community* (Edinburgh, 1993), 82–113.

Stringer, K.J., 'State-building in Twelfth-Century Britain: David I, King of Scots, and Northern England', in J.C. Appleby and P. Dalton (eds), *Government, Religion and Society in Northern England, 1000-1700* (Stroud, 1997), 40–62.

Thomson, W.P.L., *History of Orkney* (Edinburgh, 1987).

Toorians, L., 'Twelfth-century Flemish Settlement in Scotland', in G.G. Simpson (ed.), *Scotland and the Low Countries 1124–1994* (East Linton, 1996), 1–14.

Topping, P., 'Harald Maddadson, Earl of Orkney and Caithness, 1139-1206', *SHR*, lxii (1983), 105-120.

Tytler, P.F., *History of Scotland*, i (Edinburgh, 1828).

Veitch, K., 'The Scottish material in *De domibus religiosis*: date and provenance', *Innes Review*, xlvii (1996).

Warren, W.L., *Henry II* (London, 1973).

Watt, D.E.R. (ed.), *Fasti Ecclesiae Scoticanae Medii Aevii ad annum 1638* (Scottish Record Society, 1969).

Watt, D.E.R., and Shead, N.F., (eds), *The Heads of Religious Houses in Scotland from Twelfth to Sixteenth Centuries* (Edinburgh, 2001).

Williams, A., *The English and the Norman Conquest* (Woodbridge, 1995).

Wilson, J., 'Foundation of the Austin Priories of Nostell and Scone', *Scottish Historical Review*, vii (1910), 157–58.

Winchester, A.J.L., 'The Multiple Estate: A Framework for the Evolution of Settlement in Anglo-Saxon and Scandinavian Cumbria', in J.R. Baldwin and I.D. Whyte (eds), *The Scandinavians in Cumbria* (Edinburgh, 1985), 89–101.

Woolf, A., 'The Diocese of the Sudreyar', in S. Imsen (ed.), *Saertrykk fra Ecclesias Nidrosiensis 1153–1537: Sokelys pa Nidaroskirkens og Nidarosprovinsens historie* (Senter for Middelalderstudier, 2003), 171–181.

List of Illustrations

All illustrations from the author's collection

About the Author

Richard Oram is Senior Lecturer in Scottish History at the University of Stirling, editor of *History Scotland* the popular Scottish history magazine, and the series editor of Tempus' *Scottish Monarchs* biography series of which *David I* is the launch volume. His other books include *Lordship of Galloway*, *Scottish Prehistory*, *Melrose Abbey* and *The Kings & Queens of Scotland* (also published by Tempus).

Praise for *The Kings & Queens of Scotland*:

'It's all here – all the drama, all the passion, all the crises which make up the extraordinary panorama of royal hopes and failures and achievements down the turbulent centuries of Scotland's nationhood'
Magnus Magnusson

'The colourful, complex and frequently bloody story of Scottish rulers... an exciting if rarely edifying tale, told in a clear and elegant format'
BBC History Magazine

'A serious, readable work that sweeps across a vast historical landscape to help dispel the often shaming ignorance surrounding this ancient monarchy in its own land'
The Daily Mail (Scottish edition)

Index

TEMPUS SCOTTISH MONARCHS

A series of scholarly yet accessible biographies of the kings and queens of Scotland

Representing the oldest of the constituent components of the United Kingdom and providing the modern British monarchy with the longest pedigree in Europe, Scotland traces its origins from the sixth-century Argyll-based kingdom of the Scots. Its history can be presented as a long tale of triumph over adversity, characterised by the personal achievements of its truly remarkable rulers who transformed their fragile kingdom into the master of northern Britain. This series will chart that process, tracing through the lives of the men and women whose ambitions drove it forward the often rocky path from its semi-mythical foundations to its integration into the Stuart kingdom of Great Britain. It is a route way-marked by such towering personalities as Macbeth, Robert Bruce and Mary, Queen of Scots, whose lives have made an indelible imprint in world history, but directed also by a host of less well-known figures, such as Causantin mac Aeda, who challenged the heirs of Alfred for the mastery of Britain, David I, who extended his kingdom almost to the gates of York, or James IV, builder of the finest navy in northern Europe. Their will and ambition, successes and failures shaped not only modern Scotland, but have left their mark throughout Britain and the wider world.

PUBLISHED
Richard Oram, *David I: The King Who Made Scotland*

FORTHCOMING
Maureen M. Meikle, *Anna, Queen of Scots*
Alasdair Ross, *William I: Lion of the Scots*
Fiona Watson, *Robert the Bruce*

Further titles are in preparation